Islamic Philosophy

Islamic Philosophy
An Introduction

Oliver Leaman

Polity

First published in 2009 by Polity Press

Polity Press
65 Bridge Street
Cambridge CB2 1UR, UK

Polity Press
350 Main Street
Malden, MA 02148, USA

ISBN-13: 978-0-7456-4598-8
ISBN-13: 978-0-7456-4599-5(pb)

A catalogue record for this book is available from the British Library.

Typeset in 10.5 on 12 pt Sabon
by Servis Filmsetting Ltd, Stockport, Cheshire
Printed and bound by MPG Books Group, UK

The publisher has used its best endeavours to ensure that the URLs for external websites referred to in this book are correct and active at the time of going to press. However, the publisher has no responsibility for the websites and can make no guarantee that a site will remain live or that the content is or will remain appropriate.

Every effort has been made to trace all copyright holders, but if any have been inadvertently overlooked the publishers will be pleased to include any necessary credits in any subsequent reprint or edition.

For further information on Polity, visit our website: www.politybooks.com

Contents

Preface to the Second Edition

This is not the first introductory text which I have written on Islamic philosophy, which raises the obvious question of why there should be a need for another one, and by the same author. Whether, ultimately, this book has been worth the effort of writing and reading is of course something that the reader will have to decide; but from my point of view it has been worthwhile, because I have changed my ideas about some of the ways in which I formerly saw the main issues. In the past I had what seems to me now to be a rather narrow view of the discipline. I prioritized Islamic philosophy in the Peripatetic or Greek tradition, Islamic philosophy based on logic and the sort of analysis with which most philosophers in the Anglo-American world feel at home. I still think that this is the most important strain of Islamic philosophy; but I now think that the other two main schools – the mystical, or Sufi, school and the illuminationist, or ishraqi, school – produce interesting and important arguments that have to be assessed as parts of the whole enterprise. Ignoring these traditions does an injustice to the breadth of the enterprise of Islamic philosophy. In any case, very few of those writing within the Peripatetic tradition of *falsafa* restricted themselves to this type of writing; they merely saw it as playing a role in the rational understanding of our place in a world created by God – not the only role, but just one role among many others. Moreover, these other roles, especially those of mysticism or illuminationist thought, are also important ways in which we can know who we are and how far we can understand what is above us. I think it is true of any general philosophical movement that we go awry if we concentrate merely on one aspect of it. In this book I present a more rounded and comprehensive guide to the topic than I could have in the past.

Another difference from some of my earlier work is that I now think that it is not so obvious who the heroes and the villains are or were. It is not uncommon to point to 'conservatives' and 'progressives' in the Islamic world, just as today we can divide Muslims into 'traditionalists' and 'modernists'. Although in the past I always thought that the quality of the arguments of the opponents of philosophy was high, I thought that the arguments of the defenders of philosophy were higher. Now I am not so sure. It seems to me that often those Muslim thinkers who seek to emphasize their faith at the expense of what they see as philosophy produce better philosophical arguments than do the defenders of philosophy. I think this brings out nicely the ways in which Islamic philosophy is really part and parcel of the general working-out of the implications of Islam itself, as a consequence of which any attempt at artificially segregating philosophy from faith is too one-dimensional to do justice to Islamic philosophy. On the other hand, I have written this book on the assumption that one does not need to be committed to any particular religion, or indeed any religion at all, to understand Islamic philosophy. Nor does one have to know much about Islam itself. I have kept the technical vocabulary to a minimum, and have tried to explain whatever cultural and religious details are important for an understanding of Islamic philosophy. I have also on occasion used Islamic philosophy to pursue controversies in the modern Islamic world, to bring to the attention of the reader the contemporary relevance and interest of the ideas and arguments discussed within Islamic philosophy. Because I presuppose no knowledge of either Islam or philosophy, I start with a brief history of Islamic philosophy that also introduces the reader to some of the basic concepts of Islam, and throughout the text ideas in Islam and philosophy are discussed together. There are omissions from the book that should be found in a more comprehensive account of the topic, of course; logic in particular is a notable absentee, but I did not feel that this was a particularly appropriate topic for the general reader. Logic aside, I hope I have included most of the main categories of Islamic philosophy, and have given sufficient bibliographical details for those interested in pursuing the subject further.

Despite what I hope is a more inclusive account of Islamic philosophy than hitherto, there is no doubt about whom I regard as the major thinker in the subject, and that is Ibn Rushd (Averroes). I make no excuse for my choice, and hope that in this eight-hundredth anniversary of his death the exceptional interest of his arguments will impress the reader. The difficult life of Ibn Rushd, who brought forth great theoretical works while suffering intermittent political disruption, reminds those of us who work in more comfortable conditions of the essentially radical nature of the philosophical enterprise when it confronts, or even tries to coexist with, tradition.

I have added a couple of new chapters and generally updated what remains, but the structure of the book is similar to the first edition, in that this is not primarily a historical introduction to the topic but is rather based on topics and issues, very much how I see Islamic philosophy as needing to be done. Not of course that there is anything wrong with history, but it can be very limiting in its attitude to its subject matter, when that subject matter consists of arguments and debates. One of the new chapters looks at some modern Islamic philosophers, and here I have only been able to discuss a few of the relevant thinkers. The other considers the frequent assertion that Islam needs an enlightenment, and missed out on it, since this is primarily a philosophical claim, although it is often given a political and theological direction.

Many of the arguments in this book were originally presented to various audiences in different countries, and I must thank all those who made comments on such occasions, who are too many to enumerate, and especially the students with whom I have been privileged to work. No one is to be held responsible for my views here, of course, except their author.

Oliver Leaman
Lexington, 2009

Author's Note and Abbreviations

Dates are generally given in this form: AH / CE. AH refers to the *hijra*, when in 622 CE the Prophet Muhammad moved to Medina and established a political community. This marks the first Muslim year in the lunar calendar.

Transliteration from Arabic and Persian is partial, omitting diacritics and macrons, but otherwise using ordinary conventions.

Quotations from the Qur'an are generally from the Arberry version, with occasional alterations, and carry the normal form of references to the original text.

Readers should note that the dates provided for books relate to the date of publication, and not of course to when they were written.

The following abbreviation has been used:

A = Leaman (1997a), *Averroes and his Philosophy*, 2nd edn, Richmond: Curzon (1st edn, 1988, Oxford: Clarendon Press).

Glossary

For more detail on theological terms, see Leaman, O. (ed.), *The Qur'an: An Encyclopedia*, London: Routledge, and on philosophical terms, see Groff, P., in *Islamic Philosophy A–Z*, Edinburgh: Edinburgh University Press.

ahadith	Traditions, plural of *hadith*
'alam al-ghayb	hidden world
'alam al-khayal	world of imagination
'alam al-mithal	world of images
'alam al-shahada	visible world
anniya	being
'aql al-awwal	first intellect
'aql al-fa''al	active intellect
asalat al-wujud	priority of being
asbab al-nuzul	occasions of revelation
ayat	signs, verses of the Qur'an
barzakh	isthmus, passage between this world and the next
bi-la kayfa	without asking how
dar al-ahd	land of truce
dar al-aman	land of safety
dar al-harb	land of war
dar al-islam	land of Islam, i.e., peace
dar al-sulh	land of peace
dhat	essence
dhawq	taste

dhikr	remembrance
dhimmi	protected subject, i.e., non-Muslim
falasifa, falsafa, faylasuf	philosophers, philosophy, philosopher
fana'	annihilation
faqih	lawyer
fasad	corruption
fayd	emanation
fiqh	jurisprudence
fitra	innate nature; destiny
hadith	Tradition, report of something said by the Prophet or his Companions
	haqiqa truth
al-haraka al-jawhariya	substantial motion
harakat al-tanwir	enlightenment movement
haskala	enlightenment
hikma	wisdom, philosophy
hikma mashraqiya	Eastern wisdom
huwiyya	being
ihya'	revival
i'jaz al-qur'an	miracle of the Qur'an
ijma'	consensus
'ilm	knowledge
'ilm al-tasawwuf	mystical knowledge, science of mysticism
inhitat	decadence
insan al-kamil	perfect man, i.e., Muhammad
ishraqi	Illuminative (philosophy)
isnad	chain (of transmitters of *ahadith*)
isti'ghrab	occidentalism
jahada	struggle
jihad	a struggle, war
jihad al-nafs	struggle with the soul
jism al-khayali	imaginal bodies
kalam	theology
kana	being
kashf	unveiling, i.e., to open the heart to mystical illumination
khilafa	caliphate
ma'arifa	knowledge/esoteric knowledge
malaki	angelic
mashsha'i	Peripatetic (philosophy)
maskilim	enlightened, i.e., modern scholars
mawjud	existence

mutakallimun	theologians
nahda	(Arab) renaissance
nawabit	weeds
qalb	heart
qudsi	sacred
salaf, salafi	ancestors, original, i.e., orthodox
shari'a	religious law
shaykh	leader
shaykh al-ra'is	the first master
shi'at 'Ali	the party of Ali
shirk	idolatry
shura	consultation
al-sirat al-mustaqim	the straight path
sunna	tradition
surah	chapter of the Qur'an
tajdid	renewal
ta'lim	education
taqlid	imitation
tasawwur	conception
tasdiq	assent, judgement
tashkik	equivocation
tashkik al-wujud	equivocality of being
tawhid	unity
ta'wil	interpretation
umma	community
'ulama	scholars
usul	principles
velayet-i faqih	rule by the clergy
wahdat al-shuhud	unity of consciousness
wahdat al-wujud	unity of being
wali	friend

I

A Short History of Islamic Philosophy

Adherents of religion often start off by thinking that the religion provides everything they need in order to understand reality. Not practical or scientific knowledge, perhaps, but certainly knowledge of how to live and what the real nature of the world is (Islam does also provide scientific information in the view of some believers, see Shamsher Ali 2006). It is interesting to speculate about why a religious movement should feel the need to take on systems of theoretical thought which come from outside that movement. After all, many such movements possess a considerable theoretical machinery of their own. Believers might well feel that there is enough within the system of thought of Islam itself to encompass any conceptual problems or issues which could arise. Within the system of Islam itself there exists, first and foremost, the Qur'an, with its detailed analysis of the nature of reality and its advice to readers. The Qur'an stresses that it is written in a simple Arabic and the implication is that it is then not difficult to understand (19: 97; 54: 17). Then there exist for many Muslims the practices (*sunna*) of the Prophet and his Companions, and his community (*umma*), while for others there is the continuing guidance of a spiritual leader (imam). The former acquire their name of Sunni Muslims from the fact that they are committed to using the reports of the practices of the Prophet and his close Companions as a source of information about how to behave. The latter are the Shi'ites, or Shi'i, who derive their name from the term *shi'at 'Ali* (the party of 'Ali), because they pay particular attention to the Prophet's son-in-law, 'Ali, and his successors as sources of spiritual knowledge (Muhajirani 1996; Lalani 2006). As sources of authority there are also the traditions (*ahadith*, sing. *hadith*) that reproduce important sayings of the Prophet and his Companions, and a methodology for distinguishing between reliable and suspect traditions. On this basis, a superstructure of theology (*kalam*) was constructed, which investigates the theoretical problems in understanding the combination of all the former techniques, and jurisprudence (*fiqh*), which specifies what actions are acceptable or otherwise. Finally, there is the grammar of the Arabic language, the language in which the Qur'an itself was transmitted, the speech of God himself, so crucially important for understanding the meaning of the message in the text. It is hardly surprising that many Muslims felt, and continue to feel, that there is more than enough within Islam and its systems of knowledge, often called the Islamic sciences, to deal with any problem which might arise, and hence that there is no need for any additional source of theoretical information to be employed. This is a common reaction of adherents to many religions which have a sophisticated system of explanation, who, as a result, resent the idea of going outside the religion in order to resolve theoretical and even practical problems (Leaman 1988b, 2000c).

The growth of Islam

Once the Islamic empire expanded into areas of the Middle East which were imbued with Greek culture, the question immediately arose as to whether any use could be found for that culture. A similar issue arose with the conquests in the East, which brought the Islamic world into contact with Indian and Persian cultures (Nomanul Haq 1996). This is not just an issue about what sorts of knowledge are useful and important but even more, perhaps, about identity. Is the identity of Muslims so self-sufficient that they do not need any theoretical information from outside Islam itself? Obviously not, since there is a lot of information which is neutral in religious terms, but which it is important to know. However, there are also many theoretical issues where Islamic and Greek thought seem to be in opposition or, at the least, offer answers which are different. Even where they agree, Islamic and Greek thought stem from distinct bases, so any concurrence between them might appear to be a matter of chance. Where Islam conflicts with any other theoretical system, the conclusion for a Muslim seems to be obvious: that the other system must be rejected.

This is not the conclusion that was always drawn, though. Greek philosophy is so powerful in what it can do and explain that it proved a temptation too powerful to resist. Why not, then, just incorporate it in the Islamic view of the nature of reality? One reason not to do this would be if aspects of that philosophy contradicted Islam in some way; but, as we shall see, it was often argued that such contradictions were more apparent than real. Another reason would be the xeno-phobic one of rejecting the foreign, of asserting a specifically Islamic identity that excludes other cultural frameworks, except perhaps those of the other people of the Book. The other people of the Book are generally taken to be the Christians and the Jews, although on occasion other religions have also been included, their allegiance to a book based on an earlier prophecy providing them with a higher status in the Islamic world than those entirely bereft of prophecy. There were, and continue to be today, powerful political and cultural forces which seek to reject knowledge from non-Islamic sources. On the other hand, there were, and are, Muslims who are so confident of their identity as Muslims that they are prepared to consider using alternative methodologies in combination with their religious beliefs to throw light on the structure of reality. They are relaxed enough about their identity to take on board the idea that other ways of viewing the world may be significant and should be explored. Since they often operate within a context in which their peers do not share their attitudes on this, they have to be careful how they express themselves and what sort of audience they are likely to have. But this problem can be, and often has been, exaggerated (Leaman 1980a). Islamic philosophers, like philosophers everywhere, wrote in ways that they hoped would resonate with their local intellectual com-munities. They naturally expressed themselves as Muslims, or within a Christian or Jewish context, and used the language and culture of their religion to explore and explain ideas and arguments that were often originally mediated by Greek thought.

Neoplatonism

One of the interesting aspects of the influence of Greek thought on Islamic philosophy is the application of a form of Neoplatonism, which was the leading way of doing philosophy within what was left of the Greek cultural realm. Since Neoplatonism is rather different from the thought of Plato and Aristotle themselves, it is intriguing to see those two philosophers credited with ideas which are in fact very different from those we now know them to have proffered. A particularly popular work at the time was the so-called *Theology of Aristotle*, which was in fact part of Plotinus's *Enneads* plus some additions. In any case, it is far better to talk of Neoplatonisms rather than Neoplatonism, since the latter was far from a definitive system with a common party line. Although many Neoplatonists were atheists, Neoplatonism does as a doctrine fit rather neatly into religion, especially a religion such as Islam. For instance, there is an emphasis on the existence of one supreme being or principle, out of which everything else emerges in such a way as not to interfere with the absolute unity of the One. This philosophical issue mimics a theological problem in Islam: namely, how we should link the one God of revelation with the multiplicity of existence without compromising God's absolute perfection and self-subsistence. Can we even say that God has properties, or is this to associate God with other things, the sin of idolatry (*shirk*)? There were heated theological debates around this issue, so it is hardly surprising that the language of Neoplatonism struck a chord within Islamic culture (Leaman 2002).

One of the problems with Neoplatonism from a religious point of view is that it does not treat seriously the idea of God creating the world out of nothing at a particular time. On the contrary, creation is generally identified with emanation (*fayd*), a continual process of generation which has no beginning or end, and which is automatic. This picture of the natural world has everything connected with everything else in a determined way, and this pattern of determination is necessary from a logical point of view. That is, at least at the higher levels of reality, the way in which interaction takes place is determined by the most rational way in which it can take place. It is pretty obvious that this is going to cause problems with the traditional Islamic notion of God, but it is worth pointing to the advantages of this sort of philosophical theory. It does trace the production and reproduction of everything back to a source and a single source at that, and it establishes a rational structure behind the universe. Thus the various Neoplatonic thinkers did provide a suitable set of principles for use by Muslim thinkers, albeit those principles often clashed with Islam itself. What is important, though, is not so much whether there is agreement between Neoplatonism, in whatever form, and Islam, but whether both systems of thought speak a language with some common points (Morewedge 1995).

A point that many commentators on Islamic philosophy make about its use of Neoplatonism is that it reproduces the syncretism of that doctrine or, rather, series of related doctrines. Neoplatonism appears to be a less 'pure' theory as compared with the philosophy of Plato and Aristotle, for example; in addition, Islamic thinkers often shared a great deal of interest in philosophers such as Empedocles and

Pythagoras. It is said that there was an attempt to make many of these thinkers, who actually had quite disparate views, agree on central philosophical points. This does not accurately describe the situation, however, despite the existence of occasional texts that did try to link the different Greek thinkers in ways that do not reflect their real views. There were eclectic thinkers, and it is worth mentioning here the Ikhwan al-Safa', the Brethren of Purity (fourth or fifth to tenth or eleventh centuries), who constructed an encyclopaedic work which discussed a route to spiritual liberation through philosophical perfection (Netton 1982, 1996). There were other thinkers like al-Farabi who occasionally explored the scope for agreement in Plato and Aristotle; but Islamic philosophy entailed far more than just combining the ideas and arguments of the various Greek thinkers. Overall, a very real attempt was made to group the varying arguments in Greek philosophy into common positions, then analyse the strength and weakness of those positions, while at the same time relating those arguments to contemporary issues in Islam. Far from it being the case that Islamic philosophers were unable to distinguish Plato from Aristotle, they were able even to distinguish Plato from Socrates, often regarding the latter as a more spiritual thinker as compared to both Plato and Aristotle (Alon 1991).

Major thinkers

Al-Kindi (died between 252/866 and 260/873) is often called the first philosopher of the Arabs, and he followed a Neoplatonic path, albeit attempting to argue for the creation of the world as against the theory of constant production and reproduction. He was working at a time when the philosophical curriculum and vocabulary were still being constructed, and it is noticeable how difficult he sometimes found it to express a point that he wished to make. The Arabic language of his time had not yet really taken on board the sorts of distinctions which were later to become commonplace in theoretical discussion (Klein-Franke 1996; Kennedy-Day 2003). He was followed by a group of philosophers centred on Baghdad that reached its acme in al-Farabi (b. c.257/870), a thinker who was highly influential on subsequent thought (Black 1996; Fakhry 2004). Al-Farabi not only established the sorts of topics which were going to be the focus of Islamic philosophy for the next few centuries; he also played a large part in refining the vocabulary, to enable it to be used far more subtly than had been the case up to his time. He provided the theoretical basis for an aspect of Islamic philosophy which is not going to be explored in any depth in this book, but which was very important, the study of logic (Street 2005). A great deal of the Greek work that was translated into Arabic dealt with logic, and this was greeted with great initial enthusiasm in the Arabic-speaking world. For one thing, it could be used in debates with non-Muslims in an attempt to persuade them of the merits of Islam through rational debate. Second, it fitted well with the translation project's concentration on scientific manuscripts, since logic seeks to organize our ideas on the topic of thinking itself, while natural science organizes the phenomena of nature systematically.

Perhaps the most controversial aspect of logic was that it seemed to challenge what had hitherto been taken to be the leading role of grammar as an explanation of how language works. Since the grammar of the Arabic language is the grammar of the language that God used in transmitting his final revelation, it was taken to represent formally the structure of what can be said and how it can be said. The miracle of the Qur'an (i'jaz al-qur'an) lies to a degree in the language itself, and one of the proofs of Islam is taken to be the purity and beauty of the form of expression of the text itself. It is hardly surprising, therefore, that the grammar of that language is accorded high status as an explanatory vehicle also. Al-Farabi argued that grammar did not really represent deep structure; it merely expressed the rules for the surface structure of the language, and even more basic than these rules are the principles of logic itself. This became a highly controversial topic, and it is not difficult to see why. The argument was really about power. Who has access to the more profound analysis of language, the grammarian or the logician? If al-Farabi was right, then the grammarians were dethroned from their previous crucial role. All they could comment on were the particular rules of an individual language, while the logicians could establish the principles of any and every language (Abed 1991; Mahdi 1970). This represented the spirit of the philosophers over the next few centuries, a spirit of ambition and confidence in their ability to express rationally the basic principles upon which all other forms of thought and expression are built.

An especially creative thinker who followed in this tradition was Ibn Sina (Avicenna) (370/980–429/1037). It is impossible to summarize his huge corpus, but for our purposes what is of particular interest is his development of the argument that the universe (apart from God) consists entirely of determined and necessitated events (Goodman 1992; Inati 1996b). God is the exception; God is the only thing that is not brought about by something else; and he represents the starting point of the series of causes and effects which make up the structure of reality. Now, this sounds quite compatible with religion; yet, when one looks a bit more closely, one sees that Ibn Sina does not leave God much of a role. God does not know about the world of generation and corruption – our world – since transitory and material events cannot be apprehended by an eternal and perfect consciousness. God cannot change anything in existence, since whatever happens does so because of something else causing it to happen, and although God is the nominal ultimate cause, he does not really seem to have the power to do anything to interfere with how things will turn out anyway. This attitude to the deity led to the fierce attack on philosophy by al-Ghazali (450/1058–505/1111), which is commonly credited with having destroyed it (Campanini 1996). Al-Ghazali brought two main charges against philosophy, both of which are interesting. The first is that philosophy offends against its own principles, since it cannot establish its conclusions on the basis of its premises. Second, philosophy is irreconcilable with religion, since the former leaves no room for the latter. That is, however much the philosophers may talk about God, they treat him as the name for a vacuous notion, since they give him nothing to do.

It is wrong to think of al-Ghazali as having brought philosophy to an end within the Islamic world, although it is true that after his attack philosophy fell into disrepute in much of the west of the Islamic world. He was answered by perhaps the greatest Islamic philosopher in the West, Ibn Rushd (Averroes) (520/1126–595/1198), the best representative of Andalusi thought (Urvoy 1996). Within al-Andalus (the Muslim part of the Iberian peninsula) a particularly significant strain of philosophy flourished. It will be argued later that there is a specifically Andalusi character to philosophy, and here we will only skim the surface of thinkers such as Ibn Bajja (d. 537/1138) and Ibn Tufayl (d. 581/1185–6), philosophers who both pursued the Peripatetic tradition, yet also placed it within a broader philosophical context (Goodman 1996a, c). The latter's *Hayy ibn Yaqzan* (Living Son of the Awake), which will be discussed later, provides an account of how an individual in complete isolation can use intellect alone to understand the important things about reality, knowledge which is later shown to be in accordance with the details of revelation. Ibn Rushd set out to refute al-Ghazali's critique, and at the same time tried to refine philosophy. That is, he tried to return it to its Aristotelian roots, since he suspected that a good deal of the curriculum up to his time was infected (in his view) by Neoplatonic and Avicennan impurities. His main contribution to Islamic philosophy, and to philosophy in Christian and Jewish Europe, is the thesis that there are different routes to the same truth, and that all these routes are equally acceptable. The theory of meaning on which this is based is highly original and rich in its metaphysical implications, as we shall see.

Ibn Rushd is unusual in the world of Islamic philosophy in that he is one of the very few thinkers who was at best neutral about mysticism (Urvoy 1998). Most Peripatetic thinkers found no difficulty in combining their Greek-style philosophy with the mystical tradition. This is put nicely by Ibn Sina when he compares Peripatetic philosophy with what he calls 'oriental' philosophy, the idea being that the latter is far more significant than the former (Nasr 1996a). That is, Peripatetic thought exists within a more limited perspective than the sort of wisdom that is capable of putting its followers in experiential touch with the source of reality. So Peripatetic (*mashsha'i*) philosophy is often regarded as a part of the wider *hikma*, or wisdom, or as an alternative form of organized thought. This idea of there being alternative routes to knowledge is an important one within Islamic intellectual life, and many thinkers start their intellectual biographies by running briefly through the options which they saw as available to them. For example, al-Ghazali states in his work *Munqidh min al-dalal* (What Saves from Error):

> I came to regard the various seekers (after truth) as comprising four groups: (i) The Theologians (*mutakallimun*), who claim that they are the exponents of thought and intellectual speculations; (ii) the Batiniyah, who consider that they, as the party of 'authoritative instruction' (*ta'lim*), alone derive truth from an infallible Imam; (iii) the Philosophers, who regard themselves as the exponents of logic and demonstration; (iv) the Sufis or Mystics, who claim that they alone enter into the 'presence' (of God) and possess vision and intuitive understanding. (1953: 267)

These groups should not be seen as necessarily exclusive, of course; but what this sort of proposition does is to set out the varieties of intellectual routes that were seen as available. Thinkers would be expected to make a conscious decision about which route they were going to take, and why. Al-Ghazali is quite right in explaining these alternatives in ways that emphasize their competing claims to authority. But there is no reason why a particular thinker should not combine all four approaches, and many did.

Sufism, as a form of mysticism, became very important in Islamic philosophy, sometimes as an alternative to other kinds of philosophy, and sometimes as an accompaniment (Nasr 1996c; Kılıç 1996). Al-Ghazali did a great deal to make Sufism respectable, but its systematization was really initiated by Ibn al-'Arabi (560/1164–638/1240).

The whole point of mysticism is to provide a taste (*dhawq*) of ultimate reality, and there has been a wide variety of accounts of how to do this. One of the most powerful mystical traditions in Islamic philosophy is found in Isma'ili thought, the sort of thought referred to in al-Ghazali's statement above as supporting *ta'lim* (Nasir Khusraw 1998; al-Din Tusi 1998; Nanji 1996). The imam, the spiritual and intellectual guide of the community, is able to understand the meaning of the message of God, and communicates that meaning to his followers. There is no route to the real meaning of the message except through the imam; only he has access to the appropriate form of interpretation (*ta'wil*) which reveals its inner (*batin*) nature. Persian thinkers were often concerned to differentiate their approach to reality from Sufism; so, instead of calling their approach *'ilm al-tasawwuf* (which would identify it too closely with Sufism), they sometimes used the expression *'ilm al-'irfan*, the science of gnosis. The Sufis came in for a great deal of criticism for their antinomian tendencies – that is, for the idea that once one knew how to experience ultimate reality, one did not need to obey the rules and regulations of public religion. However, there are a lot of similarities between the Shi'i, and in particular the Isma'ili, accounts of the approach to mystical truth and that described by the Sufis. The Isma'ilis insist on the necessity of a guide, the imam, and the Sufis on a spiritual leader, a *shaykh*.

One of the main topics of concern to those interested in mysticism is the nature of *tawhid*, or the unity of God. Ibn Sab'in (b. 614/1217) used this concept as the basis of his attack on Aristotelian logic. The trouble with such a system of classification, he argues, is that it breaks down and makes distinctions within what is essentially one, a reflection of the unity of God. Logic implies the acceptability of knowledge that is other than knowledge of God, so must be ruled out. It is worth pointing out that the reason for ruling out logic is itself logical – that it does not produce knowledge of God, so does not produce knowledge (Taftazani and Leaman 1996). These reflections on the nature of unity are very much discussed also in the works of Ibn al-'Arabi, who produces the doctrine of *wahdat al-wujud*, the unity of being, as the only feasible implication of the unity of God (Chittick 1996a).

These arguments were countered by Ahmad Sirhindi (971/1564–1033/1624) with his doctrine of *wahdat al-shuhud*, the unity of consciousness. According to Ibn al-'Arabi, God and the world are identical, so that when we differentiate between them, we are just adopting an uncritical way of speaking which does not capture the true state of reality. Sirhindi argues, by contrast, that God and nature are distinct, and that the latter is a reflection of aspects of the former. Shah Waliullah of Delhi (1114/1703–1176/1762), the outstanding

Muslim thinker of the Indian subcontinent, argued that this debate was really more about language than about philosophical concepts, and that these two views are easily reconcilable (Kemal and Kemal 1996). As we shall see, the notion of being was an extremely controversial one in Islamic philosophy.

An interesting blend of mystical and Peripatetic philosophy was initiated by al-Suhrawardi (549/1154–587/1191), the originator of *ishraqi*, or illuminationist philosophy (Ziai 1996a, c). The point of the word 'illumination' is to bring out the idea that if we perfect ourselves, we put ourselves in a position to be illuminated by the principle, or source, of reality. Al-Suhrawardi replaced the notion of reality as consisting of objects with a view of reality in terms of varying degrees of light; he saw real knowledge as occurring when we are illuminated by light which derives from the source of light itself, the source of reality. This does not in any way oppose Peripatetic thought, which is accepted as a valid approach to conceptual knowledge, albeit limited to that sort of knowledge (and it is worth pointing out that al-Suhrawardi criticized, on logical grounds, many aspects of Aristotelianism). Illuminationist philosophy is able to go further than this; it argues, and provides immediate and perfect knowledge (Amin Razavi 1997; Ha'iri Yazdi 1992).

In the western part of the Islamic world, philosophy came very much under a cloud after the attack of al-Ghazali, and did not reappear in any significant sense until the nineteenth century, with the inauguration of the *Nahda*, or renaissance (Abu Rabiʿ 1996). In the East, however, it continued, and continues today, in an unbroken tradition of commentary and supplementation (Amin Razavi 1996). The major figures who influenced this Eastern pursuit of philosophy were Ibn Sina, al-Suhrawardi and Ibn al-ʿArabi. The outstanding intellectual movement was the School of Isfahan, whose foremost thinkers were Mir Damad (d.1041/1631) and Mulla Sadra (979/80/1571/2–1050/1640) (Dabashi 1996a, b; Ziai 1996b; Nasr 1996f). This school of thought followed classical illuminationist lines, but really made some very creative points about the nature of Islamic metaphysics, as we shall see. In contemporary Persian philosophy the influence of the School of Isfahan is very important, and its thought is often combined with some version of the thought of Ibn al-ʿArabi and his followers. A good example of how integrated this kind of thought has become in modern Iran is provided by the figure of the spiritual and political leader of the Islamic revolution, Khumayni (Khomeini), who was himself a not inconsiderable philosopher within the tradition of thought which flourished in Iran. As a member of the School of Qom, he participated in a philosophical movement that sought to challenge the ubiquity of Western thought, yet which at the same time was very open to ideas and concepts from Western philosophy. Even modern thinkers such as Said Nursi (1877–1960), the important theologian in Turkey, felt the need to refute the idea that what he regarded as the materialist Western philosophical approach should replace Islam.

Of course, the impression that Europe was seeking to dominate the Islamic world intellectually as well as physically contributed to this suspicion of Western philosophy, and the latter's generally secular ideology can easily be viewed as an attempt to persuade the Muslim intellectual of the irrelevance of Islam along with the other religions. Nursi presents powerful arguments, albeit more theological than philosophical in tone, to refute the arguments of the philosophers, and to insist on the divine nature of the world. This provides evidence of a long-standing influence which philosophy has had on the Islamic world, in that even those who are opposed to the conclusions and methodology of philosophy will nonetheless use philosophy to try to establish their point. Or at the very least philosophy will be identified as a problematic area of enquiry, raising issues and, more importantly, doubts that need to be isolated and refuted.

Within contemporary philosophy in the Islamic world, a whole variety of schools of thought exist; moreover, the discipline received a huge boost from the impact of earlier thinkers such as al-Afghani (1838–97) and Muhammad 'Abduh (1849–1905) who took on the modernist agenda of trying to link Islam with forms of life suited to modern scientific society. The debate between Islam and modernity has been something of an ongoing topic in the last century or so, and the Indian thinker Muhammad Iqbal (1877–1938) made an original contribution to it. The controversy entails coming to a new understanding of the past, in order to revive Islamic culture from what is seen as a period of decadence, and then linking this new perspective to the major achievements of modern Western civilization. It is no exaggeration to say that a large part of the most interesting work carried out this century in the Arab world deals with reactions to the West. This should not be taken as a patronizing description since much earlier Western philosophy, by which is meant here philosophy in the Christian and Jewish worlds, was structured in terms of its relationship with Islamic philosophy, in particular the metaphysics of Ibn Sina and the theory of meaning evolved by Ibn Rushd. Perhaps the best-known Islamic philosopher today is Seyyed Hossein Nasr, a Persian thinker living in the United States, who has criticized Western thought and science for their atomistic and material bias. He argues for the significance of the mystical tradition within world religions, as a counter to the scientism of the West, and has shown in detail how sophisticated the mystical tradition within Islam is.

It may be that in the future this discussion of the confrontation with modernity will be regarded as overdone, but there is no denying its continuing fascination within the Islamic world. As at the beginning of the meeting of Islam with the rest of the world, a question of identity arises. How can Islam preserve its distinctiveness while acquiring much of the culture of the non-Islamic world? Should Islam reject foreign cultures, or should it incorporate them within its structure? A distinction between the situation now and that of a thousand years ago is that then Islam was full of confidence, as a result of continuing military and political successes, and perhaps could take on a more variegated identity as a result. Today Muslims are often on the defensive, seeing themselves as living in the wake of a long period of decline, in a cultural climate that may not be appropriate for philosophical creativity. However, the history of Islamic philosophy reveals it to be a highly creative, significant aspect of the discipline of philosophy as a whole, and we shall see in the rest of the book how intriguing many of the arguments of the philosophers in the Islamic world are.

2

Main Controversies

What is Islamic philosophy?

It might seem strange, but it is often felt necessary first of all to define the precise nature of Islamic philosophy (Nasr 1996b). It is always a rather worrying feature of an area of enquiry when its practitioners spend a lot of time trying to justify what they do; but it can also reveal that those practitioners have taken seriously the conceptual problems involved in what they are doing. Some would argue that philosophy and religion are so different in nature that there cannot be a philosophy of a particular religion. There can certainly be a philosophy of religion, and a theology of a particular religion, but not a philosophy of a particular religion. After all, philosophy deals in generalities, in concepts with universal validity, and we cannot expect it to be of use when dealing with a particular religion. There is also the problem that a particular religion will hold certain propositions to be true on the basis of factors that are quite specific to that religion, and not generalizable. The standards of proof and truth in religion and philosophy are quite distinct, and so the notion of Islamic philosophy seems to be something of an oxymoron.

The position is not that serious, though. We can make a fairly sharp distinction between philosophy and theology even within a particular religious context. Theology relates to the particular principles of a religion, while philosophy is more general, dealing with the arguments which have been produced within the context of that religion that are universal (Leaman 2008). In fact, this distinction was frequently made by Islamic philosophers themselves. The idea of arguments being produced within the context of a religion is taken quite broadly in this book, to include all philosophical arguments and trends produced in the cultural context of Islam, not only those by Muslims. There is certainly a potential conflict between religion and philosophy; and, indeed, that became an often discussed topic within Islamic philosophy itself, though that should not be taken to rule out the possibility of an Islamic philosophy. If those thinkers were to abandon rational argument because it seemed to end up in conclusions contrary to those of faith, then they could hardly be referred to as philosophers. What makes them philosophers and interesting philosophers at that is their ability to use rational argument to defend their views and attack competing views.

In approaching philosophy stemming from a cultural context with which one is initially unfamiliar, there is a tendency to see it as being either very much the same as the sort of philosophy which one does know something about, or as very different. For instance, there is a widespread belief in the West that Indian philosophy consists entirely of discussions among mystically inclined thinkers about issues relating to salvation. So if someone refers to a particular Indian thinker as a philosopher, many would snort derisively. In recent years, however, understanding of Indian philosophy has become far better known, and one can only be impressed with the extraordinary conceptual richness of the material it contains. It is certainly the case that much of it is closely connected with particular religions, but not to the extent that this interferes with the rigour of the arguments or the universality of the conclusions (Leaman 1999a; Smart 2008). Many people I meet who find out that I write on Islamic philosophy give me a rather strange and nervous look, and wonder how fanatical Muslims, who have become the stereotype of all Muslims, can possibly have any interest in philosophy. The very negative stereotypes of Islam today in what is often called the West are frequently applied to everything labelled Islamic. For some reason, those within the Islamic world who carry out terrorist murders for some declared religious motive are labelled 'Islamists', while Catholics and Orthodox Christians in the former Yugoslavia, for example, who perform similar deeds are not called 'Christianists'. Westerners tend to operate with quite simple cultural descriptions – Indians are other-worldly, Muslims are aggressive, Chinese are practical – and their views of these people's philosophies are correspondingly impoverished.

Although in this book I am discussing aspects of Islamic philosophy only, it is with the attitude that it is high time that those of us whose primary philosophical orientation is to the Anglo-American or continental traditions learned a lot more about the character and riches of other traditions (Leaman 1998a). It is rather strange to suggest that Islamic philosophy is alien to the Western traditions of philosophy, because Islamic philosophy has been so strongly influenced by Greek thought, and in turn has had much influence on the development of philosophy in Christian Europe. It is worth pointing out that many of the sources of Islamic philosophy are to be found in the links between the growth of the religion of Islam and Greek culture (Peters 1996; Shayegan 1996). This is not in any way to disparage what one might see as the philosophical character of the original Islamic texts themselves. Within the Qur'an and the other sources of the religion there exists a great deal of material which is highly philosophical in the sense that it raises theoretical issues which explicitly call for a rational response. I do not know if it is ever useful to rank systems of thought with respect to rationality, or whether it is plausible to think of rationality as a universal concept, but were this to be done, there is little doubt that Islam would score highly. There are many references to the importance of knowledge and reason in the Qur'an (Mohamed 2006), and Islam seems to take pride, at least in its early years, in presenting itself as highly rational. What this implied was that people approaching Islam should use analytical reason in assessing the religion, in the sense that they should consider whether what the religion regarded as evidence for its truth is in fact evidence. We need to remember that Islam had to persuade members of other religions, and of none, to accept its validity, and what grounds could there be for such acceptance except reason? Force, after all, is officially ruled out, although it was often employed, and Islam is not very enthusiastic about miracles, except for the miracle of its own form and matter. We often pay inadequate attention to the significant ways in which religions emphasize reason, preferring to set up a faith versus religion conflict which often owes more to a particular period of religion than to its nature as a whole. The original Islamic sciences, the study of the Qur'an, the traditions, grammar, jurisprudence and theology, are highly rational in structure (Nasr 1996g) – hence the early bitter debate between the enthusiasts for the new thinking of philosophy and the advocates of the Islamic sciences. This is not, it is important to grasp, a debate between philosophy and religion, but rather a debate between two different ways of reasoning.

It is interesting to speculate on the motivation behind the original push to translate Greek philosophy into Arabic. To a certain extent it came in on the coat-tails of works about science and technology, practical texts which directly showed how life could be made better and healthier (Leaman 1999b). Within Greek culture a sharp distinction was rarely made between the natural sciences and philosophy, and the latter was introduced into the Arabic world along with the former. This was not entirely fortuitous, though, since it was thought that the same remarkable culture that had produced natural science of such quality must also have produced rules of thought worth studying. We should remember that at the time Muslims were seeking to persuade others of the truths of their religion, and for this they had to debate with followers of other religions who had at their disposal the very sophisticated toolkit of Greek logic. It is hardly surprising that Muslims should have sought to use that logic against those who had used it against them. Only that type of logic would work when arguing with those who were used to its employment. The problem was that it proved impossible to use this form of reasoning only against one group of non-believers. Why not also use it within Islam itself, since it represents a highly effective and powerful form of thought?

There are a variety of sources of Islamic philosophy, and a range of ways of interpreting it. In this book the notion of Islamic philosophy will be identified with a range of theoretical issues which arise within thought and which are often closely linked with theological and religious controversies. From the early years of Islam a number of important conceptual difficulties arose which clearly represent philosophical problems, although they were not always recognized as such. It is important to realize that, like all religions, Islam leaves wide scope for interpretation of the appropriate religious understanding of a whole range of topics. We are not going to concentrate on theology here, but for an appropriate understanding of Islamic philosophy it is important to have some grasp of the main issues in Islamic theology. Philosophy often emerges out of what were originally theological disputes, and we shall see that many theological debates are highly philosophical in nature.

The first source of argument within any religion is the nature of the source of authority. How can we tell whether something or someone is to be regarded as relevant from a religious point of view? Who has the right to expect to be obeyed or followed within the religion? These are far from arbitrary questions, since satisfactory answers will determine the whole basis of the religion.

The particular role of the Pope in Roman Catholicism is a case in point, as is the Talmud in orthodox Judaism. One might wonder why the basic religious text is not enough. Why do we need to look to other areas of authority? This inevitably leads us into disputes about what counts as an authority. The answer is that, however clear and useful the basic text, it requires interpreting if we are going to apply it to all aspects of our lives, and to every contingency which may arise in the future. The Qur'an is no exception here. It is a beautiful and often very clear text; yet it equally often calls for interpretation if one wants to discover the point of a particular passage. In any case, the views of the Qur'an on issues which are not found explicitly in it – say, on fertility treatment for childless couples – obviously need to be determined by argument based on what is there. How can one tell the difference between good and poor arguments on such a point? How does one know whom to trust in producing such arguments? What additional sources can one consult in trying to discover the true Muslim path, which is often referred to as the 'straight path' by Muslim thinkers?

Apart from the Qur'an, a good deal of reliance may be placed on the *sunna*, which is often translated 'tradition'. The Tradition refers to the ways of the Prophet and his close Companions, the sorts of things that he did and said, and these are a source of inspiration and information for those who come after him and wish to know how to act. Such accounts are found in vast bodies of reports known as *hadith*, which describe what was said or done on particular occasions. As one might expect, the reliability of some of these reports is rather dubious; but there is a methodology often called a science for working out which are the more reliable that is accepted by many Muslims, and each *hadith* has an *isnad*, a line of transmission which represents its provenance, its route from the Prophet or one of his close Companions to the time at which it was formally noted and written down. As with all attributions of authorship, the reliability of such reports is sometimes challenged, and arguments are provided for replacing them with other reports which perhaps give a different answer to the particular issue being discussed.

On the basis of the Qur'an and the Traditions, the principles of Islamic law (*shari'a*) arose. This law regulates the interactions of people with each other, and with God. From an ethical point of view, it recognizes five kinds of action: the obligatory, the meritorious, the neutral, the reprehensible and the forbidden. While there is broad agreement about the moral character of some activities, there is also wide disagreement about the precise moral nature of other activities, which is discussed within the schools of jurisprudence (*fiqh*). These differ in many ways, but their attitudes concerning how to conduct legal argument are of particular interest here. Some schools support the use of logical methods of argument – in particular, analogy from one case to another – while others are far more restrictive on what they accept as an appropriate hermeneutical technique. Some accept innovations, while others do not. The schools also differ on the precise nature of acceptable legal reasoning, so they each presuppose a philosophical position of some sort on the issue of how to proceed argumentatively from a particular set of initial premises. Many of these controversies tie in with particular theological problems, such as whether the Qur'an is created in time (by God) or whether it is eternal.

Perhaps the most significant conflict between those who take different positions on the nature of authority is that between the Sunnis and the Shi'is. The Sunnis, as their name suggests, base their interpretation of authority on the traditional view (in their opinion) that such authority reposes in the consensus (*ijma'*) of the community (sometimes interpreted as the community of scholars or religious leaders), as well as in the Qur'an and the Traditions. Consensus may be invoked to select the religious leaders of the community, as it was in the case of the first four caliphs, ranging from Abu Bakr to 'Ali ibn Abi Taleb (10/632–41/661). The Shi'is disagree, and claim that the only valid successor of the Prophet was 'Ali, For them, authority reposes in the Qur'an, the Traditions (of which they have their own compilation) and the unbroken train of spiritual successors of the Prophet. The notion of a hidden imam, or religious authority, is important for many Shi'ites, and they repose confidence in the figures who are taken to be in communication with this individual. The majority of Muslims are Sunni, while about one in seven are Shi'i, and the latter are further subdivided into different groups that interpret the source of religious authority in a variety of ways.

All Muslims accept five main principles of religion. The first is the unity (*tawhid*) of God, which is far from an uncomplicated notion, as we shall see. They also accept that there is a chain of prophets or messengers of God, a day of judgement and a resurrection. The Shi'i add to this list of *usul*, or principles, the existence of the imamate and a belief in the justice of God. Following from these principles are the belief in Muhammad as the Prophet of God, and for the Shi'i in 'Ali as the prince of the believers, the performance of daily prayers, fasting during the month of Ramadan, pilgrimage to Mecca, payment of taxes for the poor (and for some of the Shi'i financial support for the descendants of the Prophet), together with the importance of struggle (*jihad*), to spread the message of Islam. This last should not be confused with holy war, with which it is sometimes identified, since this is only one aspect of it. There are two types of *jihad*, and the greater *jihad* is the struggle that we all have to undertake to reassert our basically spiritual nature in the face of the claims of the material and secular world.

These religious principles and their implementation led to a variety of legal and theological controversies over their interpretation right from the start of Islam. Many of the questions that arose were philosophical without anyone even realizing it. For example, the arguments about the nature of divine unity often dealt with the difficulties of relating a completely simple being to a highly complex creation. If the principle of reality is one, why is it that there is more than one thing in existence? Why would one cause bring about so many different effects? If God is the ultimate cause of everything, how can we speak of our bringing things about also? Surely what we think we do is merely a reflection of something that he does. Does this mean, then, that we cannot really act at all? If God knows everything, does he know that I am going to write this even before I do? If so, am I free not to write it? More importantly, is the sinner able to avoid sin? And, if not, what is the justice in punishing him or her for it? These sorts of issues were debated with considerable theoretical sophistication in the early years of Islam; but it was not until some time later that they came in for a technical philosophical treatment.

The engagement with philosophy came about when the Islamic conquests reached the centres of civilization in the Middle East which were within the ambit of Greek culture. The expansion into what is today Syria and Iraq meant contact with highly sophisticated Christians and Jews, and the conquest of Persia involved encounters with Zoroastrianism, and led to the necessity to debate and argue with the intellectual representatives of these faiths. The latter used the techniques of Greek philosophy in their arguments and literature, so the Islamic conquerors had to acquire this also if they were to argue on an equal level. Philosophy was only part of the exciting cultural spoils; a whole range of knowledge was available in the new territories, dealing with engineering, natural science, mathematics, astronomy and astrology, and medicine. The new rulers could have ignored all this knowledge, arguing that it was inessential and poor compared to the truths of Islam, and some obviously took this line, as we shall see when we look at the debates between the logicians and the grammarians. But, on the whole, there was enthusiasm among the governing classes for the new knowledge, which was, in reality, very old (often referred to in Arabic as *al-'ulum al-awa'il*, the first sciences) and this was encouraged by a comprehensive translation project from Greek into Arabic, often via Syriac, the language of the largely Christian intermediaries. This project resulted in the availability in Arabic of a range of philosophical texts, including much Aristotle, some Plato and a good deal of the Neoplatonic curriculum which dominated the Greek world after the death of Aristotle. In accordance with that tradition, there was frequently confusion as to the precise authorship of certain works, so Aristotle was credited with several Neoplatonic texts that we now know were not his at all.

As one might expect, the arrival of Greek philosophy provided a great impetus for the growth of Islamic philosophy. It was not that the Islamic thinkers slavishly followed the ideas of the Greeks; had they done so, they would have been rather poor thinkers. Rather, they set about the task of applying Greek thought as a methodology to Islamic subject matter. Since there were apparent inconsistencies between arguments that, on the basis of Greek thought, seemed to be solid and the principles of Islam, or at least some of those principles, a great stimulus to intellectual debate was created. For example, according to the Qur'an, the nature of the afterlife is determined by God, and our individual fate in the next life is determined by God examining our conduct in this life. In Aristotelian thought, the afterlife seems to be something about which it is difficult to say anything at all, since once the soul has left the body, there is no longer any personal identity left, and the idea of that identity becoming miraculously reconstituted in the afterlife is regarded as going against the principles of the rational construction of the universe. In fact, Greek philosophy has severe problems with the existence of miracles as a whole, so one can imagine that this set up serious problems for Islamic philosophers. Their problem was that they were persuaded of the validity of at least some of the arguments which Greek philosophers produced on these issues (although of course they criticized many of those arguments too), while also accepting the truth of Islam; so it became necessary to think of some way to hold on to both sets of beliefs. It was the apparent contradiction that led to so much theoretical creativity within Islamic philosophy. This is generally the way that philosophy operates. It produces a conclusion that goes against some proposition that we firmly believe, and we then need to find a way to reconcile both claims. For example, we tend to believe that things in our world have real power to affect other things, as right now my fingers are affecting the keyboard of the computer I am typing on. Yet many philosophers have criticized this idea, arguing that things have no power in themselves to affect anything at all, since it is conceivable for the keys on my computer to move of their own accord. It would never happen, we think, and never has happened in our experience, but it could be imagined to happen. That suggests it is possible, and if it is possible, then no necessity lies in the connection between events such as my hitting the keys and the consequences, the words being produced. We may be convinced by this argument, and many philosophers were, and yet find it difficult to reconcile with our everyday experience of the world, a world after all in which we constantly do things and expect other things to happen. This is where philosophy really gets going, in finding a way, indeed, a variety of ways, of bringing together two beliefs that appear to be incompatible. The so-called clash between faith and reason in Islamic philosophy is no more than the normal grinding away of this process within the Islamic world.

What is often expressed as a clash between philosophy and religion, or between reason and faith, is something far less dramatic. It was not that these thinkers had a blind faith in Islam and a rational faith in philosophy that they then had to reconcile somehow. They saw their faith in Islam as a rational enterprise also, and the ways in which Islam portrays itself make this quite feasible. The Qur'an frequently refers to evidence for its claims (and, indeed, its verses are called *ayat*, or signs, the idea being that they point quite rationally in a particular direction); and as the newest and freshest of the three monotheistic religions, Islam sees itself as the modern, up-to-date version of the truths referred to in the earlier religions. Becoming a Muslim, as opposed to remaining a Jew or a Christian, might be seen as rather like having an option between three kinds of computer: an old version, a slightly newer one and the best, most efficient model available. Of course, there are people who prefer to stick with their old machine; but this is hardly rational, the argument would go, if there is something better available. It is not that the new machine does anything radically different from the old one, in so far as it incorporates the main principles of software that are present in all the machines; but it does it in the best possible way. Moses and Jesus were great prophets, but Muhammad is the greatest, and indeed the seal of the prophets (i.e., the last prophet), and this can be seen by considering the nature of his message and the ways in which he put it. As Ibn Rushd expressed it, the difference between Muhammad and the earlier prophets lies entirely in the fact that Muhammad was a supreme politician, able to encapsulate the truth in ways that were more perfect and more attractive than his predecessors (Rosenthal 1968). So the implication is that there are good arguments for adherence to Islam, and one of the uses to which Greek philosophy was put was extending those arguments to make them more persuasive to even more people.

It might be thought that this sort of argument does not do justice to the phenomenon of revelation, but again it is a mistake to see revelation as exclusively a matter of faith rather than reason. A revelation that is accepted is accepted because there are grounds for believing it. If there are grounds for believing it, then these can be rational grounds. If I accept the Qur'an, then I do so because I find its presentation of the truth to be based on a reasonable interpretation of the nature of reality (although as the Prophet says in a famous *hadith*, we tend to follow the religion we are brought up in when he refers to *fitra* or destiny – Kahteran 2006). Even if the basis of my faith is a personal experience of God – perhaps a personal revelation – I must still have grounds for accepting the experience as genuine, as compared with any other experiences that I might have. As we shall see when we look at some of the theories produced by the Sufis, the mystics in the Islamic world, there was no question of their just blindly accepting that what seemed to be experience of the divine was genuine. They required evidence and criteria of the validity of that experience.

Early reactions to Greek philosophy in Islamic culture: the Great Debate

The difficulty of accepting the main principles and techniques of Greek philosophy is that this would seem to imply that the Islamic sciences are not up to the task of handling theoretical questions, so one has to import a methodology from an entirely different culture, one which pre-dates the arrival of Islam. This might not have been too serious a matter had that culture at least been monotheistic. But, of course, Greek culture was often exuberantly quite the reverse, and seemed to manage quite well to produce impressive theoretical techniques without benefit of any kind of revelation at all. The opponents of Greek thought argued that there are two plausible objections to its use of logic. One is that logic is more than just a tool, which can be applied to any language at all. The other is that the most appropriate tools to use for the study of conceptual issues in a culture are the tools of that culture, not something imported from elsewhere. This might look like an attempt at a reactionary, xenophobic response to the new philosophy; but it should not really be considered in such a negative light. There was in Islamic philosophy a long and interesting debate on the precise nature of the links between logic and language. Is the former part of the latter, so that each language has a particular logic that is its own logic? Or is logic merely a technique for discussing the deep structure underlying languages? The famous debate in Baghdad between al-Sirafi and Ibn Matta in 320/932 goes into this issue in depth. The Christian translator, Ibn Matta, argues for the view of logic as common to all means of expression, so that a study of logic in one culture is useful in another since it is eminently transferable (Leaman 1997e). Al-Sirafi, by contrast, suggests that each language has its own structure, which

is essentially a grammatical, not a logical, structure, and that structure in Arabic does not need, and cannot use, the grammar implicit
in Greek (Abed 1996). There is a tendency to see Ibn Matta as on
the side of philosophy and progress in this controversy, but it is his
opponent who is more in line with many of the leading thinkers on
this issue today. It is often argued that it is an error to see meaning
as an essential aspect of the deep structure of a language, something
that can be transferred to another language through translation and
interpretation. There are objections to this view, on the grounds
that it seems to be possible for other language-users to understand a
different language when its rules have been explained, but that this
does not show that they grasp the inner meaning of the statements
of that language. We could not know that they do, since we cannot
compare those meanings without going to yet another language to
do it in, and thus set out on an infinite regress of meaning. There
is no reason why one should not be just as sceptical of meanings
in language as one might be of knowledge of the external world.
The fact that we seem to understand, as we seem to know, does not
show that we do in fact understand or know. Pragmatic success is no
guarantee of identity of meanings. So al-Sirafi may well have more
philosophical right on his side than is ordinarily admitted. This is
not the place to enter into all the details of the debate between him
and Ibn Matta; but it is worth pointing out how crucial it is to give
appropriate respect to both sides.

There was a related debate in Islamic philosophy over the nature
of logic itself (Leaman 2000b). Is logic a part of language or philosophy, or is it a tool of language and philosophy? This is more than
just an argument about words, since if logic is merely a tool, then it
should be capable of being applied to any language, and should be
acceptable regardless of its origins. This is a point made by two very
different thinkers. Ibn Rushd used it to argue in the first chapter of
his *Decisive Treatise* that it does not matter where logic comes from,
since it is like the instrument of an unbeliever that may legally be
used in a ritual context provided the appropriate rules of the ritual
are maintained. Al-Ghazali, the constant critic of philosophy, argued
that although philosophy is itself suspect, there is nothing wrong with
logic, which represents the rules of thought, and that logic should be
employed to introduce clarity into all our thought, especially in the
fields of theology and jurisprudence. He suggests that what is wrong
with philosophy is not its inclusion of logic, but, on the contrary, the
illegitimate way in which it uses logic, since the leading arguments
in philosophy do not work even if we accept their premises and
principles.

The main objection to philosophy was often not to philosophy as a way of acquiring knowledge, but to the way in which philosophy was applied to particular religious issues which were not regarded as benefiting from philosophical treatment. Now, there was a trend in Islamic thought which often goes under the label *bi-la kayfa*, and which means that if there are issues left open by Islam, there is no need to enquire into them (Abrahamov 1995). That is, the Qur'an is sufficient, along with the other Islamic sciences, in resolving major theoretical disputes, and there is no need to ponder any further things that those religious sciences do not resolve. This also seems to be a reactionary and anti-philosophical stance, but it need not be seen that way. Many major philosophical theories rule out ways of resolving particular metaphysical issues if they cannot be resolved within the theory itself. That is, the theory is taken to be a system of meaning that establishes the rules of what makes sense, and any questions that arise outside that system literally do not make sense, so do not require examination. The grounds for believing that this is the case for a system that is divinely established are rather strong, one might think, so there is certainly nothing wrong with presenting such a theory. The theory becomes even stronger if it can be argued that when we examine the ideas of philosophy, we come across inconsistencies and contradictions. Of course, that is what one would expect if philosophy goes further than the limits of sense.

Al-Ghazali and philosophy: the question of creation

The claim that philosophy goes further than it is entitled to is precisely the charge of al-Ghazali's critique; and by 'philosophy' he really meant the sort of philosophy developed by Ibn Sina. When he considers this form of thought in his *Incoherence of the Philosophers*, al-Ghazali (1997) makes it look as though he is bringing theological objections against philosophy, since he suggests that, on a number of issues, philosophers present theories which represent unbelief, not just innovation (A 15–41). That is, those theories go against basic Islamic principles, and do not try only to extend or reinterpret those principles. This would be a valid objection for someone interested in theology perhaps, but is surely of little theoretical concern to a philosopher per se. What makes it of concern here is the brilliant way in which al-Ghazali tried to take on the philosophers at their own game, and to show that their conclusions do not follow from their arguments – hence any impious conclusions that might be drawn are invalid as well as being heretical.

Al-Ghazali's main objection to Ibn Sina is that, while he and the other philosophers speak endlessly about God, they actually give God no role to perform. Since they give God nothing to do, God is not actually the sort of being that can be called 'God'. It is not enough to talk about God if what one means by 'God' is very different from the God of religion. The point here is that if the language about God is really language about God, and not a new kind of talking about a slimmed-down notion of a deity, then certain rules have to be followed. The most important rule for al-Ghazali is that God be treated as a real agent. What is involved in being a real agent? Al-Ghazali argues, very plausibly, that what is needed here is the ability to make one's own decisions, to do whatever one wants to do within one's capacity, and to have a genuine influence on the world. He accepts that even God has to operate within the laws of logic, but, apart from those limits, if God is a real agent, then he must have the power to act in whatever way he wishes. In his *Tahafut al-falasifa* (Incoherence of the Philosophers) he pokes fun at the ways in which the philosophers give God what he regards as a pseudo-role with respect to the world.

Why does he think that the philosophers do not regard God as an agent? Take one of the issues that plays a large part in his book, the creation of the world (A 42–6). The ordinary interpretation of how the world came into existence is that God decided to create a world, and then he created it. Were he to wish to bring it to an end, he could easily do so, and he has similar total control over everything in the world. Nature takes a certain form, but there is nothing necessary about this form, and God could easily change it, or even intervene to change natural events on particular occasions. These latter occurrences are called 'miracles', and they are explained as a result of God's direct intervention in his creation. The Qur'an refers to God saying to creation, when he wants something to happen, 'Be', and it then comes into existence, which accords precisely with the normal view of divine creation (36: 84; 16: 40).

Many of the philosophers reject this approach to creation. They argue that there are a number of excellent reasons for thinking that the world is eternal, just as eternal as God. First, if the world is worth creating, as it obviously is, since it was created, why should God delay creating it? In our own case, there is a gap between thinking about something and doing it; that is because we are finite creatures. This cannot be the case with God, though, since if the world is worth creating, it always was worth creating, and nothing could explain a delay in that creation by an omnipotent and perfect being. Moreover, there is a problem in explaining what kind of time could exist before the world was created. With us, there is a gap in time between considering an action and actually carrying it out. There is no such gap for God, since before the world was created, were there to be such a time, there would not have been time as we understand it. Time is itself a measure of changing events, and before the world was created, there were no changing events, so there was no time. If there was no time, then there was no time at which the world itself was created. It follows that the world must always have existed, since there cannot have been a time before it was created. This goes against the idea to which al-Ghazali alludes on a number of occasions that, first of all, God existed by himself, and then he existed with his creation, the world (A 15–46).

The nature of time

One way in which al-Ghazali could have argued for his view would have been to give a different account of the nature of time. He could have argued that time is not a measure of change, but that, instead, it is an independently existing framework in which change takes place. This would have been a far easier notion of time to reconcile with his idea of the link between God and the world. He makes life harder for himself by accepting the relative definition of time, but this is because he wants to show that even on the premises that the philosophers accept, they go awry. Can we not imagine, he suggests, a time before time, as it were, during which God existed by himself, with proper time starting when he created the world? This implies the existence of two notions of time: ordinary time, which starts with the creation of the world, and supernatural time, which exists eternally. A rather unusual idea is thus produced, involving the combination of both the framework and the relative notions of time, which does appear to be incoherent. We need some argument to show why we are entitled to use these two contrary notions, and we do not really get one, though this is clearly a picture which we can hold in our minds, which we shall come to see is a very important indication of meaning for al-Ghazali (Leaman 1985, 1997c).

Let us put this difficulty behind us for a moment, and consider whether there are any problems with the notion of a perfect creator delaying his creation. For al-Ghazali, this is not a problem, since we can form the idea of someone delaying his action, even though he has decided to do it, since it is an aspect of being an agent that one can decide when an action will take place. He gives examples from our ordinary behaviour to suggest that this is something we do all the time, and if we can do it, then God can certainly do it. Of course, the objection will be made that we have to delay, because we lack perfection, so often have to wait, or wait until we see what transpires. God is not in this position – all times are the same for him so why should he delay? Al-Ghazali throws this question back, and asks, why should he not? We often make arbitrary decisions, and it is an aspect of being an agent that one can do so. He gives the example of a hungry man being offered two identical dates, where he has to choose which one to eat. Since there is nothing to distinguish the dates from each other, they represent the decision that God made about the time at which to create the world. In just the same way that we can choose one date over another, so God can choose one time over another. There need be nothing about the particular date we choose first which makes it the date we have to select, in just the same way that there need be nothing about a particular time which makes it the time at which the world ought to be created. In his criticism of this point, Ibn Rushd points out that what the hungry individual is deciding is not, primarily, which date to eat, but whether to eat or not, so it does not matter to him which date he selects (Ibn Rushd 1961). They are literally identical as far as satisfying his hunger goes, and this brings out a rather worrying aspect of the analogy, the idea that an agent wants or needs something to be achieved through his action. Surely this idea is not appropriate for God, who does not need anything, and, if he acts, does so out of pure grace. What al-Ghazali would argue in response to such an objection is probably that – apart from the fact that God is unlike us in so far as he needs nothing as a result of his action, and of course this is an aspect of his perfection as compared with our imperfection – if he is a real agent, then there must be strong links between what he does and what we do. If we can choose between two identical things, as we can, then so can he. Ibn Rushd would argue that if we choose something, then there must be something about it which makes us choose it, and, whatever that is, it can be used to explain why we choose one thing rather than something else very similar. For Ibn Rushd, the choice is between eating and not eating, so there is no genuine problem; but surely al-Ghazali is correct in arguing that, while this is indeed an aspect of the choice, it is not what the choice is primarily about. The choice really is quite arbitrary, in that either date would do, but the chooser has to select one, and the ability to make such a choice is indeed characteristic of being an agent. It is more characteristic of agency even than the normal case of being motivated by a clear aim to select an obvious action, since that tends to be carried out in a habitual and unconsidered manner; but when we have the choice between identical alternatives, we are completely free to decide which way to go. So this is actually quite a strong argument for the idea that God could have created the world at any time he wanted, even though all times are the same to him. He could have decided when to create, even though it made no difference to him when that was.

Perhaps the more difficult problem which al-Ghazali has to explain is why God would delay a decision to create the world. If God could create the world at any time, and if the world is worth creating, why wait? Al-Ghazali interprets this objection as a challenge to the ability of God to wait, and suggests that if God wants to wait, he will wait. Why should he not wait if it is appropriate to wait? The problem is, as the *falasifa* often point out, that they can see no circumstances in which it would be appropriate to wait. This is not like the previous problem of explaining how God could decide between two identical alternatives. The decision here is between creating or not creating. Although in a sense both alternatives are the same for God, since he is not creating to satisfy some purpose he has, we clearly need some explanation of why something that should be done and could be done is not done. Al-Ghazali wishes to preserve the links between God and humanity, and suggests that just as we can delay our actions, so can God. But this surely will not work in quite the same way, since when we delay, we have some reason for the delay, which God could not. Once the world is created, we can certainly make sense of God waiting before making a particular intervention, since he would then be waiting for something to happen. Although he would know that it was going to happen before it happened, he might wait for it to take place before taking whatever subsequent action is appropriate. Before the world is created, though, there is nothing else in existence that could explain delay, so why should a perfect being delay?

Mulla Sadra on change

One solution to this difficulty is produced by Mulla Sadra with his theory of change. Ibn Sina and Ibn Rushd suggest that there are two kinds of change: essential change from one substance to another, which is sudden, and gradual change, which takes place when accidents in the sense of properties like quantity or quality alter. This seems plausible. After all, when one thing changes entirely into something else, this happens all at once. At one time a block of stone is just a block of stone; but when the sculptor has finished with it, it is a statue. On the other hand, when it is moved from one spot to another, this does not change its essence, but only its position, and such a process may take a lot of time. Change requires an unchanging basis, a substrate that remains the same, and it is by reference to this permanent thing that we can talk about movement and change. Mulla Sadra rejects this theory, arguing that, were it true, then movement would be equivalent to a series of unmoving spatio-temporal events. When something moves from potentiality to actuality, we need to refer both to an abstract mental idea and to a material thing that is in constant flux. He called this *al-haraka al-jawhariya*, substantial movement, and claimed that it is perpetually operating, bringing into existence the phenomena of the world.

For Mulla Sadra there is no connection between the essences of the world, only between those things that actually exist. We tend to ignore the small changes which occur in existents, since they are so small, and we create essences which represent a type of stability more mental than real. Substantive motion operates all the time, so that something is never the same at two separate moments. This movement is always in the direction of higher forms, and out of it we create the concept of time, which in itself is not real. Time is itself a measure of change, a feature of things that we construct, and so it shares at least one characteristic of space. We tend to identify things in our imagination, since it is helpful to us to do so, but in reality we abstract over what is in fact constantly changing, so that what we regard as things are really just aspects of motion. Time is the measure of this continual change, not an independent space-like dimension in which change takes place. Hence the world may be seen as eternal, in the sense that it represents the continual bringing into existence of things. On the other hand, there is continual change and movement, and everything that comes about is produced at a particular time. So the world consists of events, all of which take place in time, yet is eternal, since it has no beginning or end. Time is not something independent of the world of change, so we cannot speak of a time before the time when the changes started.

Iqbal on time

This dynamic account of the nature of being was enthusiastically taken up by many modern thinkers who were impressed with the boldness of the thought of Persian thinkers such as Mulla Sadra. The great Indian philosopher-poet Muhammad Iqbal created a theory of the self that follows directly from this sort of metaphysics. He starts out by criticizing the Christian idea of humanity being excluded from Paradise through sin, and suggests that the symbol of Adam is of the concept of self-conscious humanity, not a particular individual. The Fall is a matter of the transition from 'a primitive state of instinctive appetite to the conscious possession of a free self, capable of doubt and disobedience' (Iqbal 1930: 85). Human beings are a mixture of matter and spirit, the matter coming from the earth, the spirit from God; so it is hardly surprising that there should be occasions of conflict between these two very disparate kinds of things. What is important is that we should evolve and develop our notion of who we are, within a context of recognizing that we are dependent upon God. As we increase in our knowledge of ourselves and other beings, including nature, we become increasingly self-conscious; and the notion of God is precisely of a being who is entirely self-conscious, without any barriers to his understanding and awareness of himself, since he is without the limitations of materiality.

It is a mistake to think of the creation of the world as something that happened in the past, a past action of God. For Iqbal, God is always acting, and the creation is an ongoing project. It is also a mistake to think of ourselves as finished products, since we are constantly changing and developing in terms of levels of consciousness. This is even the case at the rather banal level of our everyday activities, since we have to work out our relationship with what surrounds us in the material world, and this is not a finished, completed relationship. More important, though, is the self which is abstracted from the empirical world, and which encompasses the pure notion of our individuality. This is the pure self, the self which pertains to who we really are, as compared with our empirical selves, and which operates almost independently of the body. One way in which Iqbal clarifies this distinction is by contrasting two different conceptions of time: ordinary serial time and what he calls 'pure duration'. Serial time is the ordinary flow of events, often represented in a spatialized form, so that we experience the changing nature of the world, and indeed of ourselves as physical beings in the world. Yet there is also, he argues, a deeper notion of time, in accordance with which everything has some form of eternal and constant being. This is like the feeling that we may achieve during meditation, when the whole of reality is seen as being present all at the same time, in the sense that its main features are observed all at once. Presumably, this is the way in which God sees our world, as the constant playing and replaying of themes and patterns which we experience with surprise as the changing nature of our world. In meditation, we have the feeling that what we customarily regard as in motion is fixed, and this is the deeper self and the more perfect notion of time that is available to us, at least in principle, through the development of our spiritual capacities to accept and understand such experience.

Iqbal draws some interesting conclusions from this theory. One conclusion is that there is no point in Islam seeking to 'freeze' itself in a certain political and theological position. There existed in the past a plethora of legal and theological points of view, and vigorous debates within the Islamic world about the appropriate understanding of the most important aspects of the faith. A significant number of what are often called *salafi* thinkers, by which is meant those who hark back to a purer, more perfect age in the distant past – better known in the West as 'fundamentalists' – seek to do what Iqbal criticizes here. They see the world as a finished product, and the issue now is how to return to an earlier, happier state of affairs, to a more fundamental understanding of Islam. Iqbal spent much of his time arguing for Islam as of continuing relevance to the modern age of the twentieth century. Yet he was opposed to the sort of harking back to a golden age when everything was clear and perfect. In fact, he does hark back to a golden age, albeit of a different sort: the world of Islam during the period when it was tolerant and interested in other ideas, and in particular in scientific ideas and theories. While certain fundamental truths may be acknowledged as eternally true, it is a mistake to try to fix them for ever within a particular political and legal structure, since the main principle of reality is that it changes all the time. Even when we are dead and, hopefully, in heaven, we shall not be able to relax, he suggests, since heaven is not a holiday. Even there we shall continue to develop our selves, and will use the others who are with us to come to ever-increasing awareness of what and who we are. Whatever one may think of the political implications that Iqbal draws from his metaphysics, it is worth pointing out the ways in which different accounts of the nature of time are an important feature of how the nature of reality is characterized.

Ibn Rushd on time

Ibn Rushd declared his allegiance to a rather similar theory. He claimed that the Ash'arites accept there are things which are brought about through the actions of other things, and which take place in time. Then there is a being who is not brought about through something else, and who may be said to be not in time, and that is God.

Finally, there are beings that fall between these two extremes, and these are neither made from anything nor in time, and this is the world as a whole. It cannot be made from anything, because there is no stuff that it could be made out of, since the world is all the stuff there is. It is not in time, since time is the measure of its changes, and before it exists it cannot change. As Ibn Rushd points out, the world considered as a whole both looks as though it has been brought about by another thing, and also seems to be eternal. It cannot be both, since what is brought about through something else is itself finite, and what exists out of time has nothing which brings it into existence (Hourani 1976: 55–6). Ibn Rushd suggests that the theologians differ from the philosophers only in the question of the origin of time. The former hold that time is finite, and only past time at that, while the latter argue that it is infinite. But really there is no contradiction in holding both that the world is infinite, since it is not produced in time, and that it is originated, since it is in some unspecified way dependent on God. He has a point, although whether he correctly identifies the theological argument is debatable. One proposition which he ascribes to the theologians is that future time and being are infinite, on which they surely would not agree, since they were as determined to argue that the world can come to an end as that it had a beginning (A 25–9, 42–6).

Where Mulla Sadra and Ibn Rushd are on firm ground is in pointing out how complex the question of the origin of the world is, and how the eternity versus finitude debate is not as simple as it might seem. As Ibn Rushd indicates on more than one occasion, there is no explicit statement in the Qur'an that the world is finite and was created out of nothing at a particular time. Why should the world not be seen as eternal, since this does not rule out its dependence on God? On the principle of emanation, which is so important in the philosophy of Ibn Sina, and which Ibn Rushd fought against, though he had little alternative but to use it much of the time, there is no time at which God exists but then brings the world into existence later. On the contrary, God always exists and always produces thoughts, and these have the consequences for our world that we have seen already, since his thoughts lead to a number of different levels of reality and existence, which eventually ended up with our world. Since time is the measure of change, and change involves matter for Ibn Rushd, we can say that our world is later than God, since what led up to our world did not occur in time, because it did not occur with respect to matter. That is why the theory of change which Mulla Sadra produces is so interesting, for he insists that change occurs right from the start of the creative process, and does not require matter, so time has always been in operation. Time is infinite, since the world is infinite, and the world is infinite in the sense that there has always been change. But the world is also finite in the sense that all the changes that take place occur in time, so that the world is characterized by impermanence and finitude. Again we have got some way from the ordinary idea of God creating the world and time after a period during which he existed entirely by himself. On the other hand, the notion of God that survives does seem usable by religion, and in particular by Islam. Even if this notion passes the test of the concept of time, the question still arises as to whether it fulfils the other criteria that must be satisfied by the God of Islam.

What can God do?

What really irritates al-Ghazali is the suggestion that there can be anything necessary limiting God's scope for action. God can do anything logically possible; therefore, since it seems logically possible for him to create the world whenever he wishes, why should we question this possibility? A very similar problem arises when it comes to analysing the nature of the world itself. The *falasifa*, and Ibn Sina in particular, interpret the world as consisting of facts and events linked in terms of causes and effects, where the causes necessitate the effects (A 46–52). The only cause which is not itself an effect of some prior cause is God himself, who is necessary in himself and the ground of the possibility of everything else. Everything apart from God is necessary, given its cause, and, once the cause operates, the effect must follow in accordance with the normal laws of nature (Leaman 1985; A 52–63, 113–14). Ibn Sina interprets the universe as the physical representation of a series of syllogisms, logical forms of argument, which enable us to work from particular instances to general conclusions. The structure of the world is entirely rational, and, although it may not seem like that to us, this is merely due to our limited grasp of the nature of reality. There are some people who understand the logical structure of the world; they possess the general principles according to which the world operates and so, when they are presented with particular facts, they know how to derive the consequences from those facts. Ibn Sina equates this ability with that of many prophets, since the prophet is someone who can predict what is going to happen. The normal religious understanding of prophecy is that God makes anyone he chooses prophesy; but the normal philosophical understanding at the time is that the prophet is a special kind of person who is able, through his intellectual and practical perfection, to become aware of the ways in which the logic of the world is structured, as a result of which he knows what will happen in the future. He is also politically skilled, in that he can express that logic of the world in such a way as to resonate with the community at large.

Miracles and meaning

Let us contrast this with the theological view of nature with which al-Ghazali was for many years aligned, the Ash'arite view. According to this, the basic structure of reality consists of atoms which can take any form at all. When change takes place, this comes about through God arranging the atoms in particular ways, but in themselves the atoms could be organized in any way whatsoever. Of course, we experience the world as rule-bound, but this is because God, being kind, makes life easier for us. Unfortunately, this generosity can lead to confusion, since we may think that what happens had to happen because of what preceded it, or even that when we act, what happens takes place because of what we do. In reality, when we act, our action is brought about through God, and when change in the universe occurs, it is God who is behind it all, holding together the atoms in certain ways, in order to give the impression of change and also the idea that the universe operates in accordance with rules. This makes life much easier for us, since unless there were such regularity, we should have no idea how to behave or what was going to happen. The idea of necessity that we use is a very useful idea in a practical sense, and there is no reason why we should not use it; but what we should not do is to think of the world as operating in terms of its own necessity. The world is as it is because God makes it appear to be like that, and nothing forces him to do it in one way rather than another. He could do it in any way he chooses, or not at all.

This might seem to be an extreme interpretation of giving God the status of an agent. It is one thing to insist that for God to be God, he must have the status of an agent, and quite another to claim that he must be as active as al-Ghazali seems to require. On the other hand, what al-Ghazali has his finger on here are the implications of the view of nature as necessary in the sense defended by Ibn Sina. On that account, there has to be a complete reinterpretation of doctrines such as prophecy and miracles, as indeed there was. As we have seen, the normal idea of prophecy is that a particularly upright person is chosen by God to be a prophet, and has prophecy conferred on him.

God makes someone into a prophet who was not a prophet, and unless God did it, it would not happen. But on the view of nature presented by the *falasifa*, this is far from the case. A prophet is someone who has the natural qualities appropriate to that role, and God has no alternative but to allow him to prophesy. God can no more stop a prophet from prophesying than he can stop a cat from having fleas. In both cases the natural state of affairs must come into being once the appropriate set of prior conditions is in existence.

Similarly with miracles. On the normal understanding of miracles, God intervenes in nature on occasion, to overturn the normal rules by which phenomena operate. He wants to make some point, perhaps, or to provide directly an example of his power. Since God is the author of nature, there should be no problem about his intervention to change it, especially if the change is temporary and affects only a particular time and place. Yet, if the sequence of causes and effects is necessary, this is ruled out. How could God intervene and change what is a necessary process? Al-Ghazali replies that the only form of necessity which constrains God is logical necessity; so, if we can think of a way in which natural events may be reversed, contrary to the law of cause and effect, then we can see that such a change would be logically, albeit not physically, possible. And in many cases it is not difficult to think of ways in which events may change. For example, I am at the moment typing these words on a machine, and although I can see my fingers hitting particular keys, it is quite possible for divine intervention to make different words and letters appear on the screen in front of me. When this happens normally, I assume I have made a mistake; but suppose that, even after an exhaustive investigation of the machinery, I discover that there can be no ordinary explanation for what is happening; then I may conclude that a miracle has occurred. It would be even more plausible, within a religious context, if the words that keep on appearing in front of me were of a significant spiritual nature. Surely there is no difficulty in imagining this happening. Indeed, I can easily imagine it happening, for I have just imagined it now while typing out the words that have appeared.

The point which al-Ghazali is making is that there is something very strange in believing that God cannot make a real difference to the world if he really is God. He must be able to make a difference to the way in which things would happen without his intervention. A way to work out which things he can do and which he cannot is to try to imagine a change in the normal state of affairs. If we can do this, then it is something he can do. If we cannot, as in the case of turning a circle into a square, then it is something he cannot do; but it is no criticism of his agency that he is unable to do things that logically cannot be done. On the other hand, it is a sign of mental laziness if we insist that the way in which the world is presently organized is the only way in which we can think of it being organized. It may be difficult to imagine things being different, but if the difficulty is only a matter of being used to things being a certain way, then such difficulty does not prove anything at all about what is necessary.

Let us take two more examples of states of affairs we can imagine, yet which the *falasifa* deny are possible. I can certainly imagine God being aware of everything which goes on in the world, and the Qur'an even encourages me in this belief, by claiming that God is so close to us that he understands our thoughts, and sees every leaf that falls. As al-Ghazali suggests, if God does not know everything that takes place, he is in a difficult position when it comes to rewarding and punishing us. The other notion which the *falasifa* treat with suspicion is that of a personal and physical afterlife. Yet I can imagine myself living after my death, and the Qur'an presents graphic accounts of what is involved here, depending on what level of behaviour I achieve in this life. The fact that I can imagine these states of affairs suggests that they are logically possible, so God should have no problem in carrying them out.

The afterlife

What problems do the *falasifa* have with these ideas? The basic difficulty with the notion of a personal afterlife concerns issues of what is meant by personal identity after the disappearance of the body (*A* 82–96). If a soul survives the death of the body, something that was accepted by many *falasifa*, we have the difficulty of working out whose soul it is. It might seem clear that the soul is the soul of the person whose body has perished, and that the soul carries on surviving in some form or another. But what makes one soul different from another soul? The obvious answer is that it is the body that the soul originally belonged to, and also the unique memories and thoughts of that soul; so, on death, the particular soul can continue in existence with its thoughts and memories, knowing that it has left behind a particular body which represented its life during its stay in the world of generation and corruption.

The problem, though, is that for the soul to be a thing, as Aristotle argued, it requires some matter, and, if resurrection is only spiritual, there is nothing for the form of the person, the soul, to inform and shape. It is interesting that the precise objection which al-Ghazali makes to the *falasifa* is not that they deny an afterlife, but that they deny a physical afterlife, and the ways in which he describes their position make it fairly clear that he agrees that something has to be said about the nature of the matter in that afterlife, which is why the Qur'an describes in highly corporeal terms the nature of the after-life. We still have the problem of explaining how a natural process, the death and decay of the body, can be reversed by God. It is, as always, quite feasible to imagine that, after I am buried in my grave, I am resurrected by God, and wander off with both body and soul to wherever I deserve to go; but does this feat of imagination prove that this is possible? What would be involved here would be a miracle, and we have seen that the *falasifa* do not allow the ordinary conception of miracles to be possible.

What can God know?

What is the problem with God's knowledge of events in the world? There is no problem in thinking of God having knowledge; but the *falasifa* limit this knowledge to abstract and necessary truths (*A* 71–81). How could God know what I am doing now unless he has a body? We know that he does not have a body, so he cannot know. As al-Ghazali points out, this implies that God does not even know that Muhammad prophesied! We have little difficulty in imagining what is involved in God knowing everything, including temporary and finite facts, since we just extend what we call knowledge to someone whose knowledge is not limited by his finitude.

In just the same way that I know what the contents of my room are, God knows the contents of everyone's room, everywhere and for all time. The problem, however, is this means he has as knowledge infor-mation that changes and varies, and how can a perfect consciousness which is itself immutable include as part of its content the mutable, the changeable? In a more banal version of this question, how could someone without senses know things that can only be known by a creature with senses? Yet it is important that God does know every-day events, since he is going to reward or punish us for them, and we may expect that when we pray, there is the possibility of being heard. We expect God to take an interest in his creation, not to be in the position of the distant managing director of a company who knows none of his employees, or what they do.

The crucial issue here is whether it is part of the meaning of 'God' that he can know particulars, and can resurrect us physically in the afterlife. According to the *falasifa*, the problem with the idea of his knowing particulars is to explain how a being who is perfect can come to know things which are imperfect. What is involved in omniscience, in knowing everything? Does this mean really knowing everything, no matter how trivial or impermanent the object of knowledge is? Or does it, rather, mean knowing the principles that lie behind the world of generation and corruption? It is the latter, according to the *falasifa*, and they would argue that it is inappropriate for God to know absolutely everything, no matter how trivial. This might be illustrated by different views of what is involved in management. Some accounts of management insist that the manager should know everything that goes on in her organization, and that, as a result, she is responsible for everything which takes place. That used to be the understanding of the British government, so a minister would be obliged to resign if one of his civil servants did something that should not have been done. In the 1990s a new model of managerial responsibility has become the norm, such that a minister is responsible only for the general organization of the business of the department, and not for the day-to-day running of it. Which view is appropriate for God? According to al-Ghazali, it has to be the former, while the *falasifa* advocate the more relaxed approach to responsibility. They would argue that just as a manager cannot be expected to know everything, God should not be thought to know everything about his world. But the objection might be made that God is very different from a mortal manager. While the latter is of course restricted as we all are by finitude, this is not the case with God, and there is no reason why we should feel the need to draw boundaries around his knowledge.

However, the human manager's failure to find out everything about her organization is not owing to an inability to do so, but rather because it is not important to do so. What is important is policy and the implementation of policy, not the nitty-gritty of the actual workings of every aspect of that policy. As Ibn Rushd puts it, God's knowledge is both like our knowledge and at the same time very different. It is like our knowledge in that it consists of true and justified statements of which he is aware. It is different in the sense that, unlike us, God actually constructs the objects of his knowledge, so he has an entirely different access to those objects compared with us. It is not as though he has to wait to find out what is going to happen, or what the contents of his knowledge are going to be. He knows immediately what there is to be known, but this does not mean that he knows everything that we know. How could he know what the smell of a just-opened packet of coffee was like, without having a nose? What he does know, and knows perfectly, is the structure of the world, the basic principles that lie at the core of everything, and he knows this with the sort of knowledge that a maker has of what he has created. Is it a restriction on God's knowledge that he cannot know the sorts of things which we can know because he has no body? In a sense it is, although it is in a rather strange sense, since the body is a source of both knowledge and limitation, and what we call knowledge is really a pale reflection of what God has. Ibn Rushd suggests that what God has is the paradigmatic notion of knowledge, the perfect example of knowledge, while what we have is a pale reflection. Objecting that God must share our sort of knowledge is like insisting that he must share our limitations, which is surely not required of the deity.

Philosophical accounts of religious concepts

The case of the afterlife is rather different from that of knowledge, but is linked to the concept of miracles, in that the issue here is whether God can overturn the laws of nature. We have already seen that the *falasifa,* at least in the persons of al-Farabi and Ibn Sina, doubt whether this is possible, and we might extend the argument about God's knowledge to show why. The laws of nature are not just an arbitrary organization of facts; they represent the working out of abstract and rational principles. In terms of those principles, we can work out what is going on, who we are, and what sorts of things we might expect to happen. As part of this, we know that we are a combination of form and matter, where the form is the soul and the matter is the body, and we know that without the matter there is nothing for the form to shape. If there is nothing for the form to shape, then there is nothing except the form itself, and this consists of ideas and abstract knowledge, entirely general principles, and certainly nothing that can of itself constitute a new thing. This tends to be the line pursued by Ibn Rushd, but Ibn Sina takes a different view, talking about the continuing existence of souls in the afterlife. Even if we think this is possible, though, it is clear that the sorts of afterlife being discussed here are very different from those described in highly physical terms in the Qur'an, and even al-Ghazali suggests that the religious texts on the afterlife should not be interpreted literally for all believers. That is, it is not out of a desire to incur physical pleasures and avoid physical pains that the good Muslim acts, but entirely out of a desire to serve God. On the other hand, material language suits some people and that is why it is appropriate to make it available, in other words, to use it.

But this does not really address the issue of whether the apparent inability of God to revive us physically is a problem for his omnipotence or not. Al-Ghazali suggests that it is a problem, and that there is no difficulty in thinking of us continuing in an afterlife in much the same way that we live in this life. Not only do we have the objections about personal identity that Ibn Rushd and others produce; we also have the problem of how such an image of an afterlife might skew our behaviour. If we act well in order to benefit in the next life, then this gives our behaviour a self-interested aspect that is surely inappropriate, given our ability to act out of spiritual motives. Ibn Rushd suggests, as we shall see, that accounts of the physicality of the afterlife are devised in order to impress the majority of the community with the idea that what we do in this life has effects that extend further than this life. For most people, this idea has meaning only if it can be connected to their narrow, personal interests; but this is no bad thing if it helps them to act well and perhaps serves as a springboard for more sophisticated moral motivation. The philosopher realizes that what the afterlife means is that our actions continue their effect after our death, in the sense that what we do has implications for what continues to happen in this world, and that the abstract ideas which we manage to produce, and which are in themselves eternal, continue in existence. We cannot expect an afterlife in a more personal sense than this, though, and this is not a reflection of the limitations of God's power. God could have arranged matter and form in such a way that the literal interpretation of the Qur'an actually came into existence, but he chose not to do so, since this would have given undue importance to the physical aspects of our lives, and would have made it difficult to act out of pure love for him. It is no restriction on God's power to suggest that there are things that he cannot do once he has decided to produce a certain sort of world with particular kinds of creatures in it.

How free is God?

But how free is God to act? On the account of creation provided by Ibn Sina, he seems to be rather unfree in this respect. The description of creation has it taking place on the model of emanation. The start of the process has God thinking, and the appropriate object of his thought is himself. We start off with just one thing, God, and then when God starts to think, we get the creation both of the object of his thought and the thinking itself, which brings into existence two more things. This results in further triads coming into existence, continuing the process of thought leading to the existence of something else, but at increasingly less abstract and pure levels, until we reach this world, which is the most impure of all, since it consists of matter which provides a real obstruction to the ability of thought to inform its matter. That is, since matter has its own obdurate being, it prevents ideas from completely shaping it, but manages only to achieve a partial imposition of rationality on what is already there. The whole process remains in operation because God always thinks, and it is worth pointing out that there are many levels of reality separating this world from the level of God's thought, which does indeed appear to cut God off from direct awareness of what is going on in this world, and from direct intervention in our world. After all, although he is at the source of the process, he is concerned with a far higher level of pure abstraction than has any direct application to this world. How free is he even to think about what he wants to consider? Not very, apparently, since he can only think about what is true and pure, though it would be difficult to argue that this is a sign of imperfection. Why should a perfect being think about what is imperfect? It is also worth pointing out that God does indirectly think about the imperfect, in the sense that the latter follows from his perfection, albeit in a rather extended way. To give an example, God cannot make mistakes in understanding the laws of mathematics, but since his thinking about those laws leads to our world, albeit indirectly, and our world has people in it who make such mathematical mistakes, he is connected with those mistakes. To acknowledge such connections is very different from claiming that he himself knows what it is like to make mistakes, or that he should be able to understand what that would be like.

Essence, existence and miracles

It might be thought in vindication of God's agency that this is firmly present even in the metaphysics of the *falasifa*. After all, for Ibn Sina, God is the only existing being which is necessary in itself, and everything else in existence is in existence only because God has brought it into existence (*A* 104–16). Everything that can exist is logically possible as an existent, but it needs something to move it from potentiality to actuality, and this ultimately is God. God puts in train a sequence of change which eventually results in everything which really could exist finally existing. This might seem to be wrong, since surely there are things that could exist, but never will, since they will never be moved into existence, as it were. This is certainly the case for Ibn

Sina; there are possible things that remain possible forever, since they are never going to be brought into existence. To exist, a thing needs something to bring it into existence. There is an interesting similarity between this theory and that of his chief opponent, al-Ghazali, who also argues that for something to exist, something must move it into existence, and that something is also ultimately God. Both Ibn Sina and al-Ghazali make a firm distinction between existence and essence. For the former, only God has an essence that makes it inevitable that he will exist; everything else in existence has been brought into existence by something else. For al-Ghazali, there can also never have been a time when God did not exist, and everything that does exist is both brought into existence and kept in existence through the power of God. If God decided not to maintain the force for existence, as it were, then the things that previously existed would go out of existence, in just the same way that if someone does not keep up the payments on a house mortgage, the house will be repossessed.

Ibn Rushd criticizes both these views. According to him, while it is true that a logical distinction can be made between existence and essence, a distinction should also be made between formal possibility and real possibility (A 104–16). If the world is infinite in time, as Ibn Rushd argued, then anything that really could come into existence will come into existence at some time or other. But surely, it will be argued, something could be possible but never come into existence, because nothing may move it into existence. Ibn Rushd argues against this view; he points out that if we see the world as a rational, organized structure, what exists and what does not is specified by its role in the structure. To take an example which al-Ghazali uses for a different purpose, if one puts a piece of cotton wool into a flame, then what comes into existence is burnt matter. Is it possible for the result to be something else? Well, it is formally possible, in the sense that there is no logical impossibility between putting the cotton wool in the flame and its not burning, or its turning into a dove. This is what magicians do: they make something that we expect to change, or not change, in a particular way, and we admire their skill because they produce an unexpected result. If we thought that they really were able to perform magic, in the sense of radically changing the natures of things, then we would have to re-examine our ideas about what things are. If an egg could suddenly become a rabbit, for example, this would radically change our ideas about what an egg is, and also what a rabbit is. We can certainly imagine an egg becoming a rabbit, and we even 'see' it happen when magicians do it, or even more extraordinary things, but this does not show that it can be done. All it shows is that we can be fooled into thinking that it can be done.

Ibn Rushd argues that the distinction between existence and essence made by Ibn Sina and al-Ghazali suggests that something has to come from outside a thing, as it were, to bring that thing into existence. For example, when the cotton wool is put in the flame, and we get ash, something produces that ash which, ultimately, is different from the cotton wool and the flame themselves. According to al-Ghazali, what creates the ash is really God, and anything could lead to ash, were God to command it. But Ibn Rushd counters this with the argument that what is meant by ash is something which is produced in a certain way, so that its existence is very much part of its essence. What happens to the ash has to happen to the ash, since it is ash, and there is nothing outside it that could lead to a different state of affairs. One cannot, except in a logical sense, distinguish between what things are and whether they exist, since whether they exist is a part of what they are. Given its essence, cotton wool will burn when put in a flame, and given the essence of a flame, ash will result. Nothing is required from outside of the cotton wool, the flame and the atmosphere to explain the existence of the ash. That existence is part of the essences of what led up to it. If the ash is really possible, then it has to come into existence. Of course, we can imagine it not coming into existence, which shows that it is not logically necessary as a result of the prior causes and conditions. We can certainly think about everything appropriate being done to produce ash, without ash resulting, even if we cannot find anything about the situation that prevents it happening. But if we think that what we are imagining shows that there is no connection in meaning between ash and its prior conditions, we err. If we seriously contemplate ash not coming about in the conditions that should make it come about, then we should have to change our ideas about what ash is, and the whole notion of ash would become different. Facts certainly affect what we can say about the meanings of terms, and if we can imagine the facts radically different, then we might well have to change our meanings as well.

The trouble with distinguishing between essence and existence is that it suggests that we can distinguish usefully between what something is and whether it is. Such a distinction is logically feasible, but has dangerous metaphysical implications. These are that something apart from how things are is necessary to make them exist, and of course we have seen that the traditional interpretation of this ultimate cause is that it is God. Does relieving God of this task lead to difficulties in acknowledging his agency? Ibn Rushd would claim that it does not. God is responsible for the organization of the world in the first place, but that does not mean that he could have created any sort of world at all. He obviously created a world that is rational and well structured, a world that provides us with guidance as to how to live and what to believe. Could he have created another sort of world, one in which there is neither order nor a user-friendly structure? If God is really what we mean by God, he is obliged to produce a world which embodies intelligence and general benevolence; he cannot do anything else. The view of God's links with the world that Ibn Rushd has is even more restricted than that of Ibn Sina. For the latter, God is the ultimate cause of everything which exists; but it is not clear whether, once a thing has passed the test of possibility, God can prevent it from coming into existence. God is rather in the position of a constitutional monarch, who is required to sign the legislation passed by parliament, which makes the legislation 'royal', so legal. But all that the crown does in this sort of situation is rubber-stamp, as it were, a decision which has already been taken elsewhere.

It is far from clear whether God has even this role in Ibn Rushd's account of the world. Since both God and the world are eternal, they coexist; but what links there are between them is unspecified. Sometimes the name 'God' seems to be more or less another name for the world, a name that makes it easier for ordinary people to work out how to behave and think. We shall see later on how this is explained, but it is clear that Ibn Rushd is operating with a very different theory of meaning from al-Ghazali. For the latter, meaning is univocal, which means that it is impossible to stretch it very far. We know what an agent is; so when we say that God is an agent, we have to mean that he is, as far as his agency goes, rather like us. Of course, it would be the height of unbelief to claim that God is like us in the sense of having a body and being imperfect; but enough of the ordinary notion of agency must survive in the application of the term to God as compared with our use of it. For Ibn Rushd, by contrast, meaning is equivocal, and there are only faint resonances of a term when it is applied to God as compared with our use of it. He argues that its use when applied to God is the paradigmatic or perfect use, and that when applied to us, it is only a pale reflection of that use.

Take the case we have been discussing here, the concept of agency. God is a perfect agent, in that there is nothing to prevent him acting when he wishes to act, and no deficiencies of knowledge or motivation either. A divine action is perfect, in that it is carried out entirely rationally, with no desire for personal gain and in total understanding of the situation to which the action is applied. It follows that the notion of agency that constitutes the perfect concept is in fact rather thin, since it is distant from what we would call agency. For example, we might do something just to prove that we can do it, and since we act in a context of incomplete information, our actions are often misplaced and inefficient in attaining their ends. This is very different from God's actions, which are in complete accordance with a perfect view of the situation, and which are not restricted by problems of finitude and materiality.

The meaning of words

Al-Ghazali worries that this sort of description of God as an agent does not leave him with enough to do to be a real agent. Ibn Rushd worries that a more human description of God as an agent makes him too much like us to be a divine agent. This is not primarily a dispute about the nature of God, but more about the nature of meaning (Leaman 1997c; A 179–96). It is not at all clear which of the pro-tagonists is correct. The advantage of al-Ghazali's view is that it fits far better with the approach to religion of the ordinary member of the community, who tends to interpret religious language as rather similar to ordinary language. It thus connects with the living faith of the participants in Islam – no bad thing for a theory of language that is supposed to reflect the meaning of that language. But Ibn Rushd also manages to make sense of the beliefs of ordinary people, since he has a theory of language that is broad enough to include a variety of views of the same object, in this case God. The ordinary believer is allowed to view God in rather (for Ibn Rushd) crude terms, this being the appropriate way for him to work out his religious duties and beliefs. The more sophisticated believer, by contrast, needs to go beyond this and grasp intellectually the nature of God as the paradig-matic knower and agent, which means seeing God as knowing and acting in very different ways from us. So Ibn Rushd would argue that he has managed to encapsulate al-Ghazali's theory within his own system as an example of the theory of the ordinary believer, a theory which is certainly important and valid, but which will not do for a more sophisticated attitude to God.

There are good reasons for thinking that Ibn Rushd has a point here, especially as al-Ghazali himself seems to allow for different routes to knowledge of God, in particular the mystical route, which is not available to the ordinary believer. The philosophy of Sufism has been very important in the history of Islamic philosophy, and during the last part of his life al-Ghazali committed himself to this approach, understanding that his earlier, more literal approach to Islam was limited to only a part, albeit the largest part, of the com-munity. It was possibly because of these sorts of arguments over the appropriate attitude to the meaning of religious concepts that Ibn al-ʿArabi developed his extensive theory of mysticism. He reports that during a debate with Ibn Rushd, he trounced the latter's arguments, and his journey back to Cordoba with Ibn Rushd's body is obviously supposed to symbolize the burying of the old philosophy by the new. What is wrong with the old philosophy, according to Ibn al-ʿArabi, is that it fails to represent accurately the phenomenon of *tawhid*, the oneness of God. If we take this idea seriously, we have to conclude that all being is one, and the phrase which is often used to characterize Ibn al-ʿArabi's philosophy is *wahdat al-wujud*, the unity of being.

The main characteristic of this theory is the idea that previous accounts of both God and his creation have failed to acknowledge the essential unity that exists between them. That is, God's creation is just a reflection of God's being, and has no possibility of existence without God; thus, strictly speaking, we should not talk of God and a world, but just of God. Similarly, when we examine the world, we come across what appears to be a wide variety of different things, things that change and go in and out of existence. This makes us think that there are a lot of different objects in the world, whereas in fact, since the world is merely a reflection of the being of God, there is really only one thing, God, which we interpret in a range of varying ways. Does this mean that our impression of the existence of a variety is wrong? Ibn al-ʿArabi suggests that this is not the case; of course, we are right to think that there are many things in the world, but we are wrong if we think that this represents how the world really is. We are right in thinking that God is prepared to allow himself to be reflected by variety in this way, and this means that such a view of him is in a sense quite real. It misleads us only if we confuse these impressions with reality. This account of the link between God and the world as just two ways of seeing the same thing is a neat solution to some of the difficulties that arise within the *falsafa* tradition employed by al-Ghazali and Ibn Rushd. It leads to a transcending of the question as to when the universe was created, for it has existed for exactly the same length of time as God has existed, and in that sense is infinite. On the other hand, the things in the universe appear to be finite, and they are indeed finite, although, as aspects of God, they are linked to the infinite.

Meaning and unity

Seeing the universe as one is not an easy undertaking, of course. According to the Sufis, one has to undergo a long, strenuous process of preparation and purification before one can see the world as one, and in this way unite or make contact with God. Two forms of relationship with God are possible here, one of which is much more dramatic and potentially dangerous from a theological point of view than the other. The idea of making contact with God is bold, but not that difficult to accept, since when one person makes contact with another, both are unchanged except to the extent that the relationship changes them. The idea of uniting with God is far harder to understand, since it results in the thinker becoming God, and God becoming the thinker, in what might be thought to be rather difficult ways to accept in Islam. For Ibn al-ʿArabi there is not a great problem in understanding this notion of unity, because we are already the same as God, in the sense that we are just a reflection of God's being, and God allows himself to be represented by us; but the actual attainment of an understanding of how this is possible is more than an intellectual task. The trouble with intellectual thinking is that it tends to be analytical; it breaks reality down into parts, and treats those parts as though they are the basic constituents of reality. What we must do if we are to grasp appropriately the divine basis of reality is to think synthetically; we must put together what is otherwise disparate, and recognize the basic unity between everything we experience and its ultimate resting place in the transcendental. This grasp of the oneness of everything is not something that is attained lightly: it involves relearning how to look at the world, as it were.

From the point of view of whether God is an agent, and what it means to use the notion of God in an account of the world, Ibn al-ʿArabi has a point in thinking that his theory provides a useful resolution of some of the long-standing problems. It has the advantage of reconciling the unity of God with the diversity of the phenomenal world; for although God is not an ordinary sort of agent, he clearly acts, and his acts have consequences for our world. On the other hand, we still have the difficulty that the access of most believers to ultimate reality is strictly limited, since only a few have the mystical capacity to attain this level of awareness of the unity of being. We also have the difficulty of explaining what criteria determine whether the appropriate level of awareness has in fact been attained. The trouble with placing an experience at the apex of individual spiritual growth is that experiences are irreducibly subjective. How can one tell that the experience one has is a genuine awareness of the unity of being or only an apparent such awareness? It would be wrong to think that the Sufis ignored this problem; on the contrary, many of their books go into great detail about how to tell the difference between a genuine experience of the unity of being and what is bogus. As we shall see, the illuminationist tradition argued for a particular way of knowing which could not be mistaken, in which case we could feel confidence in the genuineness of the experience; but the Sufis also spent a lot of time wondering how the validity of the experience could be guaranteed (Leaman 1992). Ibn al-'Arabi certainly makes room in his theory for the experiential aspect of religion, but perhaps not enough to resolve questions about its reliability.

These difficulties in distinguishing between God and the world have led to a similar, but contrasting, theory, that of *wahdat al-shuhud*, unity of consciousness. On this view there does indeed really exist only one sort of being, God, and our impression that there are many things is just an artefact of the way in which we view the one reality. The unity of consciousness refers to the way in which we can, if appropriately trained, think of reality as just one thing, and can then link the unity of consciousness with that of being. If we fail to make that identification, we end up with the view that God and his creation are distinct, in that the latter is only a reflection, so not identical with God, which means that while the divine is eternal, the world is not. Shah Waliullah argues that such a view comes about through a defect in consciousness, which, when it is working at its peak, is capable of treating consciousness as though it is one, and in line with the unity of being. This linking of thought with being is attainable only at the highest level of spiritual awareness. At lower levels, we are impressed by the reality of the things in the world, and we find it difficult to see them as parts of just one thing, and a divinely constructed thing at that. The higher up the mystical scale we manage to move, the easier it is for us to see how consciousness and being are both united as describing one object ultimately, the object of God.

bi-la kayfa

When one considers all these complications in trying to understand what initially appears to be quite simple, the relationship of God with the world, one can understand the attractions of the *bi-la kayfa* slogan: the response that there are problems to which the appropriate response is to say that one does not know. The implication is not only that one does not know, but also that one does not care. This slogan appeared originally as a way of dealing with problems in understanding the anthropomorphic language of the Qur'an, the relevant passages being those which refer to God having hands and a face, sitting on a throne, and having feelings. Since the Qur'an also tells us that God is unlike anything in his world, we obviously cannot interpret these references literally, most Muslims suggested, although there were some who did accept the literal truth of these statements. Still others took these passages in the *bi-la kayfa* sense, which means accepting the text without enquiring into precisely how (*kayfiyya*) it can be true. The idea is that the *bi-la kayfa* doctrine is a moderate position, between that of the literalists (who hold that God really has a body) and that of the demythologizers (who think we need to interpret these verses allegorically) (Abrahamov 1998).

The interesting question is whether this middle position is a coherent one. That is, one can see good arguments for accepting the verses that refer to God's body as they stand, and also good reasons for not taking them as they stand; but it does not seem possible to reconcile these positions. It is all very well to suggest that one should not interpret a passage allegorically if there is an acceptable literal interpretation, but given the many warnings in the Qur'an against anthropomorphism, one might think that all literal references to God's body are ruled out as they stand.

Ibn Taymiyya on talking about God

The most persuasive arguments in favour of *bi-la kayfa* were produced by Ibn Taymiyya (d. 728/1328), often seen as the great enemy of philosophy and logic (Hallaq 1993; Leaman 2000b; Pavlin 1996), who nevertheless consistently used philosophical and logical methods to prove his point. He criticizes al-Ghazali's interpretation of God knowing everything that a person thinks, being nearer to us even than our jugular vein (50: 16), which is, in terms of divine omniscience, not actually proximity. Ibn Taymiyya argues very plausibly that there are many references in the Book to God's omniscience, so nothing is being added by referring to proximity in this sense, if all it means is knowledge. The problem is that we cannot really understand the way in which God exists unless we know what God is, and vice versa. So what we need to do to understand these references to God's attributes is, first of all, to understand what they mean in connection with the sorts of creatures that we do understand, and then to acknowledge that we cannot understand how they can be extended to a being who completely transcends his creatures. Al-Ghazali does not accept this, arguing that the *bi-la kayfa* doctrine is applicable only to ordinary believers, while more sophisticated thinkers could use figurative interpretation. This position is taken to its logical conclusion by Ibn

Rushd, who criticized the use of interpretation (*ta'wil*) by theologians as unnecessary and confusing to ordinary believers. The only people who are entitled to engage in interpretation, he suggested, are the philosophers, since it is only the philosophers who are able to come to a demonstrable or final conclusion about these issues.

What we need to remember when examining Ibn Rushd's position is that he is a determinedly anti-mystical thinker. The point of Scripture for most people is to provide them with some indication as to how to live; while for the more sophisticated there is a need to use more technical methods to derive the meaning of the text. Ultimately, the philosopher can see what the real meaning of the text is, but only the philosopher can see this in such a way that the whole question of the meaning is entirely resolved. For Ibn Taymiyya, by contrast, there is no such perspicuous grasp of the meaning of many religious texts, since we can only try to come a bit closer to understanding the mystery of the divinity by thinking about the meaning of the words in the text. There is no problem for him in accepting that we cannot ultimately understand many texts, since this replicates our weakness with respect to God and the meaning of the world. How could we expect to come any closer than we do to the meaning of the text? This gives the *bi-la kayfa* doctrine a far more attractive appearance, not as the redoubt of religious reactionaries, but as an entirely rational reaction to some of the difficulties of coming close to a transcendent being for prospective knowers who are finite. Our understanding of the text is then seen as a task, a process rather than a product, and one we need to bear in mind when considering the meaning of the text.

3

Knowledge

There are a very large number of references in the Qur'an and the *hadith* to knowledge, both the desirability of acquiring knowledge and the limitations of knowledge (Nuseibeh 1996; Mohamed 2006). As we have seen, there are problems in understanding the notion of God having knowledge, especially knowledge of everything, since this would involve him knowing things which change, and this is not easy to reconcile with his immutability. In this chapter, however, we are going to concentrate not on what God can know, but on what we can know.

An interesting question arises within Islam: namely, is all knowledge valuable? It has been suggested that there was some resistance in the early years of Islam to the importation of the 'first sciences', by which is generally meant Greek philosophy and science. There was resistance to the secular idea that knowledge can be compartmentalized, since this is inconsistent with the principle of *tawhid*, the unity of the deity. If there is really only God, and the world is just an aspect of his being, then what we count as knowledge is really only an aspect of what is knowledge for God, the perfect and perspicuous grasp of the nature of reality – namely, himself. The whole project of reconciling Scripture and philosophy or science is based on the notion that there is really just one truth, which may be approached in different ways. This is not a specifically Islamic project, but may be pursued in a variety of religions, and not only the monotheistic ones, where there are different levels of authority.

The notion of Islamic science

Some Muslims have argued that Islam is more compatible with science than other religions, pointing out that the Islamic world saw in the past a great flourishing of the natural sciences (Bakar 1996; Nasr 1996; Shamsher Ali 2006). In any case, there is something rather questionable about the implication that we need to show that science is compatible with religion, since the normal way of interpreting the latter is to see it as an eternal repository of truth, while natural science is always tentative and changeable. Although the truths of science may strike us as impressive, they are surely not as impressive as the constant, basic truths of religions, if we regard the latter as truths. In recent times Muslims have become more critical of science, and have tried to interpret it within an Islamic perspective, since it is a principle of Islam (and indeed all religions) that every aspect of life is to be interpreted in accordance with faith. One cannot go about science as though it were an entirely independent area of knowledge, since this would be to promote the secular values of science to at least an equal status with religion. Rather, science needs to be understood in terms of the values of Islam; only then will it be capable of attracting the adherence of Muslims. In any case, the idea that natural science represents a system of pure, unmediated truth is no longer as popular as it was in the past, and science is often viewed as just as ideological as religion itself.

This might seem a strange idea, since surely science is just a series of truths and theories that operates in accordance with its own rules, although for a religious believer these rules no doubt exist within a broader spiritual context. But the problem with seeing science as an entirely independent area of inquiry is that nothing is really completely independent from a religious point of view, since the world was brought into existence by God and its constitution is formed by God (Leaman 1996h). Creating a strict dichotomy between science and religion is tantamount to elevating the secular values of science to equal standing with religion, or even to promote them over religion. After all, one can actually see the products of science, and benefit from its successes, whereas religion requires belief in the unseen, and does not provide us with any obvious evidence of its truth. If, on the other hand, we set about reinterpreting science in Islamic terms, we put it in its place, and see it as functioning within the boundaries of Islam. Some thinkers have used this argument to support a call for a new understanding of what knowledge involves, looking back to the tradition of seeing knowledge as basically spiritual and experiential,

as against the positivism and secularism of modern science. There is
certainly scope for such a reinterpretation of knowledge, since the
present positivist principles may be argued to have illegitimately
divorced humanity from its spiritual roots, and as a result brought
into existence an atomized concept of both science and humanity.
The most persistent supporter of this view in modern times is Seyyed
Hossein Nasr, who argues not only that we should support a new
form of science, but that we should also see that the account of philosophy on which the secular notion of science rests is only one aspect
of Islamic philosophy and its account of reason, not the whole of that
tradition, and as such it is too restricted in scope to make sense of the
role of humanity in the world. It is hardly surprising that the form
of philosophy that we have called *falsafa* should accept the truths of
natural science, since its Aristotelian basis is entirely in line with the
principles of that science; as far as it goes, this is acceptable, but only
in so far as we are looking for a theory of natural science. What such
a philosophy cannot do is to provide space for the development of
humanity's links with the spiritual; it cannot help us understand in an
emotional and personal way what our place in the world is, so should
not be taken as the only way to look at the world. On the contrary, it
should be seen as part of knowledge, and we need to see this part of
knowledge as valid, but not the last word.

We might accept the theory behind the reintroduction of a religious
perspective into science, but we still require some indication as to
how it might work in detail. There need to be principles of Islamic
science that differ in some way from the principles of non-Islamic
science, and we need to be able to specify what they are. Some argue
that, by contrast with the monolithic structure of Western science,
Islamic science is pluralistic and inclusive of different approaches
to scientific work. But this is contradicted by some of the putative
differences between the two approaches to science. Western science
is positivistic, and insists on complete freedom to do as it wishes.
The Western scientist is individualistic, and believes that whatever
she wishes to study is acceptable as an object of study. The Islamic
approach, by contrast, argues that science is really just an alternative
form of worship, that it operates within a social and spiritual context,
and outside that context has no value. Given the principle of *tawhid*,
the unity of God, there is no scope for claiming that a part of our lives
– our scientific lives perhaps – is independent of considerations of the
divine nature of the universe. We are in the position of *khilafa*, trus-
tees of the welfare of the world, as a result of our divinely sanctioned
role. The point is that we are not allowed to dominate the world or
treat it as an external object. On the contrary, we are obliged to treat

both the world and ourselves as parts of divine creation, so we must treat possible objects of enquiry with the respect that their ultimate nature requires. Knowledge, then, is not a neutral attempt to grasp an external object, as it is for positivist science, but, rather, an aspect of worship, an activity carried out for a purpose, and this leads to the conclusion that there are forms of knowledge that are not worth pursuing.

What knowledge is not worth pursuing? There is a variety of answers here. It is knowledge that is spiritually and physically destructive of both humanity and faith. Such knowledge has nothing to do with the preservation of social justice, or of the natural world itself, and should be discouraged from an Islamic perspective. Only knowledge that is useful is worth having, so there is no justification of knowledge for knowledge's sake. It is rather difficult to say precisely how this distinction results in actual practical differences. One of the problems with laying down rules about how science should be done is that it is not possible to predict before research takes place what the consequences of that research might be for humanity. To take an example, there is a lively debate in many Western countries about how far we are justified in using animals in experiments designed to help human beings. Some people argue that there is no such justification, since animals and human beings are entirely on all fours, as it were, morally, and that just because animals do not share our humanity, it does not follow that their capacity to feel pain should be disregarded or assigned less moral value than human pain.

How would this come out on the Islamic approach to science? Some Muslims might argue it is humanity that is specifically mentioned with respect to *khilafa*, as God's representatives on earth, so animals are a lower form of creation, and are there for the use of humanity. Others might extend the meaning of the Qur'an to suggest that animals are just as much a part of God's creation as we are, and that we are not entitled to exploit them for our welfare. Is there a specifically Islamic line on this? Alternatively, take the issue of research on destructive weapons. One position might be that this is ruled out by Islam since it entails working on means to destroy God's creation, which is to interfere with his plan for the world and for the unity of all creation. On the other hand, are Muslims not allowed to defend themselves? They are. Indeed, the Qur'an goes into considerable detail on rules of conflict and war, and there is the implication that there is nothing wrong with ensuring that Muslims go into conflict with appropriate weapons. Since Islam does not demand pacifism, there seems to be nothing wrong with research on weapons. Are there restrictions on the weapons that might be developed? Some might say that weapons of mass destruction are ruled out, since they go further than is required by the rules of just war (*jihad*); but suppose that the other side has such weapons? It is hardly obvious what sorts of science Muslims should pursue, and which they should avoid.

It is worth being sceptical of the practical implications of the idea of an Islamic science, since the Qur'anic pronouncements on the topic are so general. Natural phenomena are signs (*ayat*) of the existence and nature of God (16: 66; 41: 53; 51: 20–1; 88: 17–20) and so are flawless (67: 3). The world is organized and has a direction (3: 191; 21: 16; 38: 27). Human beings are God's *khalifa* (2: 30; 6: 165) and there are certainly warnings against waste and mismanagement of those things that God has provided, but what these directions actually mean is far from obvious (Leaman 2003a). These notions are explored and developed in more detail of course in the *hadith* and Islamic law, but here, as one would expect, one finds a wide variety of views on what constitutes treating and studying the natural world appropriately.

Science and rationality

When we get away from looking for specific Islamic answers, we are on surer ground. The main point which modern defenders of Islamic science make is that both Islam and natural science rest on a particular attitude towards rationality. The sort of rationality employed by science involves faith just as much as does religion. At different times there are different approaches to science, and these have a lot to do with the sort of society in which science is produced. In that sense, then, science rests on nothing more secure than does religion. Both involve faith in a set of principles which in themselves lack justification. One might say that science seems to work, but one could say exactly the same thing about religion. The main advantage of the notion of an Islamic science is that it is permissive with respect to methodology, in that it broadens the concept of knowledge to allow a wide variety of different understandings of what knowledge is, so that at the same time it permits a variety of different kinds of science. Islam validates a whole range of different ways of knowing, and these different ways are all equally valid, even though some of them may be quite personal and apparently subjective. Another advantage is that religion sees science as a way of knowing and working within a broader perspective, and science cannot itself set out rules for how it is to be done, because it is a set of techniques, not a moral philosophy.

The principles which science uses to carry out its work cannot be justified by science itself, since scientific methodology is all about how to achieve certain results and understandings of the world. It is not about the nature of how the world ought to be or what activities are morally acceptable.

This basic distinction between science and religion is accepted by most scientists. Suppose that a baby is born with a large number of deformities, and with no possibility of living what might be deemed an acceptable life. Let us take it that it will live for only a relatively short time, and can only be kept alive by extensive medical intervention that will be both unpleasant and painful. During its short life the baby will never develop into anything even close to an ordinary child, so the question arises of what should be done. Ought it to be left to die without major intervention, which, we must remember, in a world short of resources, will mean that the resources available can be used for babies who stand more of a chance of an acceptable future life? Or ought the baby to be kept alive for as long as possible, regardless of expense and the use of resources, since allowing it to die is to interfere illegitimately in the decision of the Almighty as to who lives or dies? It is not clear that there is a specifically Islamic answer to this question. After all, the doctors might want to keep the baby alive to see what sorts of interventions are most effective in prolonging its life, or they might wish to conserve resources by allowing it to die. They might think that since it has no long-term viability, the kindest thing to do is to discontinue treatment. This is a decision that is taken every day in hospitals, with respect both to the recently born and to those soon to die. It is not at all clear that the actions of a Muslim physician, say, inspired by the motives of religion would be any different from those of an entirely secular doctor. It is not even clear how Muslim versus non-Muslim parents might decide, or which decisions would be right ones. These sorts of examples suggest that the apparent conflict between the positivistic scientist and the holistic Muslim have often been overplayed.

The nature of knowledge

Let us look at what can be known according to Islam. First of all, we need to examine the references in the Qur'an to two realms of knowledge, one seen and one unseen. The former can be understood by human beings, and is the object of science. The unseen world can also be known, although in a different way from the seen world, and is the province of revelation. This is reasonable, since there is no physical evidence that we can receive about the unseen world. The Qur'an talks of a faculty we possess, which is like physical hearing, yet different, and it is with this faculty that we can approach the unseen world. The faculty is called *qalb*, which could be translated as 'heart'. There are two kinds of knowledge: *'ilm*, which describes the *'alam al-shahada*, the world with which we are familiar and which is described by natural science, and *ma'arifa*, which describes the *'alam al-ghayb*, the hidden world, and which is more than propositional knowledge. The way to attain this knowledge is through revelation, and the relevant faculty is the heart, which brings in nicely the personal and experiential nature of our links with the unseen world. A danger with this sort of understanding which results from its unseen nature is that it may be pseudo-understanding, since subjective feeling can masquerade as objective knowledge. We therefore need to be very careful in what we say about the unseen realm, because only God really knows what the constitution of this realm is; but it is all too easy for us to think that we have gained admittance. We have hearts to think with (*qulubun ya'qiluna biha* – 22: 46), which means that we have to balance the emotional subjectivity of the heart with the propositional objectivity of reason. But we can achieve this sort of balance if we are prepared to adhere to the teaching of Islam and the guidance of the Prophet's message.

One of the interesting features of accounts of knowledge in Islamic philosophy is the frequent stress on the necessity of a guide. The seal of the prophets, the Prophet Muhammad, is obviously the paradigmatic guide; but there is a tradition that God has always provided humanity with a guide. This point has been taken to an interesting conclusion by Isma'ili thinkers, who go further and argue that without a current guide it is impossible to know how to act. Some thinkers, by contrast, suggest that an individual who is sufficiently well developed intellectually and personally can do without a guide and, indeed, can guide himself. The famous example is the story by Ibn Tufayl of Hayy ibn Yaqzan, the baby who survives a shipwreck and floats to an island, where he is brought up by a deer, and his only companions are other animals and nature itself. He manages to work out by himself the principles underlying the nature of the world and the meaning of human life, even before he knows that there are other human beings, since he is able to think rationally about what must have brought this world into existence, and what our obligations to that being are. Through a combination of rational thought and quiet meditation, Hayy is able to worship his creator, albeit without any direct intervention by a guide to assist him. One might think that nature itself is a guide, and likewise the reason which he applies to it, and there is a lot to be said for such an interpretation, though the important point here is that he is not the recipient of a prophecy, nor is one available to him. When he eventually meets another human being and goes with him to the city in which Muslims live, he is repelled by the hypocrisy and banality of ritual and social life, and soon returns to the island to continue his devotions in a relatively solitary yet perfect manner. He already has a well-developed knowledge both of his duties and of the nature of reality, in so far as the latter can be attained by human beings, and he does not need to approach God in the symbolic and imperfect way which is common in the Islamic community.

What is knowledge for?

What is the point of knowledge? It is not as easy to answer this question as one might think. Some would argue that knowledge is valuable for its own sake, but this is a strange proposition as it stands. Very little is valuable for its own sake, and we generally seek some other explanation for thinking anything is worth pursuing. In the case of knowledge the ultimate end is salvation, and although the sorts of knowledge which interest us might seem very distant from information which is useful for salvation, it is all part and parcel of what leads to improving our lives and our ultimate futures. From a philosophical point of view, knowledge is generally identified with grasping the immaterial form or essence of things, as opposed to their material embodiment. A very important distinction is that between conception (*tasawwur*) and assent (*tasdiq*). The former is the grasp of an object without a judgement being made about it, whereas the latter involves a judgement, and in fact represents a relationship between the mental representation and the object that it represents. Concepts are the matter of knowledge, and assent is its form, in a sense. We cannot determine issues of truth or falsity unless we first have concepts, but just having concepts does not in itself raise questions of truth or falsity. A knowledge claim involves both concepts and truth claims.

We can divide concepts into the known and the unknown, where the former are actual objects of the mind, the latter being merely potential objects. Assent can be similarly divided up into the known and the unknown. Some of the former – that is, true propositions – are acquired through our experience of the structure of the world, while some are necessary and known through reason itself. There are different ways of moving from the known to the unknown, which is what is meant by the growth of knowledge. The most popular method among the Peripatetic philosophers, the *falasifa*, is demonstrative reasoning (*burhan*), and we need to operate here in accordance with the rules of syllogistic logic, which in itself is a perfect example of how to move from the known to the unknown. One starts with a premise that one knows, adds it to another premise that one also knows, and then arrives validly at another premise that, as a result of this process, is now known. The trouble with logic, one might think, is its very abstraction, and the fact that although it can deal with premises that describe matters of fact, what it involves is actually an interplay between concepts, not facts themselves. This is really not a problem, since the ordinary coming and going of events in the world is far too lowly an activity for us to bother with as far as our epistemic efforts are concerned, when we could concentrate on the essences of things through logic. Even when logic uses individuals in its premises, these are only representatives of general ideas and concepts; so the conclusions of such reasoning may appear to be about individuals, but in fact are entirely universal. It is worth pointing out that the controversy about whether God can know particulars is often misunderstood when it is formulated as God being unable to do something which we can do, since for the *falasifa* not even we can really know particulars. An understanding of particulars would not be dignified with the designation 'knowledge' for anyone.

When we approach the phenomenal world, there is of course scope for awareness of its material aspects, and we abstract from these to extract the universals, the general concepts that they embody. The imagination, which is often identified with the internal senses, has an important role in working with the ideas we identify as organizing material objects and linking them with more abstract ideas, while at the same time using material images to describe those ideas. After we have looked at our ideas through imagination, there remains much scope for their continuing abstraction. There exists next a series of intelligences with which our ideas can come into contact, and the most discussed is undoubtedly the agent intellect (*al-'aql al-fa''al*), sometimes called the 'active intellect', in Arabic the first intellect (*al-'aql al-awwal*). This is the notion of a faculty that provides us with the forms of thought we employ when thinking about both matters of fact and more intellectual topics. This is often identified with the moon, in so far as it is the lowest of the moving bodies in the heavens, and so the lowest development of reason before it becomes irretrievably caught up in the matter of the world of generation and corruption. The active intellect is slightly higher than the acquired intellect, which is the repository of thought about concepts that no longer have any connection with matter. The active intellect is more important than this, since it not only works with concepts, but actually creates them. It is often regarded as the highest level of knowledge which we can attain, and it plays an important role as a bridge between our world and the yet more abstract and perfect world which is higher than it. We shall see that this notion of a bridge (*barzakh*), which is really a Qur'anic concept, plays a vital role in Islamic philosophy.

A distinction needs to be made between the ways in which different philosophers used the key notion of the active or agent intellect. One line of interpretation popular with Ibn Bajja and Ibn Rushd is that our thought is rendered more abstract by the general ideas produced in the imagination becoming increasingly purified by what is often referred to as the light of the agent intellect, which then makes them completely theoretical and abstract (although it has to be said that Ibn Rushd came to be critical of this view in his later work on Aristotle's *De anima*). Al-Farabi and Ibn Sina, by contrast, often argue that the concepts are already completely abstract and theoretical, and what happens is that the active intellect shines on the imagination, casting a shadow on the theoretical intellect, which then creates ideas very similar or identical to the ideas already in existence. This is a useful description of how knowledge can come about, in that the effect of the attempt to understand the structure of the world results in ideas that are found to replicate abstract ideas that the mind already possesses. Hence we say that what we find in the world is merely an instance of what we already possess in our mind, and, indeed, unless we already possessed it, we should be unable to find it in the world in the first (or perhaps it should be the second) place.

Imagination

How important are symbols in the pursuit of knowledge? Are the universal concepts that we discover in the world a clear representation of how things are, or are they instead only something that stands between us and reality? In a sense it is true that concepts get in the way of reality, since they are not reality itself, but a way of organizing our ideas to grasp that reality. In Islamic philosophy, individuals with a strong imagination are said to be capable of receiving prophecy, and the ways in which they receive that prophetic knowledge are thoroughly tied in with the effects of the imagination. That is one reason why Ibn Rushd called the Prophet Muhammad the 'final prophet', because of his political skill having reached the highest possible human level. As a politician, he was able to translate the formal knowledge that the philosophers understood only theoretically into imaginative and figurative language that the community at large could understand. Ordinary people require symbols to help them know how to behave and what to believe, and the prophet, with his imagination, is well placed to provide these symbols. The prophet and the philosopher know the same thing, but they know it in different ways, and this variety makes it possible for the less sophisticated members of the community to share such knowledge, albeit to a lesser degree, since they are probably not interested in spending a great deal of time in acquiring knowledge.

What is the highest level of knowledge that we can achieve? The penultimate stage on this journey is that involving the acquired intellect, which is given that name (and also the name of the 'holy intellect') because it is the source of knowledge that appears to come from outside us and so is something we acquire. This level of knowledge comes about when the active intellect and the theoretical intellect are in alignment, and there was an extended argument about whether this theoretical intellect is only potential or is actual. Ibn Sina took the latter position, for the reason that unless the theoretical truths are actually always in existence, it is difficult to see how we could use them as we do to make judgements about both them and the material world. For Ibn Rushd and Ibn Bajja, following on from al-Farabi, the theoretical intellect is only potential, and exists only in so far as it is applied in our thinking. What we need to remember here is that for Ibn Sina the most important part of knowledge is our grasp of the middle terms in our reasoning processes. This is what the prophet understands all at once, as it were, and what the philosopher comes to understand gradually. The contrast comes out nicely in the language we use to describe prophetic revelation, which is often referred to as 'inspiration', as like a flash of understanding in which everything is revealed suddenly. This seems to be wrong, in that one might think that one could acquire abstract knowledge from our experience of the material world itself. This is the view of the empiricists, but it is rejected firmly by Ibn Sina. One reason for rejecting it is precisely this phenomenon of prophecy, which entails the principles of knowledge being made known immediately, which is surely incompatible with the idea that they are acquired only gradually, through our experience of the material world.

Such a rejection of empiricism might seem a bit quick, for, even if we accept the way it is for the prophet, what about everyone else?

Could they not abstract from experience to form ideas of universal concepts? This is possible, especially if we see the abstract ideas as built up from the contrast between major and minor premises in processes of reasoning. But if it is possible for some to grasp these abstract ideas all at once, then, although most of us would tend to acquire them by working our way up from the world of experience, those ideas themselves cannot be based on such a method. When we acquire those ideas from experience, what we are doing is following a slow route to their acquisition that merely replicates a set of ideas that already exist, and that potentially exist in our minds also. How we acquire those ideas is not relevant to their status, because, if they are to be the real object of knowledge, they must already exist. We cannot know something that is not really there, in the sense that it has not yet been produced. So the objects of knowledge must already exist, even if we are only potentially, and not actually, aware of them. Of course, we need to recall that the notion of having knowledge of particulars is a suspect one in much Islamic philosophy, since the world is a place in which things are frequently changing and inauthentic, whereas the world of ideas is entirely logically regulated and is structured in terms of permanent and eternal truth.

To take an example, there is a well-developed distinction in logic between a subject and a predicate, between what a statement is about and what is said about it, though in our experience this is far less secure. What we take to be the subject may not turn out really to be a subject at all, but just a property of some other subject, and the nature of the predicates that apply to a subject in the world of experience is variable and loose. By contrast, in logic there is a firm notion of what is involved in being a subject, and in that subject having predicates, and it is this logical notion that genuinely comprises knowledge, not the changing matter of the world. It was on this point, and in particular on the Aristotelian notion of definition, that the structure of Aristotelian knowledge rested, and thinkers as diverse as al-Suhrawardi and Ibn Taymiyya based their critique of logic on it. They argued that the starting point of logic and science is not capable of doing what it claims, since a definition along Aristotelian lines does not lay down forever what the essential qualities of a thing are. A definition tells us in a stipulative fashion, they argue, what something has to have if it is to be a particular sort of thing. But how can we know what it is unless we know precisely what its essential properties are? We see here a development of the earlier argument between al-Sirafi and Ibn Matta, in which most of the *falasifa* agree with the latter that language disguises thought (Abed 1996; Mahdi 1970). What we need to do is to peel away language to reveal the logical scaffolding of reality. This notion that there is a deeper reality that lies behind the appearance of the world of generation and corruption is also, of course, the basis of what came to be known as the science of mysticism, as we shall see.

Ibn Sina on knowledge and the 'oriental' philosophy

Ibn Sina presents a rather unusual account of knowledge by comparison with the traditional distinction. Al-Farabi, for example, argues that knowledge can be seen as the progressively more abstract development of our experiences and ordinary ideas, and when we reach the heights of the active intellect, we attain a level that represents the possibility of acquiring abstract ideas. For Ibn Sina, those ideas are already in existence, and any facility we have for acquiring such ideas comes from the ideas themselves, not from our thought about the world. Does this mean that for Ibn Sina there is no scope for using those ideas to make judgements about the material world? He would say that we can use them to make such judgements about the world, but that there is no way of telling whether they apply, since we cannot get behind them, as it were, to view the world from outside them. Hence the naive realism of al-Farabi is far too confident in its desire to rest the nature of our concepts on the reality of the material world. Another aspect of its confidence is its apparent readiness to accept that the ideas which the active intellect supplies us with are only potentially there waiting for us; in other words, they have to be supplied when we are in a fit condition to receive them, but until then it is as though they do not exist. For Ibn Sina, as we have seen, unless they already exist, we could never link up with them because they never would exist. They cannot come about through our progressive abstraction of experience.

The distinctness of Ibn Sina's theory adds credence to the argument that he really does think that there are two approaches to knowledge: the philosophical approach and the mystical. It follows from his account of knowledge that the only sort of knowledge worth having is the knowledge of the abstract ideas that lie in the active intellect. Actually, as we have seen, this is no different from the views of most other Islamic philosophers, but one important difference is that whereas for them the ideas are abstracted from the world of experience, for Ibn Sina they are not. So, for Ibn Sina, any correspondence between the ideas and phenomenal reality is purely fortuitous, while for the other thinkers it is guaranteed to some extent by the common origin of objects and ideas in the material world. It is clear that for Ibn Sina the acquisition of knowledge requires us to turn away from the world and concentrate on what is higher than the world. One is inevitably reminded of his distinction between two sorts of theoretical enquiry, one being Peripatetic (*mashsha'i*) philosophy (*falsafa*) to which he made such a distinguished contribution; the other being what he called *hikma mashraqiya*, or oriental wisdom. By this he is often taken to have meant a theory which not only sought to represent the objective truth, but which also did justice to the need for seekers after knowledge to find spiritual value in the objects of study. There is a good deal of controversy as to whether Ibn Sina really thought, as he says, that this form of mystical philosophy is a profounder version of the Greek style of philosophy, or whether it is mystical at all. There is also controversy as to whether he wrote works in the style of this oriental philosophy, since none have survived if he did, although in quite a few of his works he makes very approving references to the central concepts of mysticism.

The chief problem with this way of doing philosophy is that it appears to be irreducibly subjective. The idea that there is value in experience is unproblematic, as is even the point that there is an important aspect of knowledge that may be identified with *dhawq*, or taste. But the main problem with seeking a mystical relationship with God is that we need to raise the question as to how we know when we have achieved it. I know when I have understood Pythagoras's theorem, or even when I have grasped a law of nature, since there are objective standards of being right and wrong here, and others may agree with me or point out my errors. When it comes to establishing whether what I think is a link with God and reality is in fact such a link, or whether it is a case of self-deception, then we are in potential difficulties. It is because of this that the language of mysticism is so strange, since it claims for itself an objective status, yet at the same time insists that the subjective, the particular feeling, is a vitally important part of the process. It is a characteristic claim of Sufism, for instance, that there is available to the successful mystic a view of reality, perhaps in the sense of the unity of the world. The mystic can experience this unity; he or she can hold everything together in the mind as though they are merely aspects of one thing. In accomplishing this, one is doing more than having a feeling, and also more than acquiring some additional knowledge. The two are combined, in that the knowledge involves experience, and the experience involves knowledge. This sort of achievement would be seen by many as the crowning glory of a life of searching, and might be compared to life in the hereafter in Paradise.

Sufism, knowledge and imagination

But how do we know when we have reached such a state? It was obviously a hotly contested issue, since the various accounts of mysticism in Islamic philosophy are replete with warnings against misidentifying the nature of one's experience. Many of the books that provide accounts of how to come closer to God include indications of where one might think one was succeeding but in fact was going awry. One feature is very important, and that is the role of the *shaykh*, the spiritual guide. He will do his best to ensure that no wrong moves are made, and that one ends up in the appropriate relationship to God. However, to add to the difficulties, there is frequent confusion concerning the nature of this relationship. Some would argue that we can make contact with God, which is not in itself a wildly implausible claim, given that God has provided us with a route to make contact with him since he is apparently very interested in making contact with us. He did, after all, send a series of messengers to humanity to guide us. The more dubious claim is that we can expect not only to make contact with the deity but actually to unite with him, by which is meant becoming the same as him, and God becoming the same as us. It is this sort of claim, and its antinomianism (opposition to laws and rituals), that won Sufism such a bad name in many circles.

Disregard of laws came about through the argument that since the Sufi is capable of coming close to, or uniting with, God through his own methods, there is not much point in his following the official rules. After all, these rules are for everyone, in particular for those for whom there is no other route to God available. Those rules are also markedly less efficient in producing the desired outcome than the practices of the Sufi, so why should the latter bother with them? They are appropriate for most people, but not for those capable of realizing their goal by other and superior means.

If we consider that the successful Sufi might feel able to make the extravagant claim that he is now the same as God, since everything could be regarded as being a part of the deity, and might also feel able to disregard the customs and practices of the community on the basis of his direct knowledge of God, we need a very strong reason to think that the experience and knowledge which lie at the basis of those claims are in fact what he thinks them to be. Al-Hallaj is often taken to have made such a claim, as we shall see in the next chapter. One of the characteristics of many Sufi and *ishraqi* thinkers that would worry the *falasifa* is their predilection to value the sorts of events that take place in dreams. For example, Ibn al-ʿArabi points out that what happens in dreams is highly symbolic of the nature of our experience of the world. This experience is both varied and complex, yet its objective being is simple and merely part of God's unity. Our experience, then, is accurate in so far as it reflects what we think is the case from a common-sense point of view; but it is wrong in so far as we think that reality is just like that experience. Reality is very different, because experience, like everything else, is merely a reflection of the being of God; so we are literally wrong in thinking that it is ultimately real. On the other hand, we should not deny it, since what we experience does in fact operate as if the objects in the world that we observe exist, so we are accurately reporting the nature of our sense experience. Similarly with dreams: the story that takes place in a dream may not really be taking place, but its constituents will all be representations of real experiences, or variations thereon. So, like our everyday experience, it is both real and unreal. In fact, since we dream when we are temporarily disconnected from the conscious world, we manage to work out in dreams ideas and theories that we cannot engage with while awake; so dreams can be a very potent repository of knowledge. For both Ibn al-ʿArabi and al-Suhrawardi, the originator of illuminationism, there is a realm of knowledge which lies between our ordinary world and the higher world of abstract ideas, and that in-between realm is what Corbin called the 'imaginal world' (Lory 1996). He wanted to distinguish between 'imaginal' and 'imaginary', in the sense that the latter looks like make-belief, while the former is more respectable and refers to a different ontological realm.

The distinction is really rather bogus, since the users of the notion of the ʿalam al-khayal or ʿalam al-mithal mean that this is the world of the imagination, but they do not mean by imagination something which is unreal. Imagination is the creative faculty that enables us both to extract ideas from the world and apply ideas to our experience, and there is no reason to doubt that it can be treated as a respectable source of knowledge. We should remember that there is little point in comparing the experiences of the dreamer and those of the awake person as though the latter were real and the former unreal. The awake person is just as mistaken about the real nature of what he experiences as is the dreamer. The only difference, to use the words of the Prophet in a *hadith*, is that we wake up only when we die, in that once we have abandoned the senses and our tendency to be carried away by what we see in front of us, then we can understand the true nature of our experience and what lies behind it.

It is certainly true that many of the *falasifa* denounced the imagination, which they saw as a faculty useful in our everyday life and even important in the abstraction process, but highly liable to mislead.

Indeed, the organon, or organization, of different sorts of argument descends in order of demonstrative force, which is equivalent to increase in imaginative power. The very lowest forms of argument are those that, like rhetoric and sophistry, appeal almost entirely to the imagination, and right at the bottom comes poetry, whose argumentative value is very slight indeed. But the criterion of a good poem, unlike the criterion of a good argument, is that it be highly imaginative. There is nothing wrong with poetry – it fulfils an important social function, as does rhetoric in politics and religion – but we should not look to it for important arguments. Finally, on the deficit side of imagination, it is worth reminding ourselves of the sort of use to which al-Ghazali put it, as a source of knowledge about what ideas are logically possible and what are not. He argued that if we can imagine a state of affairs, then that state of affairs is conceivable, since that is what 'conceivable' means, something that can be imagined without contradiction. But, as we have seen, Ibn Rushd argues that this will not do as a criterion of possibility, because it does not take the whole situation into account. All it does is to put a few pictures together in our heads and then announce that this can be done; but far more is at issue in working out whether we can really put those ideas together or not. Imagination is in fact a very poor guide to possibility, he would argue, and its very vividness is an obstacle to clear, rational thought.

Knowledge by presence

The significance of the imaginal realm (I shall stick to the usual translation, although, as I have argued, I would prefer the 'realm of imagination') is that it is what links our world with the highest level of ideas and abstractions. This is, as we have seen, a useful notion, since imagination has traditionally been used in philosophy to mediate between our experiences and our ideas. A dramatic way of indicating the importance of mediation comes in the notion originally invoked by Ibn al-'Arabi of the *barzakh*, or isthmus, the passage from one level of reality to another. If we can grasp the nature of this borderline concept, as it were, we can claim with some confidence to understand both the sorts of concepts that exist at each level of reality and what transforms them and takes them on to a different level. Let us take as an example here the ordinary way of looking at the variety of things in the everyday world. Then there is a higher level of reality, which involves seeing everything as an aspect of the divine *tawhid*, or unity.

What is the isthmus between these two levels? It could be what holds together the idea of the experienced variety and the knowledge of the real unity; this bivalent notion is then the route that takes us from one level to another. Once we grasp the bridging notion, we understand the realms of discourse that are linked. Hence the importance in all types of philosophy of working out what the bridging notion is, and different kinds of philosophy will naturally interpret it in different ways.

Suppose that someone is sceptical of the possibility of grasping reality as a whole, not because he denies that there is such a unity, but rather because of doubts as to whether we as well as God can understand it. We might accept that the world is a unity, and that God can understand how it is a unity, but refuse to accept that we can understand much of its unitary nature except to say that we know that it is, *bi-la kayfa* (in a way we do not understand), one. The sceptic can be answered by evidence that we can experience this sort of unity ourselves. But this experience cannot be so subjective and personal that it is impossible to explain to someone else what it is like, or how to acquire it. This sort of problem led to the creation of the concept of *'ilm al-huduri*, or knowledge by presence, a key notion in illuminationist thought (Ha'iri Yazdi 1992). The idea is that there is a form of knowledge that is so obvious and so simple that we cannot doubt it; so the sceptic who would try to deny it is unable to insert his wedge. The wedge is the distinction between a knowledge claim and the objects that the claim purports to describe. The notion of knowledge by presence is designed to evade the wedge, since it is supposed to consist of knowledge that is so unquestionable that there is no scope for the wedge to be inserted. How could this be the case? There is already a category of knowledge that is so certain and immediate that it is incontrovertible, and this is knowledge of our pains and similar feelings. If I think I am in pain, I am in pain. There is no scope for the sceptic to doubt that I am in pain, where I am the person wondering whether I am experiencing pain. It is certainly the case that someone else may wonder whether I am in pain, but I cannot wonder what the nature of my experience is. It is too close to me for such a distinction between thinking that it is true and it being true to be made. This sort of evidence is so strong that some philosophers like Wittgenstein have even argued that it is not knowledge, since knowledge implies a contrast with doubt, and there can be no doubt in these sorts of cases.

What is it about these feelings that give them their character of incorrigibility? They share two features. One is that they are immediate; they instantly register with us if they are present. The other is that they are simple. They do not consist of parts all of which have to be present for the feeling to be evident. Yet this sort of knowledge, if it is knowledge, is restricted to rather uninteresting phenomena. Can it be broadened to include more significant material, in particular, information about the nature of the real being of the world? Some illuminationists claim that the 'I' that accompanies all our experience, the 'I' that is the framework within which the possibility of personal experience arises, is a similarly simple and indubitable idea. Everything I do, if it is something I do, is accompanied by the 'I', my 'I', and whenever I think or experience something, the 'I' is there in the background, if not in the foreground. Yet the notion of the subject is simple, since it is the bare ability to connect experiences in a particular way that ensures that they are my experiences. So I cannot doubt that I am an I, since my role as a subject is implied by that very question, and we have here the first thing which cannot be doubted, yet is important.

What follows from the nature of the subject is that there is no possibility of the user of a concept contrasting the concept and what the concept is of, because merely owning the concept means that it applies. From this position, al-Suhrawardi goes on to argue that the ontological basis of being human is itself a dimension of human knowledge. The basis of this knowledge is the reality of our awareness, where the self and what the self is aware of are the same. Since the context within which the self operates is self-certifying in this way, could it not also serve to justify the inclusion of other kinds of knowledge, knowledge that we acquire through the imposition of reality on our consciousness? What he has in mind here is the variety of mystical knowledge, which we can experience in a similar way to the manner in which we intuit our own personality. If we adhere to an illuminationist metaphysics, according to which what we know is lit up by principles and forces which lie above and beyond us, then these items of information could be illuminated in such a way that their presence is undeniable, leaving no scope for distinguishing between the concept and the object to which the concept refers.

There are problems with accepting this account of knowledge. The trouble with using the nature of personal experience to establish understanding of the self is that the only sort of self that emerges is a rather weak one. That is, all one can prove is that there is some notion of a subject which accompanies experience, but no real information about that subject is given by that sort of experience. On the other hand, what an emphasis on the subject reveals is that, to a degree, the nature of personal and private experience is significant. We should not reject personal experience merely because it has no obvious objective connection with what we tend to regard as the 'real' world. The 'real' world, from a religious point of view, often has to be regarded as merely the outer covering of what is really real, the inner truth which lies at the heart of existence. The use of light as the main technical term tends to replicate the religious position nicely. After all, according to al-Suhrawardi, the main ontological category is essence, not existence, so it is the way in which ideas are presented through illumination that gives us our notion of reality. What we take to exist as a result of that process is a secondary issue, and is one step removed from what illuminates our mind, and the notions that result through that illumination. So the argument that the gap between our idea of something and the reality disappears in knowledge through presence seems quite plausible. There is no gap, because there is no distinction between the operation of light and the light itself. So there is a level of understanding that can be taken to key in to the nature of reality itself, and where the traditional distinction between belief and knowledge no longer has to be made.

This theory suffers from a familiar problem, though: the nature of the self that is receiving the light. We can certainly accept that if we receive something that is entirely pure, and that if what does the receiving is entirely pure, then what is received is also pure. But of course our minds are not pure; they are occluded by all sorts of ideas and experiences that prevent them from receiving the light without altering it, and thereby interfere with the possibility of knowledge by presence. Part of the process of acquiring knowledge by presence is attained via an increase in self-perfection, so this type of knowledge should be seen as something to be aimed at, rather than something that happens anyway. We are again reminded of the strong links that exist between illuminationist philosophy and mysticism. It is also worth pointing to the links between such mysticism and traditional religion. After all, the way in which we perfect ourselves on the *ishraqi* account is not entirely up to us, but is dependent upon the operation of light on our souls; we do not control the operation of that light. As Ibn al-'Arabi puts the point, albeit within a different theoretical context, the Sufi can proceed as far as the door of truth, but it is up to God to open the door, or not. When it comes to knowledge, we are dependent, as ever, on God.

4

Mysticism

Mysticism as a system

One of the most pervasive trends in Islamic philosophy has been mysticism (Kılıç 1996; Nasr 1996e). It is difficult to overemphasize its significance. Virtually all of the philosophers in the Islamic world were committed to mysticism in one form or another, and those who were not, such as Ibn Rushd, stand out as a result. The links between mystical and non-mystical philosophy were made very clearly by Ibn Sina in his writings on oriental philosophy. They may be seen as two different ways of doing something rather similar, and one way (the mystical way) can easily be seen as deeper than the more analytical approach. Why deeper? The answer is probably that this is a form of thought that applies not only to reason, but also to one's personal feelings, and so hits a spot, as it were, which other ways of doing philosophy cannot reach. Is it true, though, to say that mystical philosophy can be analytical? After all, there is a tendency to see mysticism as a vague, woolly activity, in which the individual looks for a certain kind of subjective experience that he or she then dignifies with some transcendental label. Surely this cannot be called a discipline or a science?

The science of mysticism, the *'ilm al-tasawwuf* as it is often represented, is seen as far more than a subjective, personal seeking after kinds of experience. One of the characteristics of many of the works in this area is their keenness to display themselves as sensible, careful texts, making close distinctions between different aspects of mystical experience and, most importantly, discussing in detail the precise criteria by which a genuine *shaykh*, or religious leader, may be recognized. Obviously the problem with any such way of exploring the nature of reality is its ability to sink into subjectivity, something that needs to be countered by anyone who is able to lay down specific rules as to how to carry on the mystical enterprise. Often these rules mimic the rules of the other Islamic sciences, so they will, for example, present lines of transmission, in the same way that the *hadith* justify their reliability by establishing genuine sources and authoritative ways of reaching us now. It is worth adding that mystical texts do not just describe a series of experiences, but analyse those experiences and assess their reliability or otherwise and the implications which they have, or which they purport to have. It is clear from the literature that the issue of subjectivity did trouble the writers of this sort of material, and it was an issue that they addressed in their works. Whether they answered it satisfactorily is another story, though the important point is that this form of literature is not just a kind of philosophical poetry, but a real attempt at getting clear on a number of theoretical issues.

Although mysticism is an important part of Islamic philosophy, it does not follow that it is the most important part, or its only genuine aspect. We need to take seriously the diversity of Islamic philosophy, in the sense in which it is being described here. After all, there was a great deal of work done on logic, which is in its nature quite areligious and without any direct implications for the sort of claims made by the sceptics. The philosophy of logic is certainly relevant to mysticism, as we can see in the work of Ibn Sab'in, for example (Taftazani and Leaman 1996); but logic itself is not. Mysticism can be reconciled with a whole range of philosophical views, especially if one works with the theory that there are two sides to philosophy, a clearly analytical side and a more personal, subjective side. We seem to be returning to a variety of Averroism here, to the theory that there are two routes to the same truth, both equally valid and each appropriate to a different constituency. One might even say that these two routes could be appropriate to the same individual, in the sense that they might represent different ways of working which are appropriate at different times and in different ways. For example, there are times when one wishes to explore the more experiential aspects of a particular doctrine, and other times when it is its impersonal features that are of most relevance. I may wonder whether a particular relationship I have with someone is really the sort of relationship that I think it is, and to answer this question involves a combination of analytical and experiential skills. I need to be able to stand back from my particular situation and look at it objectively; yet I also have to experience particular feelings that are going to be the objects of my reflection, although not the only objects. It is this combination of tasks which is described in mysticism, or at least in much of Islamic mysticism.

Each cultural tradition has a mystical strain and it is hardly surprising that in the largely secular society of the turn-of-the-millennium West, Islamic mysticism, in the form of Sufism, should have become so important, given that many other mystical traditions might seem to have been irremediably compromised by their connections with more familiar traditional religions. The sorts of Sufism that have become popular in the West among non-Muslims are those which exist at the more subjective end of the continuum, and do not really give an accurate impression of the tradition as a whole. But that is no reason to disparage this form of writing, which serves a purpose, even a philosophical purpose when combined with its appropriate theoretical context. Nor is there much point in arguing that mysticism represents the essence of Islamic or any other kind of philosophy. It is just a way of doing philosophy, and must be treated as such.

There clearly is a big difference between mysticism and the sort of philosophy which we have described as *falsafa*, but it is of interest to ask why this did not seem to be the case for many of the *falasifa*. In modern Islamic philosophy a sharp distinction is often made between *mashsha'i* thinkers and *ishraqi* thinkers, where the latter designation is not specifically limited to those who follow the *ishraqi* School of al-Suhrawardi and the School of Isfahan, but is taken more broadly to mean mystics in general. In earlier forms of philosophy, though, these were not sharply distinguished, and perhaps, as some modern commentators like Seyyed Hossein Nasr argue, this was a leading virtue of older forms of thought (Nasr 1993, 1996h, 2006). What they had firmly in mind was that the technical purpose of philosophy is to establish the criteria of valid argumentation. It follows from this that philosophy is the only way of establishing what the real nature of being is, since everything else will only have a vague grasp of this. Philosophy, especially logic, helps us grasp firmly the real nature of reality, as opposed to less sure methods, which limit us to uncertainty and weaker links with the truth (Leaman 1992).

Is not the sort of information that we attain through sense perception a kind of knowledge that does not rely on philosophy? The answer provided here by the *mashsha'i* tradition has to be negative. All that sense experience can give us is a grasp of the particular, and knowledge is inextricably connected with the universal. The trouble with the particular is that it really refers to opinion, and only information that is capable of being expressed in terms of logical syllogisms can be graced with the description of knowledge. It is possible to place information derived from sense experience within syllogisms, but the result is some general claim about that sort of experience, not information that counts as knowledge of that particular experience. So natural science can be organized in terms of syllogisms; yet even when this is done, it is still weaker in the sense that it is less general than higher forms of reasoning, which have as their subject matter being as such. The discipline which is highest, and which precisely has nothing more than pure being as its subject, is philosophy, a point on which the *falasifa*, following Aristotle, had few disagreements.

Being

There is a problem, though, in talking of the science of being, since being itself has no genus and no differentiae; there is nothing more basic than it in terms of which it may be analysed. Ibn Sina spends some time discussing the unusual nature of being, in the sense of absolute being. It is comprehensible, to use the language of Wittgenstein in the *Tractatus*, only through what it shows, not through what it says. We have experience of being, but our conceptual terminology can only point to it; nothing it can say is able to encapsulate it. The best we can do when contemplating the cycle of reality and existence is to think about the necessary existence which is at the source of being in the world, and which ultimately brings about our very varied and inferior form of existence. How should we react to the fact that we need to contemplate something that, quite literally, cannot be contemplated?

The first thing we need to do is to refrain from confusing the nature of being with anything that lies within our sensual or conceptual repertoire. We must not identify it with the changeable and the temporary, just as we should not identify God and his attributes in this way. What we need to do is to concentrate on the notion of being, which we already know to a certain extent through our experience of ourselves and our world as aspects of being. Although we know it to a certain extent in this way, it is only to a certain extent, and if we wish to grasp it more generally and perfectly, we cannot rely on an ability to convert our partial experience into syllogistic reasoning. Pure being is too pure to be definable in terms of the syllogism, so cannot become propositional knowledge. Philosophy is important because it teaches us that philosophy is not powerful enough in itself to analyse pure being, and in having a grasp of its own limitations, it presents us clearly with a view of the limits of human knowledge. This is not to claim, though, that we are unable to explore pure being, only to argue that we cannot explore it through the techniques and concepts of logic and philosophy. We need to approach being in an entirely different way, through allowing our ability to contemplate reality directly free flow. This can only be through a form of mysticism, as a way of understanding reality in a more direct, personal manner. There is not a choice available to us between this form of understanding and propositional knowledge, since there is a limit to where we can get with propositional knowledge, and philosophy itself informs us of this. So all we have left is mysticism, in one form or another, and that is the approach we need to take.

This is the explanation of why most philosophers in the Islamic world were committed to mysticism, though naturally to varying degrees. The staunchest dissident on this point is Ibn Rushd. He does not criticize mysticism explicitly, but it is clear from his work that he has no sympathy for it. There is in his thought a thoroughgoing Aristotelian attitude to the nature of reality as something that is essentially knowable, since we are linked with it in such a way that there can be no problem in principle in understanding the nature of the world. This follows from his view of the identity of the knower, the object of thought and the act of knowing, which seems a rather strange doctrine. What it is meant to do is to show how knowledge is possible. Knowledge is only possible if there is something in its object that is like the person who is trying to know it, and an act of knowledge is only feasible if there is some essential feature that is part of both the object of knowledge and the knowing subject.

If this is not the case, then we are left with the traditional sceptical problem of explaining how an outside reality can be known via the thoughts and experiences that take place within an individual's mind. Moreover, we then have to justify our claim that what takes place within us has a reference to something real that takes place outside us. Not only do we need to establish this reference, we also need to show that what takes place within us, if it is to be knowledge, is an accurate copy of what really exists outside us. Aristotle does this by identifying the knowing subject with the object and with the act of knowledge in the case of a genuine act of knowledge. There is no problem with this on the view of reality produced by Aristotle and Ibn Rushd, since for them the world is essentially knowable, and we are essentially knowers. There is no mystery to the world; there is nothing about it in principle that we cannot know, except perhaps for those aspects which are beyond our present, past and future awareness and thought. The world is essentially knowable, and there is nothing about it that lies outside it, as it were. The meaning of the world resides in the world, and we are provided with both the faculties and the conceptual machinery to grasp that meaning. It follows that there is no need to wander into mysticism, since there is nothing non-propositional for us to seek.

Some might think that this is a view that conflicts with religion. After all, it is traditionally held that if there is a meaning to the world, then it resides with its creator, God; and unless one thinks that the world has a transcendental meaning, there is little point in talking about a deity who is its ultimate cause and source. This would only give succour to the view of those who, like al-Ghazali, accuse the philosophers of talking about God, but giving him nothing to do, so that he remains as a figurehead with no significant role to play. However, it is one thing to argue that there is a role for mysticism within religion, and quite another to insist that one cannot have religion without mysticism. That would be a difficult claim to make, especially as the role of mysticism within religion is often rather contentious. That is, there are many within Islam, and other religions, who are thoroughly hostile to mysticism and to the sorts of experiences and techniques which it uses. There is also in mysticism a further problem, which is that there is often much in common between the mysticisms of different religions, which gives support to some sort of religious universalism, hardly an attractive idea for those who are committed to the idea that there is something very special and unique about a particular religion.

Mysticism as a science

The terms in Arabic for the discipline of mysticism and for systems of thought which use mystical ideas are various, and include *'ilm al-tasawwuf, al-hikma al-muta'aliya* and *'ilm al-'irfan*. It might seem strange to refer to the pursuit of mysticism as a science, in the sense of an organized body of knowledge. There is a tendency to contrast the subjectivity of the mystical response to reality with the scientific investigation of that reality; but what is meant by 'science' here is an indication of the systematic nature of much Islamic mysticism. Many thinkers in their writings describe their particular approach to understanding the nature of reality, and they do this in the form of a spiritual autobiography. First they describe the ways in which the soul is disciplined, in an attempt to control and restrict its bodily impulses. Such a process often starts with repentance. This is more than a private spiritual journey, though, since the appropriate organization of the microcosm, the individual, brings about a powerful link with the macrocosm, the leading principles of reality. God rewards, or may reward, the spiritual seeker after truth by sending signs of his favour, or at least signs that the journey on which he is engaged is the right journey. The seeker is rewarded by indications of the correctness of the path in the form of gifts, which are often the result of developing levels of insight. How do we know that what we take to be spiritual growth really is spiritual growth, as compared with a subjective feeling that it is spiritual growth? This issue arises often in the accounts provided by the mystics. They are very aware that there is more to such growth than merely the practice of asceticism, and that there is more to gaining insight than the belief that one has done so. Many Sufis are even of the opinion that one should avoid ecstatic experience, since it is impossible to direct such experience in an appropriately Islamic direction, and may lead to loss of control in the seeker. As a result there was a long-standing debate in Sufism itself over the appropriate status of mystical experience.

The idea that there are Sufis who are suspicious of mystical experience is a useful corrective to the view that Sufism is all about people whirling around ecstatically and repeating the name of God until there is a change in the nature of their consciousness. Many Sufis are highly sceptical of such practices, charging them, quite correctly, with not having any essential links with Islam. It is certainly the case that some individuals describe themselves as Sufis, but not as Muslims, responding to the universality of ecstatic mystical experience and the particularity of Sufi routes to that experience. This shows non-ecstatic Sufis to be suspicious of the wildness of many of the claims made by ecstatic Sufis, and rightly so from an Islamic point of view in the sense that there is a tendency, on occasion, to go far beyond the limits of religion. A much-discussed case is that of the fate of al-Hallaj, who was executed on the charge of idolatry. He claimed 'I am the Truth' in such a way as to compare himself with God. From one point of view, there is no problem with such an assertion; it could mean no more than that there is a connection between the individual and his creator, and that just as the latter is the creator of my being, so in my understanding of this I share in his understanding of what it is to bring about something else. But the assertion could also mean that the individual is identical with God, in the sense of being God, and this runs right up against the rules against *shirk*, or idolatry. This brings out, yet again, the dangers of mysticism. The mystic is right to emphasize his closeness to God in the sense that everything is close to God, since there is really only God. Yet it is a slippery slope from here to identification with the deity in such a way that one fails to appreciate the immense gap that exists between us and God. This contrast between the transcendence and immanence of God is a familiar problem in many religions, of course, but particularly so in Islam, with its explicit rules against idolatry. The mystic tries to resolve this difficulty in a satisfactory way.

But can the mystic succeed? Al-Ghazali is often said to have established Sufism on a respectable religious foundation, since he insisted on a rigorous adherence to Islamic law and custom at the same time as advocating the Sufi path. Actually, al-Ghazali is a rather unusual Sufi, in that he does not indicate any particular *shaykh* as his instructor, and it is far from clear what precise form the path to spiritual development and perfection takes for him. In his remarkable encyclopaedic *Ihya' 'ulum al-din* (Revival of the Sciences of Religion), al-Ghazali sets out to do precisely what he says in the title, to revive Islam and its disciplines. There is a famous *hadith* according to which in every period someone will come to revive or breathe new life into Islam, the implication being that religion loses its freshness and vivacity over time, and requires something to get it going again in the hearts of its participants. For al-Ghazali, it is the infusion of Sufism that will give Islam a new lease of life, and he goes into extraordinary detail as to how this is possible. The work is one of the outstanding examples of Islamic and Arabic literature, and from any religious perspective at all, or none, there is a good deal in it that displays acute spiritual insight. The success of the work is often attributed not only to its style, but to its insistence on strict adherence to *shari'a*, as well as the pursuit of the Sufi path by those capable of it. Al-Ghazali is taken to have made Sufism respectable, acceptable to those in the community who were suspicious of its antinomian tendencies. That is, any form of mysticism raises the question: if access to the inner truth can be acquired through following the mystical path, what need is there of the public rituals and practices of religion?

Al-Ghazali insists on the importance of the mystic being a good Muslim, as does Ibn al-ʿArabi. Their argument was that it is only through preparing oneself along the Islamic path that one can find the higher path to experience of the reality that lies behind everything. Yet there seems to be no reason in principle why the higher path should only be accessible through religion, or even just through Islam. This is a question that was also difficult to answer for the *falasifa*, since they argued that the highest form of awareness and indeed happiness was available only to the philosophers. It would seem, then, that a philosopher could bypass the normal practices of religion and society and concentrate entirely on attaining this very highest level of happiness. Philosophers too, like the Sufis, insisted on normal life as a member of the community as necessary to the attainment of philosophical perfection. Now one can certainly see why it would be advisable to say this, and why anyone who told other people that he was abandoning ordinary social and religious activities might not find himself left alone for long enough to achieve the highest levels of awareness which are possible. Anyone in a large organization who wants to pursue his own path to some end is more likely to achieve his goal if he keeps quiet about precisely what he is doing, and what its implications are for the rules of the organization itself. But this is entirely a matter of prudence, and there seems to be no logical connection between achieving awareness of inner reality, or the highest levels of happiness, and living the life of the ordinary person.

The answer to this question is to be found by returning to the notion of the route to the truth being precisely that. There would be no merit in following the route if one were just placed on it, so to speak, or even if one were just taken to the end-point. To take an example, the mountaineer does not just want to get to the top of the mountain in the most efficient manner. What she wants to do is to discover, establish and follow a particular route, overcoming the difficulties and dangers along the way, and then get to the top. Climbing is interesting because of the dangers that are part of it. Of course, most climbers do not court danger, but unless there was some danger, the flavour of what they do would soon pall. The same might be said of our ordinary lives, that we do not on the whole put ourselves in positions of danger, yet many of us do things which are risky to some degree, and some of us take considerable and obvious risks every time we light a cigarette or ride a bicycle down a busy street. Given the vagaries of human existence, we none of us know when we shall die, whether we are going to become ill, or whether some dread disease will be diagnosed in us. If we have children, we do not know how, or whether, they will develop, and cannot predict what future problems may arise. Yet many people would say that this is what makes life interesting, and indeed more interesting than if it were completely safe and sanitized. The path of the ordinary citizen, the route taken by most of the human population, entails problems and possibilities that are part of what constitutes a valuable human life. To avoid that path is certainly to circumvent the problems, but it also implies missing the possibilities for personal growth and realization.

This is not to say that there are no circumstances in which it is appropriate to avoid society. In his *Tadbir al-mutawahhid* (Management of the Solitary) Ibn Bajja suggests that in a hostile society philosophers will be treated as *nawabit*, weeds, and that it is better for them to continue their work in isolation, since there is no point in trying to interest an essentially unfriendly community in what they are doing. Similarly, Ibn Tufayl's eponymous character in *Hayy ibn Yaqzan* leaves his solitude to participate in the life of a community, but later leaves this society, rejected and confused by the sort of reception he received. He returns to a quiet contemplative life on his island, where he can direct his life and thinking entirely towards God. In many ways this is second-best, since it is always preferable to live and work with others. For one thing, it is only through communal life that one can influence others, and it is surely better to involve others in one's journey to happiness rather than merely selfishly pursue it by oneself. Then again, for most people it is not possible to reach ultimate happiness by oneself, since one needs to work with others to get on the right path in the first place. One needs to be guided in some way, and unless there is someone there to guide, and a community to make sure that one keeps on the right path, there is little likelihood of success. The only people who can pursue this end by themselves are those of extraordinary intelligence and virtue, who have direct help from God; but it is easy for lesser mortals to deceive themselves in this respect.

The perfect man

A key concept in Islamic mysticism is that of the perfect man (*al-insan al-kamil*). He is someone who exemplifies all the virtuous moral qualities, which in turn represent the qualities that exist in God, albeit to a far stronger degree. What the perfect man symbolizes is the greatest possible human development of understanding, compassion, charity and spiritual growth, and he serves as a bridge between humanity and God. His task is to help others to span the gap that exists between this world and the next, the world of reality; and, as one might expect, the perfect man is often identified with the prophet, who has precisely this role. The perfect man represents the attributes of God in so far as humanity can accomplish this, to its greatest possible extent within the world of generation and corruption. This notion is often also identified with the friends of God, the *wali*, since they enjoy a special relationship with him (Lalani 2006). This is as a result of their maintaining within themselves a simulacrum of the perfection and balance of God himself, a state that enables them to remain unaffected by anything except God himself. The friend of God, or the perfect man, is the *barzakh* between us and God; he shares some of our qualities and also some of God's; and in his person he has the ability to lead us from where we are to where God is. In other words, he links the microcosm (us) with the macrocosm (the universe as a whole).

The important thing to realize about human beings is that we are open to a wide range of possibilities. We do not have fixed natures, and we can become more or less anything. We can become perfect, or we can become corrupt and evil. But we are more than part of the universe; rather, we are the spirit of the universe, in the sense that the universe has no meaning apart from its human beings. God brought us into existence in order that we should know him, and apart from us there is nothing in the universe that is capable of knowing him in accordance with his names. Of course, everything in the universe may be said to know God in its particular way, and imperfect human beings can grasp him in a limited way. The perfect man is able to comprehend him through an understanding of how the universe as a whole celebrates its origins in, and dependency on, God. The universe without people in it would be like the body without a soul. Everything would look the same as before, but in reality the whole meaning of the body, of the person, would be missing, and we would be left without anything meaningful.

We should not think of our links with God as something very difficult to establish, since we are all born with the natural tendency to worship him. In the words of a famous *hadith*, 'Every child is born with the original disposition, and then its parents make it a Christian, a Jew, or a Zoroastrian.' These religious deviations are seen as aspects of denying God's unity and opting for idolatry, since these religions are not as monotheistic as Islam, in the opinion of the Prophet. What the mystic seeks to do is to return to where we all started, to our original disposition to feel a simple trust in the goodness of a single God, which is often characterized precisely as *dhikr*, or remembering. The principle of reality shines on the world like light, and what we take to be reality is the result of this light, its effect on differentiated physical and mental phenomena. What we need to do if we are to understand the real nature of the real is to blend ourselves as individuals in the macrocosm, in the sense of appreciating that we are merely parts or aspects of a much larger, divinely formed whole. At the same time we need to respect the diversity and individuality of our experience, since these are also aspects of reality.

Combining these two ways of looking at the same reality is not an easy task, and requires use of the allegorical and challenging language of the mystic. It is important that we appreciate this dual nature of what is involved in grasping the real nature of the universe. It is not enough to lose ourselves in the contemplation of God; nor is it enough to lose ourselves in the contemplation of the world of generation and corruption, including ourselves. We need to bring these apparently conflicting activities together, and the difficulty of doing this explains the paradoxical language that characterizes talk about Sufism. Another term often used for mystical thought is *kashf*, or unveiling, and this brings out nicely the idea that the mystic gets to the truth by peeling away the layers of apparent reality, until one ends up at the kernel of truth. The difficulty with this, of course, is that the sort of language we use is located at the level of the layers, so we have no language to describe the experience that exists once the superficial aspects have been removed. Our language seems only to extend as far as the veiled reality itself. So any language we use to describe the end of the process is necessarily going to be unsatisfactory in a radical sense. The concept of *dhikr*, remembering, is a useful one here. It is rather like the psychological process of trying to remember something very far back in time, or something traumatic. It is often difficult to tell whether the apparent memory is a real memory, or whether it is just something that has been stimulated and indeed created by the attempt to find it. Hence there is a need for a science, or system, to reach this point. Otherwise, anything will go, and it is very important that not just anything goes, since we are describing here a route for the individual to come closer to God and to the reality that God represents. The highly systematic approach of much Islamic mystical thought is designed to avoid the charge of subjectivity.

The deepening of prayer

It is appropriate to give an example of how mysticism can be used to deepen the understanding of a religious practice, in this case prayer. As in most religions, there is an emphasis in Islam on prayer, particularly public and ritual prayer (*salat*). But there is a danger in prayer: one may think that through prayer God will help the individual, and one may pray in an automatic and inauthentic manner. Let us take these separately. The person who prays may have particular selfish concerns in mind when he prays, and he may then treat God as though he were a king or a very powerful person who has influence over the fate of those inferior to him. Of course, God is a bit like this, though far greater than any earthly potentate, and treating him as though he were just like us, but more so, is hardly considered appropriate in Islam. We should recall here the criticisms that Ibn Rushd provides of al-Ghazali's account of God, where the former argues that the latter treats God rather like a superman. Al-Ghazali would not accept that this was his concept of God, of course; but then the argument was not that this was his concept of God. Rather, it was that such an undesirable concept is the inevitable consequence of his account of how God acts and knows.

Al-Ghazali would have been just as critical as Ibn Rushd of the idea that we should communicate with God as though with a person. He would also have criticized severely the ways in which, through familiarity, prayer often becomes rather unconsidered and prosaic. Instead of making us tremble in the presence of our creator, the practice of prayer often results in a comfortable feeling that we have done our duty, or are in good standing with God. Al-Ghazali follows the Sufi doctrine that prayer can be strengthened spiritually by being associated with *dhikr*, which literally means 'remembrance'. One needs to remember one's total dependence on God, which is far from an easy task, given the ways in which the banalities of the everyday world interfere in our relationship with the deity. The different Sufi orders tended to advocate a variety of approaches to how to approach God and ultimately enjoy *fana'*, the final mystical absorption within religious experience itself. According to al-Ghazali, in his *Ihya' 'ulum al-din*, the first stage of *dhikr* is the determination to turn one's mind away from mundane matters towards God and the spiritual. This is not easy to do, especially for long periods, since concern for the world and its interests soon crowd out our memory of our basic connection with God, and at this stage we turn away from who we really are to contemplate immoral activity. Al-Ghazali advocates contemplation of one's own death as a useful approach, and goes into great detail about how repeated meditative exercises can strengthen the ability to feel the mercy of God.

There are many *hadith* in which the value of prayer as a way to avert punishment in the next world is discussed. Al-Ghazali takes this to refer more to the ways in which contemplative exercises may deepen the heart of the believer, and thereby strengthen his inner spiritual state, than anything else. What is important is not so much repeating the verbal prayer, or having the inner thought about the meaning of the prayer, but doing both together. He accepts that this form of religious behavior can lead to practices and ideas that are followed merely prosaically. The mystical impulse often seems rather overdone and mysterious, in that the mystic advocates, or even insists on, forms of knowledge and experience that many sincere believers are happy to live without. Yet the mystic is interested only in emphasizing two aspects of religion that can easily drop out of sight. One is that the most important aspect of our lives is our relationship with God. For most believers this is something they say but not something they really feel in their hearts, to use a familiar Sufi expression. How many believers really act as though they are part of a world created and controlled by God? The point of Sufism is to return religion to its roots in a simple, uncomplicated belief in God. What makes this belief simple is the other aspect of religion that the Sufi stresses, the importance of acquiring a taste of reality. It is easy to repeat a conceptual formula which establishes our commitment to a particular conception of the deity and his world, but much harder to feel that the world is actually like that. Our everyday life produces sensations that are immediate, whereas the truths of religion seem distant and obscure. The point of Sufism is to make the latter as present to us as our everyday experiences – indeed, to make God more real to us than anything else – and this is a matter of helping us come into direct experiential contact with the inner truth of our being. Although the truth that, as a result, we may capture is a simple one, the route to it is not simple, since we have allowed our lives to become very complicated through entanglement with the diversity of the world of generation and corruption. Sufism is designed to lead us back to where we started, to allow us to recover the memory of who we really are, and to reinstate our relationship with God.

Criticisms of Sufism

There are many reasons to be critical of Sufism. One is to regard it as over-elaborate and innovatory in its rituals, the sort of accusation that is brought against it by the Wahhabi ideology of Saudi Arabia. Ibn 'Abd al-Wahhab was fiercely opposed to the sorts of practices that had grown up in the Islamic world and that were more Sufi than Muslim, in his view, since they involved practices that deviated from the simple form of religion that he regarded as appropriate. Worshipping at the tombs of saints, for instance, and indeed the whole institution of saints, are very questionable in a country where even today the kings are buried in anonymous graves and sites of historical note may be destroyed for attracting visitors who pray there.

Then there is the feeling that Sufism is richer fare than is really required for the Muslim. This is very much the position of Said Nursi, who was certainly attracted very much to Sufism, and whose writings are redolent with Sufi ideas. Yet he regarded Sufism as too rich a conceptual set of ideas, since they make rather extravagant claims and demands on the believer. The implication is that Sufism is superrogatory, it goes beyond what is necessary in religion, and as such may put people off the basic set of practices and beliefs, or even encourage them in alternative beliefs and practices (Leaman 1999f).

Finally, we need to examine the reasons why the modernizers in the Islamic world like 'Abduh and Iqbal were very unenthusiastic about Sufism, and this is because they saw it as encouraging a negative approach to science and technology, and also excluding practitioners from the mainstream of social life. It is certainly true that many Sufis prioritize seclusion and privacy, turning themselves against the ordinary world, and this is hardly conducive to social and political involvement. It has to be said though that many Sufi movements in the Islamic world have had no difficulty getting heavily involved in the practical life of their countries, and even in representing serious political blocs of influence. On the other hand, it has to be admitted that this is rather contrary to the spirit of Sufism, which is oriented towards private experience and also a total trust in God, both of which might encourage passivity. But, as always in religion, we find a much more dynamic interpretation of the doctrine than a study of the basic texts would suggest might happen, and this enables Sufism to enter political life at just the same time as it advocates a contempt for such activity.

5

Ontology

We looked at the crucial role of Ibn Sina in linking what we have called *falsafa*, or philosophy, with *hikma*, or what might be called mysticism or 'wisdom'. He seems to argue that these two ways of investigating the nature of reality are inextricably linked, and that they should not be seen as in competition with each other. On the other hand, he seems to have had little doubt about *hikma* being the more central and deeper enquiry. This fits nicely with his central thesis of emanation, the idea that reality flows from a first principle, and as a result constructs the whole of the universe. It is hardly surprising that lower down the scale of being different methods of seeking understanding should be appropriate, namely those of philosophy. But if we are to gain an understanding of everything, then wider and more ambitious methods are required, hence the need for *hikma*. This might seem rather strange, since we are accustomed to think of philosophy in the sense of logical enquiry as being the most abstract possible form of enquiry. How can any other methodology be even more abstract than philosophy? The answer could well be that what philosophy cannot do, but *hikma* can, is provide direct experience of reality, a taste (*dhawq*) of how things really are. This is not to disparage philosophy, but merely to recognize that there are limits to its scope, and that if there is mystical knowledge, then there is a good argument for seeing it as extending further than the sorts of knowledge that can be obtained through philosophy.

Being and existence in Islamic philosophy

We have already seen that Mulla Sadra had a distinctive view of the nature of being and existence, and that this view played an important part in explaining his general metaphysics. Up to his time, there had been a protracted debate within Islamic philosophy on the links between being and existence, in which the former is linked with the essence or nature of a thing, the latter with its actual instantiation. A particular difficulty in the early translations of Greek philosophy arose because of the lack of a copula in Arabic (by contrast with the situation in Persian and Greek, of course), and the Arabic terms *wujud* and *mawjud*, among others, were often used to represent existence. Other popular terms for existence were *anniya*, *kana* and *huwiyya*, while essence was variously represented by *dhat*, *mahiyya* and *haqiqa*. Mulla Sadra defended the notion of the *asalat al-wujud*, the primacy of existence, by contrast with the majority of thinkers, who argued that essence comes first. The latter argued that the first question to ask of a name is what sort of name it is (its essence), and that whether that name actually exists, has a reference, is an entirely different question. Mulla Sadra, of course, accepted that such a distinction could be made; but he argued that the very consideration of that distinction presupposed the existence of the entities that are involved. Now it is often argued, in line with an Aristotelian principle, that the first question in philosophy is ontological, that is, about the nature of being. If this is true, then this particular view of the nature of being of Mulla Sadra is bound to play a crucial role in his philosophical methodology.

One of the most important theses of Ibn Sina is the priority of essence over existence, sometimes expressed in terms of existence being an attribute of being. The idea here is that what really exists is being, the notion or definition of a thing, and that its eventual instantiation is a question of whether something moves it from potentiality to actuality. This seems an entirely sensible idea, since there are many things that we can think about (so are possible) which do not actually come into existence (so are not actually existent). There seem good reasons, then, to put being first and existence second.

Ibn Rushd vs Ibn Sina on existence

As is well known, Ibn Rushd argued against this thesis. One motive for his rejection of it was its usefulness to thinkers like al-Ghazali.

The distinction between essence and existence establishes an important role for God's action. If it is the case that something is always needed to move a being from potentiality to actuality, then this role can easily be attributed to God. According to Ibn Sina, it is a prior cause that brings about existence, and ultimately this can be extended back to a first cause, or ultimate source of existence as the first principle of emanation, the Necessary Being. This is the only thing that does not require a prior cause to bring it into existence, since this Being is necessary in itself, not through something else. Unless there were such a Being, Ibn Sina argues, the search for causes would be infinite, which he suggests is absurd.

Ibn Rushd criticized this notion on the grounds that the existence of a thing may be more fruitfully regarded as being part of its essence, in which case existence can be seen as having priority over being. That is, the existence of a thing is not just an incidental aspect of it, but is essential to it, to its character and role, and cannot be regarded as something that is just added on to an idea of it. He uses this argument to suggest that many of the thought experiments which al-Ghazali employs to show how the world could be a very different place do not work. These thought experiments make sense only if we can hold an idea in our head independently of how that idea comes out in reality, and of course we can hold some such ideas in our head. The famous example is that of the griffin, which I am thinking about now, but I am unlikely to claim it has ever existed or could exist. Yet there is no problem in thinking about it existing, at least mentally, and its real existence is entirely irrelevant to the idea of it that we can grasp. Ibn Rushd would argue that the idea of a unicorn is precisely the idea of something that is non-existent, except as an idea, and the fact that we can think about it does not show that it could exist as anything more than an idea. If a unicorn really could exist, Ibn Rushd argued, then it would exist, and since it does not exist, then it could not exist.

Mulla Sadra vs al-Suhrawardi on existence

Most philosophers in the Islamic world were on the side of Ibn Sina rather than Ibn Rushd, favouring the priority of essence over existence. An exception here is Mulla Sadra, who, like Ibn Rushd, argued for the priority of existence over essence. The particular mode of being of a thing determines its instantiation, and the latter cannot be identified with essence, since essence is nothing more than a mental concept. A mental concept is nothing more than an idea in someone's head, an idea which cannot be more than an abstract formulation, so cannot make up the reality of anything more than the mental event. In presenting the relationship between essence and existence in this way, Mulla Sadra was consciously distinguishing his view from that of Ibn Sina and al-Suhrawardi, two of his predecessors with whose thought he was much concerned. The latter argued that existence itself is no more than a mental abstraction, to which nothing really corresponds. This seems a rather strange way of putting the relationship between existence and essence, since if anything is concrete and real, one would assume it to be existence. But the argument for al-Suhrawardi's view is that if existence is the source of reality, then it will itself have to exist, but then this kind of necessary existence will also have to exist, and so on, ad infinitum. This objection seems to be wrong, though. Can something not just exist, so that we can then say that it exists, and its existence is more important as an aspect of it than its essence?

This is not the case, according to al-Suhrawardi, for whom the actual instantiation of an idea requires something to bring it about, which is surely reasonable, and then an explanation of how what brought it about itself came about, and so on, returning us to the model which Ibn Sina produced. Why can we not then say that what we have here is a regress that ends up with a basic principle, which in fact is what al-Suhrawardi asserts? In his case, the basic principle is the Light of Lights, out of which the source of being in the world is created, and which itself is not illuminated by any prior or more basic principle of light. But on his view, what is important in this picture is the way in which the principle of light brings about concepts; the actual existence of those concepts is an entirely minor aspect of their reality. After all, the world in which things actually exist is the lowest world, higher worlds being those in which ideas are brought about and created. The whole point of having an imaginal realm is to have a world where questions of existence and non-existence really lose their point, since what is important is the way we can identify and use concepts, and the ways in which those concepts are constructed for us by light. The actual instantiation of anything is a poor thing by comparison.

Al-Suhrawardi particularly disapproves of the idea that there are independent things, and that they have, or may have, the properties of essences and existences. He is also entirely hostile to the idea that there can be existences that are the properties of essences. Once we start talking in this way, we get into the problem of explaining the nature of the form of existence of the essence before the existence gets to it, as it were. We also have to argue that the existing thing exists because of the addition of existence, which gets us on to an infinite regress. The critical attitude which al-Suhrawardi adopted towards Aristotelian logic runs right through his downgrading of existence at the expense of essence. For one thing, the basic distinction which Aristotle makes between genus and differentiae, between what sort of thing something is and how it exists, is criticized by al-Suhrawardi, and it is not difficult to see how that distinction mimics the essence/existence distinction. Al-Suhrawardi attacks it on account of its attempt to explain a problem in terms of something that is even more problematic, so that appealing to how a thing exists is no answer to the question of what it is. This is part of al-Suhrawardi's general critique of Aristotelian logic. According to Aristotle, we can explain the meaning of a term by reference to the properties of the term, but al-Suhrawardi objects that these properties are no better understood than the term itself, so one is attempting to explain the obscure through the equally obscure. It follows from his *ishraqi* principles, of course, that what we experience as the contingent form of existence is in fact a crude grasp by us of what has come about through its links with degrees of light, the real basis of things which we tend to misunderstand because we are wrongly fascinated by the question of what exists.

What arguments does Mulla Sadra have for the thesis that existence is, on the contrary, the basic notion of metaphysics? We need to recall here that, according to Aristotle, metaphysics is the study of being as being, which means that the proper subject matter of the most basic aspect of philosophy is being. Then, after we have discussed the nature of being, we could move on to look at the different ways in which being is expressed in existence. But Mulla Sadra argues that where we should start is not with being in this sense. Why not? First, because being is the most universal of things, so cannot be defined in terms of genus and differentiae. Any attempt at defining it in terms of something else must fail, since it is the best-known and most surely established of all notions. This might seem a rather dubious proposition, since if being is so well known as an idea, why does Aristotelian philosophy start by examining it? The point which Mulla Sadra makes is that being is the basis of all definition, so there is no point in trying to define it, except in terms in which it is the being of something that is, in terms of which it exists.

The equivocality of being

Being is just one thing, but it manifests itself in different ways in reality, and the ability of one thing to characterize many things in this way is called by Mulla Sadra the 'equivocality' (*tashkik*) of being. It is true that in so far as everything exists, then it exists in the same way; but the sort of existence there is clearly differs from thing to thing, and some things have more being than others. There is little point in using the concept of being as essence as the concept that characterizes reality, since it is far too general and equivocal to capture what it is for something to exist. What he has in mind here is that reality consists in a large number of existing things, things which actually figure as instantiated realities, and that characterizing these hard facts in terms of their essences is to misunderstand the situation. The fact that these things exist is indeed a fact that we may choose to describe in terms of being, but this tells us very little, since the amount of reality of each individual thing differs in accordance with its mode of existence. The higher up the scale of reality it occurs, the more simple and clear it is, since it will consist primarily of rational and perfect ideas. The lower down the scale it is, the more diverse it is, or, better, the more diverse they are, and saying that they exist is really to claim that they exist in very different and varied ways. Hence the equivocality of being: one is never quite sure how it is being used. This will depend on the nature of the existents that it is describing. Of course, there is a great temptation to say that the only thing that really exists is God, or the Absolute Being, and that everything else is merely a pale reflection of that form of existence (rather in the way in which Ibn Rushd describes that relationship). What makes this even more plausible is the theory of constant movement from one mode of existence to another, which Mulla Sadra sometimes characterizes as the progressive weakening and strengthening of being.

What is crucial to the theory here is that we appreciate that in change the existence of a thing both changes and also remains the same. It remains the same in that its link with the divine source of existence is unaffected, while it changes in taking up a different mode and form, and expressing the principle of Absolute Being more, or less, perfectly. This sounds very mysterious, but it is not that difficult to understand. When, for example, someone perfects their notion of love, they may come to see that this attitude is more appropriately held towards the form of a being, as compared to its matter, so that the love they feel is for something more abstract than was the case in the beginning. It is then more real love, a more refined and perfect notion of love, and the sort of love which exists has changed. It has become more like the love that God has for his creatures, and less like the desires that animals mutually experience. The sort of love which now comes into existence is in a sense the same sort of love as previously existed, since the love which existed before also had a connection with the perfect notion of love. Had it not had such a link, we could not have called it love at all. But the previous notion has changed to a more perfect notion, so it is both to a degree the same and to a degree different. This is possible given the notion of the equivocality of being.

It is important to distinguish between this notion of equivocation and ambiguity. The meaning of being is not ambiguous, but it is applied differently to different things. If I share out a handful of chocolate, then everyone gets some, but in different ways; yet they really all get some amount. The argument for this is that we perceive a similarity between the things that exist, as opposed to between them and what does not exist. Although everyone gets a different amount of chocolate, there is a closer connection between those getting different amounts as compared with those who get none, since the latter have nothing in their hands.

What enables us to say that one person is different from another person? After all, both share in the property of being human. The difference between them lies in the different ways in which they are individuated. Being becomes progressively more particularized as it spreads itself through the world, and there is an overall process from the more general and more indeterminate to the more concrete, determinate types of being, a move from imperfection to perfection, and everything is in permanent flux. The descriptions that we can provide of things are not fixed, but have to be regarded as making a reference to a certain level of being and perfection. This is an interesting model, since it contrasts with the more normal view of a decline in reality and perfection the nearer we come to this world. On this view of Mulla Sadra, the higher level of being comes from the lower, and the highest level of all, God, is equivalent to Being itself, since it is not definable in terms of anything else. Does this mean that God himself comes from some lower level of being? This would be a radical assertion indeed, but it is not Mulla Sadra's point. In so far as we naively identify God with a single being, that identification takes place at a lower level of being. This has a lot to do with the ways in which we perceive reality. The lower down the scale of reality, the easier it is to define individuals, since it is easier to apply universals to them; while the higher up we go, the harder it is to perceive essences. The equivocality of being lies in the fact that reality is dynamic, not static, so can exist in different and constantly changing ways. It is the existence of different things that produces the ideas of different things, that is, essences in our minds; but in reality it is the existence of those things that comes first. They emanate from the source of being, and any ideas about them that we produce subsequently are entirely mental, and not real. The relationship here is not entirely a matter of order, though, but a reflection of the basic constitution of reality. Existence comes about through emanation from the first cause, or Absolute Being, and it is then joined with essence. After all, that is how the whole emanationist process manages to move from just one thing to more than one thing, through the production of a thought and then the further thought that there is something about which one is thinking. These essences multiply the lower down one goes on the scale of reality, in the sense that the lower down one progresses, the more limited being becomes. The more essence there is, the less reality, as we can understand when we consider that God, the Absolute Being, has no essence and is pure.

As with Ibn Sina, we have at least two types of being: one that is contingent and depends on something else for its existence, and one that is necessary and depends on itself. One of the fascinating features of the *Asfar* (his major work on this issue; see Mulla Sadra 1967) is the complex account that he provides in it of a wide gamut of different kinds of being. He differs from Ibn Sina, though, in the definition of God, in that the latter is not to be analysed as a being whose essence implies his existence. God has no essence; he is pure being. No essence has to exist, since if an essence had to exist, its existence would follow from its essence, and hence its essence would precede or take greater significance than its existence. Mulla Sadra completely reverses Ibn Sina's ontology, so that the domain of necessity is that of existence, while the domain of essences is that of contingency.

Surely, though, it will be argued that in giving priority to existence, Mulla Sadra is challenging the fact that we can think about essences without claiming that they really exist. This is not an appropriate objection, though. He is quite happy, as is Ibn Rushd, to accept that there is a logical distinction to be made between essence and existence (he gives the example of thinking about the 'anqa, or griffin (1967: *Asfar* I.1.269)). There is a whole range of things which we can think about but which have no claims to exist at all, except in our minds. On the other hand, the fact that something exists in our minds does not mean that it exists only there, or even that its existence in the mind is not real existence. In so far as our thoughts exist in our minds, their essences and existences are the same. The point he goes on to make is that it is possible to have a number of different referring expressions, all of which refer, albeit in different ways, to the same existing thing. It does not follow that the different ways of referring to the same thing are parts of it, or aspects of it. The existence of a thing is the same as the thing that is picked out by its description; it is not something else added to the (concept of the) thing.

It might seem that we have departed some way from a proper grasp of the relationship between essence and existence here. Do we not talk of something existing as equivalent to some essence existing, in which case the essence appears to come first? Mulla Sadra allows this sort of language, but he does not allow us to claim that the existence of the essence is some factor in the essence. There is only one ontological event, as it were, when something exists, and this is equivalent to the existence of the thing and the essence of the thing. Conceptually there are two or more ideas in being, but in reality there is only one, and there are a variety of ways of understanding that one thing. The existence of Zayd, of this particular Zayd, is the same event as his determination as this precise individual. This man and this actualization of humanity are exactly the same ontological event. We can still distinguish between what Zayd is and whether he is, but this is a conceptual distinction about just one thing that exists.

It is interesting to note how both Mulla Sadra and Ibn Rushd apply the same theory of naming to underpin their hermeneutic theory of the links between different ways of approaching the same truth. For Ibn Rushd, the philosopher and the ordinary believer both describe the same truth, although they do it in different ways. They apply different descriptions to the same thing, and there is no more problem with this than there is in understanding how we can apply different predicates to one physically existing individual, for example. What comes first is the individual, and what comes after are the descriptions of the individual. It is certainly true that unless there were ways of describing the individual, we should be unable to pick him out; but it is also true that unless the individual existed, in some sense, there would be nothing for the essences to pick out.

Mulla Sadra and mysticism

One of the interesting controversies which have emerged concerning Mulla Sadra is how important it is to align his thought with mysticism to make sense of it. Some would argue that this can be overdone, since the main thrust of his thought is logical and conceptual, not mystical at all. Yet there is no doubt but that he had ongoing interest in mystical topics, given his frequent references to the thought of Ibn al-'Arabi and his many references to his teacher, Mir Damad (Nasr 1996f). On the other hand, we have already noted the similarities between his views on existence and essence and those of Ibn Rushd, the arch-opponent of mysticism, so we might question whether the mystical aspects of Mulla Sadra's approach are an integral part of his general philosophy.

It is difficult to appreciate the teaching of Mulla Sadra in its entirety without giving due attention to his mystical views. He has a view of reality that fits closely with the notion of *wahdat al-wujud*, or the unity of being, which is something he claims we can experience as we progress up the scale of awareness. The link between the unity of being and existing things is like the link between the sun and what the sun illuminates, and it is of course an error to identify the source of light with the things which are lit up by it. The idea of *tashkik al-wujud*, of the equivocality or gradations of being, explains why there is a differentiation of things in a world in which there is actually only one absolutely real thing. As we improve our understanding of reality, we come closer to appreciating the unity of everything, and we can do this at the same time as understanding how this basic unity is nonetheless diversified in the world of experience in a variety of different directions. We should recall the use of the notion of substantial motion, which plays a key role in the system here, since it is more accurate to talk in terms of events than things in the philosophy of Mulla Sadra. The world is in constant motion, and everything is changing all the time, and for this change to take place, what originally exists, or exists at a particular time, has to be seen as changing into something different. There is a basic existing being which remains the same throughout, in a sense, but it constantly acquires new properties on the route to greater perfection. This description of the process is rather misleading, since time is not real according to Mulla Sadra, being a reflection of how we think about this process, rather than a part of the process itself. Perfection comprises the progress of things to ever-increasing degrees of light, to unity with the principles that lie behind their possibility as things.

The imaginal realm

What is this level of reality to which everything is ineluctably moving? For Mulla Sadra, it is what has become known as the imaginal realm, the *'alam al-khayal*. The natural way to translate this into English would be as the imaginary realm, but many commentators have avoided this, as we have seen, because of what they take to be the negative implications of 'imaginary'. It is certainly true that we sometimes call things imaginary when we mean that they do not really exist, and when we identify ideas as imaginary, we are often using the term pejoratively.

The notion of the imaginal world is basically a product of the thought of Ibn al-ʿArabi and al-Suhrawardi. This world is designed to connect the lower world, the world of generation and corruption, with the higher levels of reality, where the perfect and pure ideas exist. One might wonder what need there is to postulate such an ontological realm, since between the ordinary ideas of our world and the purer, more abstract ideas of the world of ideas there does not necessarily have to be anything. After all, as I progressively refine my ideas of, say, number, a stage is reached at which I no longer need to make those ideas concrete. To start off with, I think in terms of a number of things, say three bananas, and I find it difficult to think of three except in terms of it characterizing some physical quantity. Then I notice that it is possible to think about the number itself, without connecting it to what it is a number of, and I start to think of the logical nature of number and the ways in which it works to define a range of abstract relationships. What need is there in such a model to have anything mediating between the physical numbers and the abstract numbers? The point of talking about an imaginal realm is to note that there is a stage in human thinking during which we play about with ideas in ways that are neither entirely determined by our experiences, nor entirely unrelated to them.

We have private and personal experiences, and these work their way into our more abstract speculations, so that, for example, if I think about the nature of love, I may think about the people whom I love myself. Yet I appreciate that the notion of love has a wider extension than is experienced by me, and that some people love things and people which I should find difficult to love. How can I understand what it is for them to love those objects? Imagination, or the imaginal realm, is what is important here, since I work from my experience of love to what I take their experience of love to be, and this is not something that can be carried out in a flash of recognition. I have to work slowly to change the way my ideas feel, to make sense of this new, unusual idea of love. For this the imaginal realm is necessary, in that I have to use my capacity to imagine what it is like to love in this new situation. This comes out nicely in al-Suhrawardi's description of the imaginal world as linking our microcosmic reality (what is important for us) with the macrocosmic nature of objective reality. The forms of the imaginal world are material in so far as they use physical imagery, but abstract in so far as they point to what is higher than it. It is more real than our world, but not as real as the higher world. In the imaginal world we have imaginal bodies (*al-jism al-khayali*), which differ from our physical bodies in that they can roam more widely across a range of ideas and experiences than our ordinary everyday bodies.

This is surely right, in that when we use our imagination, we are not limited by our personal experiences or the range of our bodies, but may extend ourselves in a variety of different, novel, directions.

This suggests that the very mysterious sorts of expression which mystics use can often be given a more down-to-earth meaning. It is even true of the *wahdat al-wujud* doctrine, which seems to be a mystical claim about the unity of existence and the necessity to develop some very special ways of understanding that unity. No doubt there are techniques which we might employ in order to see reality as one thing rather than as many different things, but the claim that everything comes down to one thing is not as difficult to understand as one might think. We need to recall the view of creation as emanation, which reflects Ibn Sina's continuing influence on Islamic philosophy, and the effect this has on the notion of being. The major contrast between Ibn Sina and Aristotle lies in the issue of the responsibility for matter, which for the latter does not belong to God. Aristotle's God is indeed the cause of the world, but not of the matter of the world; so there is something in existence apart from God and his effects, namely, matter. There is also the issue of whether this ultimate source of existence can be described in terms of substance and accident in terms, that is, of the categories. For Ibn Sina, this is impossible, because whatever brings about the form and matter of the universe cannot be defined in the same terms as the things within that universe. The source of being serves as a limiting concept, and we should not expect to be able to use the same ideas when describing such a concept as we can when describing what that concept makes possible. The only way we have of grasping the nature of the source of being is through contemplation of what it is for a perfect thing to bring about another thing.

The only proper analogy for this is the way in which a thinking thing brings about its thoughts; but it has to be in a pure and autonomous way, not as a result of the ordinary ways of thinking to which we are subjected by our everyday life. Those thoughts have to flow from our self as aspects of our contemplation of our self, a contemplation that succeeds in picking out the most important aspects of our being.

According to Ibn Sina, we cannot talk about the world and God, as though these were two different entities. Without God there is no world, and the world is merely a result of God's self-contemplation, so that in a sense there is no God without the world. It is not as if God decided to bring the world about, as if he had a choice in the matter. He had no more choice in the matter than does a good logician in working out the correct conclusion to a syllogism once he is provided with the premises, the point which irked al-Ghazali so much. Everything is one, in that it all stems from God, and plays a part in the rational structure of a reality that could not be otherwise, according to Ibn Sina. This is a point that is made even more strongly by Mulla Sadra, who goes so far as to claim that God is equivalent to existence itself. What this means is that the answer to the problem of why anything exists lies in the existence of God and his role as the source of the existence of everything in the world. Ordinary language is always going to find it difficult to explain this, since ordinary language rests on a form of existence which it cannot explain, hence mysticism. It might even be said that the move from the notion of the *wajib al-wujud*, the Necessary Existent, to the doctrine of *wahdat al-wujud*, is logically quite clear.

Different routes to one truth and the role of imagination

Is there a serious problem about reconciling different ways of looking at the same truth? There is certainly a difference in style, with some philosophers mistrusting the ability of philosophical approaches to the truth to get to completely the right result. That is, if one sees experience as being an important aspect of knowledge, then there is certainly no guarantee that any purely intellectual process will lead to that experience. One needs, perhaps, to use the theoretical machinery to come close to acquiring the experience; but then something else has to happen to make the experience possible. One thing that has to happen is that the seeker after knowledge feels dissatisfied with theoretical knowledge, in the sense of feeling that there is more to know than can be known theoretically. Some thinkers who are not convinced of the significance of mysticism present their work in rather unproblematic ways, so that once one has followed the argument, one knows as much as one can know of the nature of reality. Al-Farabi and Ibn Rushd adopt this sort of methodology, an approach that fits well with the sort of agenda that Aristotle put forward. Although it is often said, and quite rightly, that these thinkers worked within something of a Neoplatonic context, there is no doubt that their work represents much of the spirit of Aristotle, the spirit being that the universe is basically a comprehensible place, such that if one works through the right sort of principles one can accomplish a total grasp of that reality.

Individuals differ in their ability to make contact with a more developed notion of reality. For some, it is the result of a long, difficult process of working logically until they achieve some grasp of the formal structure of the world. For others, it is a matter of the occasional flash of understanding of the real nature of the world, with far more experiences that are on a lower level of understanding. Some people have purified their intellects sufficiently for them to be in contact most, or all, of the time with the active intellect, and these Ibn Sina labels holy or angelic. For such individuals, the forms of reality are as real as *qudsi, malaki* are the events and objects of the everyday world; or it might be better expressed by saying that they are as vivid. The important thing to realize about this process is that it is not automatic. For us to make contact with the intelligible world, we need something to mediate between the material world and the intelligible world, and this can be identified with the imaginal world. The imaginal world consists of concepts that share characteristics of both the material and the intelligible worlds, and unless there were such concepts, it would not be possible to explain how movement from one world to the other is conceivable. What motive would we have to seek to advance our understanding unless we could form some conception of where we could go?

Imagination is necessary to take us to a higher level, since we need to be able to visualize at a lower level of knowledge what it would be like to be at a higher level. When Ibn Tufayl's Hayy tells the narrator of *Hayy ibn Yaqzan* of the constitution of reality in highly poetic and evocative language, this is what he is doing: he is outlining to the rational intellect why it should make the effort to perfect itself, in terms which the ordinary individual will understand. In a sense, the language which Hayy uses is descriptive of a higher level of reality than this world, since although the state of affairs to which that language refers may not be exactly as he states, it is representative of a deeper truth which really does accurately describe the nature of how things are. That is one of the characteristics of imagination: that although what it suggests is the case may not be the case, it may nevertheless point to what really exists at a level of existence which is beyond what we can acquire through using just our intellect and our senses. Imagination, as a blend of intellect and senses, is capable of preparing the move to a more accurate and complete understanding of how things really are

Allegory and meaning: the imaginal realm again

There are two leading theories which seek to explain the use of allegorical and poetic stories to illustrate conceptual theses in Islamic philosophy. One theory suggests that the literary form of allegory is used to explain in simpler, more direct, ways the meaning of the philosophical theory. For those who would not understand the philosophy, a more attractive version of the truth is available in terms of a story, often heavily illustrated with attractive imagery. This is implausible as an explanation. Often such philosophical stories are so replete with imagery and ideas of a mysterious nature that they are as hard, if not harder, to unpack than the corresponding philosophical theory. One then needs the theory to understand the story; so it is not correct to say that the story is an easier version of the theory. The other account of such literary devices goes in the opposite direction, and argues that there is more in the story than there is in the theory. That is, there is an aspect of mystical awareness that is attainable through the story, and that is described in the story, and this cannot be replicated by the corresponding philosophical theory. This is a more plausible suggestion, but it is still incorrect, since it fails to do justice to the fact that the story and the theory have exactly the same meaning. It is true that the story may include some experiential information which certainly would not be found in a philosophical theory, but if it is the sort of story which accords with a theory, then there can be nothing important in it which goes beyond the theory, since the theory is its meaning. While there may be some personal information that cannot be replicated in a theory, this will only be to illustrate in a more personal way an impersonal theory.

What we need to understand by the use of stories is their imaginative role. The stories are designed to show that more is needed to come into contact with the active intellect than just improvement in intellectual ability. One needs some grasp of where one is trying to go, and why it is worth trying to get there; and the only way to get this is through imagination. That is why the notion of the imaginal realm is so important: it is the conduit (and we are immediately reminded of the notion of *barzakh*) that moves us from limitation to this world to entering the higher world. One way of understanding the imaginal realm is through imaginative stories, through illustrations that explain how our existing ideas may be extended in particular ways to bring them to an entirely different, more perfect conceptual level. In just the same way in which we need something to mediate between our physical selves and our souls, and between our souls and the idea of macrocosmic reality, we also need something to mediate between our ideas and the level which those ideas can reach if extended in the right sort of way. This is what happens in a good school, where the initial ideas of the students are extended through imagination to show them where they can get to if they go about it in the right sort of way. The sort of student who works hard but is unimaginative in that he cannot see how his present ideas can go any further is unlikely to reach the stage of the acquired intellect, where his ability to know becomes fully actualized. What happens at this stage is that one's ideas become the same as the ideas of the supremely creative principles of reality, and imagination is an important route to creativity and activity. What Ibn Sina wants to show through his stories is that it is not enough just to acquire information and apply it to syllogisms. We need also to open our minds to wider ideas and experiences, which will then permit us to be active, and not merely receptive, with respect to knowledge.

Prophecy and its psychological basis

The individual whose natural home is the imaginal realm is, of course, the prophet. His understanding is in contact with the active intellect, and he understands the nature of the universe. A prophet has the same sort of information as the philosopher, but the philosopher may, once he has passed through the imaginal realm, go on to the higher level of concentrating only on the rational nature of the information that is available there. The prophet's role is primarily political, by contrast, and he will seek to use what he has learned of imaginative language to instruct his community about the nature of the higher levels of reality, albeit in language which will accord with their ideas and habits. He will be able to do this because of his mastery of the vocabulary of the imagination. This is the language that moves us from one level of reality to another, and the prophet is the person who helps us here, since he moves us from one form of understanding of our world to another. The prophet is said to have a holy, or angelic, intellect; he is like an angel in that an angel mediates between heaven and earth. He is holy in so far as he can show us how apparently ordinary actions may have a transcendental significance through their connection with God. That is, he transforms the ordinary through imagination, to show how extraordinary it is, in just the same way in which I can view my very ordinary garden right now and, if I apply my imagination to it, see it as a blissful representation of divine purpose in the universe.

An interesting question arises here, and that is whether it is a necessary condition of attaining the level of the acquired intellect that one goes through an intermediary. Could not one's rational abilities be so well developed that one could go straight to conjunction with the active intellect, without the necessity of going through an intermediary? To give another example from education, while most children require an imaginative presentation of how a whole range of possibilities is available to them with respect, say, to a career and a lifestyle, some children may be able to appreciate this just through intellectual awareness of the facts. They also have no difficulty in making those facts a part of their personal lives, once they grasp their existence and their relevance to themselves. The answer would have to be that, while it is perfectly possible for creatures like us to find it easier to understand why certain aims in life are relevant, as compared with other similar people, while we are material creatures we are going to require some physical imagery and motivation in order to get things done. However successful we may come to be in abstracting our rational soul from our body, while we live we cannot divorce ourselves from our bodies in our thinking, so imagination becomes an essential part of that thinking. It is important that we leave imagination behind once we get to the level of formal thought, since imagination then becomes a hindrance rather than a help. For one thing, it contaminates our thought with material images that we could well do without. Yet it is necessary for us to employ imagination to get to the higher level, and that is why the imaginal realm is often described as being more real than the world of generation and corruption, although not as real as the world of forms. Imagination is like a ladder that one climbs and then discards when it no longer serves a purpose. The point of an isthmus (*barzakh*) is to get from one place to another. Once one has arrived, there is no point in lingering on the isthmus. Yet one could not have arrived at all, had one not followed the right route.

When he discusses the concept of the *barzakh*, Ibn al-ʿArabi makes it plain that we should not restrict the imagination to only part of reality. Apart from God, everything is imaginary, in a sense. The world itself is imaginary, in so far as it reflects the deeper reality of God, and has no existence in itself apart from God. We are ourselves imaginary in that we consist of varying dispositions to act, of a combination of soul and body, and even in the soul there is a variety of the spiritual and the carnal, the light and the dark, the visible and the invisible. A whole range of experience might be called 'imaginary', and yet be quite real. The links between the soul and the body are made possible by the soul employing the senses to allow us to think about the physical world. This is a crucial aspect of the imagination, the ability of the intellect to represent to itself ideas that describe the physical, which is only possible if the intellect is able to attach itself to more than the abstract and intellectual. One of the surprising comments that Ibn al-ʿArabi often makes is that he comes into contact with imaginary men whom he treats just as though they were real. He also often treats dreams as real events, in that there is experience in dreams that can be highly significant to the individual who is having them. This is a strange way of talking, since one of the first distinctions we make between reality and illusion is in terms of the world we experience through our waking senses and what we dream about. But Ibn al-ʿArabi has a point in talking this way, since it is true that the experience of a dream does have at least one foot in what we might call physical reality. A dream may be highly physical, and we sometimes awake from a nightmare trembling with fear. Presumably this is because we felt at the time of the dream that what was happening to us was very real. But were we not mistaken in this? In a sense, yes, and when we wake up, we may congratulate ourselves on not really having undergone the events described in the dream. Yet there is something real about dreams. They often portray events that could have happened in everyday life, and they may have a significance that makes them even more important than many events that happen in the everyday world.

There are many accounts by thinkers like Ibn al-ʿArabi and Mir Damad (Dabashi 1996b) of contact with imaginary people, some of whom are from the far past and some more recent; but what these meetings have in common is that they take place in dreams or visions, not in what we might call real life. This seems rather strange too, since we would tend to classify such accounts as fictional. Yet, if we see these accounts as taking place in the imaginal realm, as they are often said to do, then what we are being invited to accept is that these encounters are more real, in a sense, than the everyday encounters of our ordinary world. How plausible is this? We would normally say that they are less real. The point is that what may take place in such an encounter could have more impact on us, more meaning for us, than a similar encounter in the ordinary world. Take the case of a dramatic presentation that moves us emotionally in a particular way. What we see before us is not happening literally in the way in which it is being presented, since the hero who is suffering is an actor who is not really suffering, and the tragedy which is unfolding is not really affecting the actors. They are merely representing the tragedy; they are not participating in it. Yet that representation of a tragedy may have a stronger effect on us than a real tragedy, perhaps because of the way in which it is presented and the skill of the actors and writer in bringing out dramatically the nature of events in the play. It is a standard issue in aesthetics to explain how a fictional artifice can move us, and it can; but this is not the place to enter into this controversy. What is relevant here is to accept that many things may occur in fictional or imaginative space which we may quite legitimately take to be as real, or even more real, than similar events in our ordinary space, and it is on such an understanding that the description of contact with imaginal people makes sense. It is even more plausible if we remember that the so-called ordinary world is itself replete with a whole variety of *barzakh*, to the extent that it has within it the scope to take us to a different level of reality, since it too is an imaginative construction. The ordinary world is itself a reflection of divine reality, and if we are to have an accurate view of it, we must acknowledge this and come to terms with its multifaceted nature. What we perceive in the ordinary world is often familiar, and we feel no need to take it any further. But it is replete with the possibility of surprising us, because it is not just familiar. It has a meaning that transcends the world, as we have a meaning that transcends our physical limitations, and unless we are open to both aspects of the constitution of being in the world, we seriously misunderstand the nature of that being.

Is being really the first question in metaphysics?

We now return to the question with which we started: namely, the significance of the account of being in metaphysics. Aristotle claims that it is the first question in metaphysics; but how can it really be the first question if very different philosophies can be constructed from identical accounts of being? There is little resemblance between the general theories of Ibn Rushd and Mulla Sadra, yet they are in agreement on the priority of existence over essence. Also, as we have seen, there are considerable resemblances between the basic theory of Ibn Sina and Mulla Sadra, despite their radical disagreements on the links between essence and existence. A plausible conclusion is that the account of being is not the first question in metaphysics, but that ontology will itself vary in line with the nature of a particular theory as it develops. But this would be a mistake, since, despite the enormous differences between Ibn Rushd and Mulla Sadra, there is no doubt that their joint adherence to the priority of existence highlights a significant resemblance between their theories. They are both realists; they both argue that the basic constituents of the world are objects, in one sense or another, and that those objects have real existence. Ibn Rushd uses that approach to argue that the world could not have had a different structure from the one it does have, so the objects have to take the form they do. Mulla Sadra also argues that the objects in the world are real, although for him the notion of reality is far more complex than it is for Ibn Rushd, and he extends it to take account of a deeper sense of reality, including that which exists within the imagination.

Mulla Sadra's super-realism provides a useful explanation of the function of the imaginal realm. The contents of that realm are real because they exist, and that, by definition, makes them real. The familiar problem of the *barzakh* which links this world with some other realm, and then which leads to the question of how real this link is, is resolved by the realism of insisting that all such levels of being are in fact different kinds of existence. Since they are different kinds of existence, there is no essential difficulty in appreciating the objectivity of either the objects of the imagination or, indeed, the objects of our world. A difficulty arises here only if we see the contents of imagination as essences that may or may not be instantiated, and so may or may not be real. Mulla Sadra defiantly rejects this view by insisting on realism in ontology, and in this way brings out nicely the links which Aristotle quite rightly thought bind ontology and metaphysics together. Mulla Sadra's account of being and its application to the imagination is undoubtedly a highly significant philosophical achievement.

6

Ethics

Theological background: Muʿtazilites vs Ashʿarites

Most of the main controversies in ethics in Islamic philosophy were derived from the most prevalent and often protracted theological disputes (Fakhry 1991). One of the important theological arguments was between the Ashʿarites and the Muʿtazilites, and it related directly to the meaning of ethical propositions (Hourani 1985; Leaman 1999c). According to the former, ethical meaning is entirely subjective, in that whatever meaning it has it gets from a subject, in this case, God. The only point in acting morally lies in obeying God, and any other feature of ethics is purely superficial. That is, it might look as though there are good practical reasons for moral action, and there could be such factors, but they are not relevant to our rationale for acting morally. These factors are what Kant called 'heteronomous', in that they appeal to a side of us that is certainly worth appealing to, but not in an ethical sense. For Kant, we should do our duty out of a pure desire to do our duty, and if we do our duty out of a desire to please God, then our behaviour might be in accordance with morality, but is not done for a moral motive. The Ashʿarites make a similar claim; they insist that unless a moral action is performed out of a desire to act in accordance with God's wishes, it is not moral. This is because what morality means is action in accordance with God's wishes and commands, as opposed to immorality, which is action in line with what God forbids. Unless we understand this, we really have no chance of acting from the correct motive, which is of course crucial to the nature of virtue. We would not praise someone for his or her behaviour if it stemmed from incorrect motives, and even the wrong action carried out with the right motive is excusable (Frank 1996).

The Mu'tazilites took an entirely different approach. They maintained that while it is true that God commands us to do what is right, what is right is right independently of what God orders. He orders us to do what is right because it is right, and it is right on objective grounds, not because of what God orders. God could not order us to do something that was not right, since the rules of morality are not something that are under his control. He can certainly see much better than we can why certain actions ought to be performed, and we are often obliged to look to him for guidance; but all he knows better than us is the route to virtue. He does not know what virtue is in the sense that he creates it. So the role of religion is to help us work out how we should behave. It does this by indicating forms of conduct and advising us how to think of our duties, but it does not establish the nature of our duty. This is worked out in accordance with the nature of morality itself. Let us take as an example the situation of a good person who suffers during this life. What will happen to him after his death? According to the Mu'tazilites, God must reward him for his behaviour, since if he does not, he will be acting unfairly. God has no choice but to compensate him in the next life for what he has suffered in this one, and the reverse would be true of the evil person. God is thus forced to behave in certain ways, since if he is to be just (and he is by definition just), he must follow the rules of justice (Hourani 1971).

Ethics and divine power

According to the Ash'arites, however, God can do anything he likes. He can punish the innocent and reward the guilty. But would this not mean that he was unjust? The answer they would give is no, since whatever God does is just by definition. This is what justice means: what God does. Surely, this is an extraordinary claim, since while we might accept that God has privileged access to the nature of justice, he cannot have sole access to its definition. To give an epistemological example, while we may accept that God knows the world in ways which we cannot, since he created it and is omniscient, once the world is a certain way, then it is this way, and even God cannot prevent it from being this way. He could change it to a new state, of course, but he cannot change the cup being on the table in my room at 7.50 p.m. on Sunday, 18 May, after the time has gone.

There were arguments in Islamic philosophy about whether God could affect the past, about whether, for example, he could restore the virginity of someone who had been unwillingly deprived of it; and there were some thinkers who argued that omnipotence should mean the ability to change the past. This is not the place to enter this debate, except to say that it could generally be accepted that God may be omnipotent, yet not be able to change what has already taken place, since if it has already taken place, there is, on most views of the nature of time, no longer any way of affecting it. God could have prevented it from happening in the first place; but after it has happened, he can do nothing about it. This is even more the case on a theory of time that relates it to an independent framework, since if time is the measure of change, and if things change in a particular way, then a time interval elapses; but it could in a sense be reversed if the change were to be reversed.

But even if God managed to bring about something like this, he is not affecting what something means. He is only affecting what happens. The Ash'arite claim is much stronger than this: it is that God establishes the meaning of justice, and that this must be the case if he is to be omnipotent. Not only must he possess power over things, which is not unreasonable given that the things in the world are his creation; he must also have power over meanings. This might seem quite reasonable, since the meanings which words have might be expected to be linked to the ways in which things exist, and since God knows about the arrangement of things, he must also know about the meanings. This is uncontroversial; but what is at issue is not God's knowledge of meanings, but his control over them. We might think that the meaning of terms is conventional, that it is based on the ways in which we use words and how we wish to use them.

Al-Ghazali's attack on objectivism in ethics

It is not surprising that al-Ghazali should object to this view, since he also argues that what we take to be the conventional rules surrounding our terms do not surround them at all, in the sense of restricting them. God can extend the meanings of terms if he wishes, as we can observe if we try to think of how they might be extended. This would be the route he would follow with respect to the meaning of justice, since we should expect that God would specify what the meaning of that term is. We should remember that during the very varied intellectual career of al-Ghazali, there were some principles to which he remained true, and one of these was a basic hostility to *taqlid*, or conformism. Religions might seem at first glance to advocate blind obedience to tradition, but the point he wishes to make is that there is no religious merit in blindly following tradition. (He is also opposed to what he says is *taqlid* in our ordinary thought, like believing in causal necessity just because our experience suggests it exists.)There is only a point in following tradition if one understands why one is doing it. In just the same way as there is no merit in following tradition unthinkingly, al-Ghazali argues that there is nothing to be said for accepting the rules of language without question. After all, could not God have the power to change those rules? Although one's immediate reaction to such a suggestion might be to think that it goes too far in preserving the power of God, on further reflection it seems quite plausible. Why should God have to put up with the fixed meanings which function as parts of our language? We are limited to a particular point of view as a result of our finitude, but surely God is not. Since he sees much more than we do, he has a far better grasp of what words can be made to mean, and, as a result, he can change the meaning of words if he wishes to. Perhaps more importantly, he is the final authority on what a term means, so it is reasonable to think that the meaning of ethical terms, like all other terms, is at the total disposal of God. 'There is no changing the words of God' (10: 64), and it is his understanding of words which plays the crucial role in what they can be taken to mean (Leaman 1996e).

There are a variety of points that the proponents of the objectivity of ethics make in response to this argument (Hourani 1985). First, they point out that the ethical terms that are so important in morality actually start out as non-moral terms, and are entirely descriptive. For example, the term '*adl*, or justice, was a completely objective term for balance, as in the physical balancing of weights. So the basis of the term was objective, and it could be argued that the real meaning of the term is just as objective. It must be admitted that this is a rather weak suggestion, since all it shows is that the way in which ethical terms started off is a non-moral, objective way; but it is a very different matter to suggest that this disproves the subjective theory of ethics. After all, it is open to the subjectivists to argue that although moral terms started off in a non-moral way, this does nothing to show that in their moral form they are still characterized by their origins.

Another argument that is sometimes introduced is that it is clumsy to convert ordinary moral language into subjectivist language. For example, saying that 'lying is evil' comes out on the subjectivist account as 'God forbids lying, and it is something that he forbids'. It is even more clumsy when one has to interpret scriptural statements which refer to God and moral terms, since they tend to come out as tautologous, so that, for example, something like 'God urges us to be good' is equivalent to 'God urges us to act in the ways in which he urges us to act'. But we should not be surprised at this, since it is a commonplace of philosophy that when we analyse an expression in terms of its logical form, the result is rather awkward. For example, phenomenalists think that ordinary language sentences describing objects are logically descriptions of sense-data or experiences, so that 'I am typing this on a table' is equivalent to 'I am typing this on a collection of sense-data which when put together look like a table'. This is not the end of the analysis, which could go on to break down the concepts of typing and myself into sense-data. Now I do not wish to advocate that we accept that this is how we should go about analysing material object language, but we cannot rule it out just because it looks rather convoluted (Leaman 1985: 123–41).

A third reason for thinking that moral objectivism is plausible is the natural law theory. This suggests that any rational person could work out for himself or herself what general principles we are called upon to employ in our behaviour, even without revelation. In Jewish philosophy these are called the 'Noachide commandments', and in Christian philosophy they are linked with the rational structure of the world by thinkers like Aquinas. It might be thought that it would be unfair for God not to make it possible for anyone to work out their duty if he did not provide them with guidance in the first place, but this is not really a problem for Islam. It is an important doctrine of Islam that God has provided us with guidance at all times, and one of the features of Islam which is worth noting is that it represents itself as a very rational religion. We are to accept the logic of guidance because it is a logic; it is a form of reasoning from the evidence of the world about us, through the words of God, to conclusions about appropriate behaviour. Suppose there are no words of God? In such a case, the assumption is that there is enough evidence available in the way in which the world is organized to guide us as to how we should behave. Of course, what we could work out for ourselves has nothing to do with the ritual aspects of religion, since these are part and parcel of a particular education within a specific religious context; but these are not important to the notion of performing our duty. It does not seem implausible that, even without any ability to derive a meaning from the world through our independent judgement, we could still work out some basic rules of how to behave. We could take the analogy of a game, whereby we might manage to work out some of the basic rules using only our reason, and why should we deny as a result that the game that was subsequently played was not really the game at all, but just something that looked like the game? But this is what al-Ghazali is suggesting: that even if we work out the rules correctly, they are still not really the right rules.

Why should we agree with him? One line of defence of his argument might be derived from the problems we have in recognizing a game when it is played in a very unfamiliar context. For example, if a game of soccer is played, but the outcome of the game is rather more serious than usual, in that the losing team will all be executed, is it really the game of soccer with which we are familiar? In some ways it is, since the same rules are employed in actually playing the game. In other ways it is not, since the stakes are so high, and one might expect that this would give the game a rather unusual flavour. This is very much al-Ghazali's point: that it is not enough to show that an activity is physically the same as another activity for it to be acceptable to claim that they are the same activity. Sometimes it is easy to identify two such activities, but in many other cases it is not, as when there is something crucial which is present in one activity but not in the other. Now it is of course true that in many of these sorts of cases there can be a great deal of dispute about what the game is really all about, and perfectly sensible arguments may be proposed about whether the game is really being played in the new circumstances, or whether what is being played is an entirely new game, or a slightly different game. It is because of the looseness of the concept of game that Wittgenstein was apparently led to abandon his earlier theory of meaning in terms of determinate rules, of necessary and sufficient conditions designed to encompass completely the meaning of a term, or, to use an analogy of Frege's, as a circle encompasses a space. We shall be using these contrasting models of language again in the last chapter, to explore some of the implications of contrasting views on the nature of language for the understanding of meaning. Given his theoretical perspective, it is open to al-Ghazali to protest against the *falasifa* that there is no reason to insist on the fixed and final nature of the meaning of our language. In particular, should God have any ideas about how he would like to extend the meaning of terms, why should he not do so? Even if we feel that we have to fix the meanings of words in our language, why should God be thought to be consigned a fixed list of meanings?

Of course, the route from an attack on the idea of language as determinate to the autonomy of God in dealing with language is not that straightforward. It might be argued that if language is indeterminate, then it is indeterminate for God as well as for us. There would then be no sense in privileging his account of the meaning of ethical terms over our own. But this objection really will not do, since he is aware of the whole range of circumstances in which we live, including the structure of the universe, and one might expect with some confidence that the arrangements he makes for ethical language fit somehow with that metaphysical reality. He could decide what ethical concepts are going to mean in the sense that only he knows enough about us and our environment to lay down the law. But this is far from the uncritical and slave-like attitude to authority that some critics suggest. At the moment, I am typing this in a train, and just by sitting here, I am putting my trust in the competence and skill of the driver and all the other staff. It is not unreasonable for me to do so, since I assume that the driver knows far more about driving the train than I do, and, having spent many occasions on trains that arrived safely at their destinations, I have no reason not to trust him. It might be argued that if I am prepared to put my trust in a train driver, how much more justified I would be in putting my trust in my creator!

Trusting authority

This notion of being justified in trusting in someone is very important in Islamic philosophy. Ibn Rushd often speaks of the trust which we should repose in the physician and the lawyer, perhaps not entirely unconnected with the fact that he was at one time a member of both these professions, but his point is that if we were able to understand exactly why they give the advice they do, we would not require their services at all, since we could give ourselves the advice without going through an intermediary. Ibn Rushd actually uses this example to show that an ordinary believer need not understand precisely what the basis of his or her belief is, since there is always advice available from those who really do know. He makes the point that if we have reason to trust the source of authority, then we are justified in following its advice even if we do not understand precisely what the reasons for that advice are. Much to Ibn Rushd's disgust, no doubt, this argument could also be used to support al-Ghazali's defence of ethical subjectivism. We really cannot hope to understand what the meaning of ethical language is, since we are so limited to a particular point of view, but we may assume that God has no such problem. Whatever he tells us to do, we should do precisely because he tells us, and for no other reason. Any other reason that we could produce would only be a reflection of our limited, relative point of view.

The subjectivist view has an advantage over the objectivist position, and that lies in its opposition to antinomianism. The latter is the doctrine that one need not pay attention to laws and rules once one has acquired an understanding of the principles that lie behind those principles and rules. For example, a philosopher might think that if the purpose of a particular ritual is to bring about a particular end, and, if he knows that he can realize that end in a different way, then he need not go about attaining that end in the ways in which everyone else does. Suppose that the purpose of prayer is to acknowledge and deepen our belief in our relationship of gratitude towards and dependence on God. Most believers pray because this is a normal practice in their community, and they hardly think about the point of prayer, or what prayer is for. This is perfectly adequate, since they are carrying out their religious obligations and acquiring the appropriate attitudes towards God. But someone who is capable of understanding the purpose of prayer might think that she need not undertake it in order to achieve its end, since that end could be achieved in simpler and more perfect ways, perhaps by using her reason. This sort of attitude is common among some varieties of Sufis, who came to believe that since they had managed to identify themselves with God, there was no longer any need to pray to God, since this would have meant praying to themselves! In any case, they felt that they had achieved a far deeper and more authentic relationship with God than had ordinary believers; so they were unwilling to replace their superior link by the normal link that everyone has.

There are obviously many reasons why such an argument did not go down well with the traditional religious authorities. What we are interested in here, though, is how acceptable it is philosophically. There is one danger in it that is worth noting at the outset. How sure can one be that one is right? Suppose one has not reached the level of consciousness or the degree of self-awareness which one thinks one has. In that case the abandonment of normal practices would rest on a mistake, with very serious moral and spiritual consequences. There is always a danger on objectivist grounds that one will think incorrectly that the objective criteria of some practice can be realized in some other way, and so the practice is discontinued. There is obviously tremendous scope for self-deception here, especially when one might have reasons not to wish to perform the practice (it is tedious, it is difficult, and so on). Now the objectivists will say that it is not a good argument against their position that it is possible to be mistaken. We can always be mistaken: but unless we adhere to scepticism, this does not invalidate some form of confidence in our own judgements. But the subjectivist point here is that we are very likely to be mistaken if we think that we can work out the meaning of ethical terms by means of our own reason. It may even be that when we think we can do without the practice, we are in even more need of the practice than ever, since the practice is capable of damping our arrogance and pride. Thus, there may be people who are able to achieve the spiritual end without undergoing the practice, but will never fail to participate in the practice, since they will never feel confident enough in their own ability to judge these matters.

This might seem to be unnecessarily deferential towards God, and overly suspicious of human reason. The objectivist would argue that God wants us to work out for ourselves, albeit not without his guidance, how we should behave, and that if we get it right, then we act in the ways in which he would like us to act. There is something about those acts that makes them acts of which he approves; it is not that they just happen to be the acts that he recommends. God encourages us to use our reason to decide on our actions. But note the use of the terms 'guidance' and 'message' as showing that he does not force people to act in a particular way, but indicates to them through hints and their natural reason how they should behave. Why should we not come to the reasonable opinion that we have transcended a particular way of seeing our duty, and go about achieving the end in a different way? For example, we might agree with Miskawayh (Leaman 1996e: l) that the point of communal prayer is to increase the links between different members of the community, and as a result strengthen friendship and feelings of being members of a community. Someone could surely come to the conclusion that they already see themselves firmly as part of the community, and have an extensive set of friends, and on top of all this they might spend a great deal of time thinking about God. As a result of all this, such an individual might decide that there is no need to pray with everyone else, or perhaps even at all, and as a result not go to the mosque on Fridays, say, and not participate in the various communal activities of the faith. The more fastidious believer might not wish to mingle with the ordinary members of the community, for example, and might not think it was incumbent upon them to do so. After all, they could pursue even higher religious activities within the privacy of their own homes. It was very much the danger of people taking this sort of approach which led al-Ghazali to counter Miskawayh's rationale of religious practice with his argument that the reason for such practices is that they have no reason. The reason we should follow them is because God has told us to, though, apart from that, we can observe nothing about them that makes them tempting. Al-Ghazali actually goes into some detail about how unpleasant many Islamic rites are, and even today the pilgrimage to Mecca (the *hajj*) is far from an easy event. There could be nothing about them that we would ourselves select if we were seeking to bring about particular ends, but we must assume that God knows what it is about them that makes them worth recommending. Who better to trust on such topics than God?

Putting God in charge of the meaning of ethical terms does not diminish the role of human reason, but it does acknowledge the difficulty that our reason has in counteracting the influence of the emotions. We tend to be swayed by our feelings, and it is often difficult to judge calmly with our reason, given those feelings. This comes out very clearly in the phenomenon of self-deception, where we know that we ought to do something, yet are swayed not to do it. It is as though we hide from ourselves our duty to act in a particular way, since we very much want not to. The subjectivist approach to ethics acknowledges this in its opposition to the objectivity of ethics, since the former view insists that the meaning of ethics is not open to all to understand, but is the perquisite of God, for whom everything is open. We can use our reason within the framework set by God and his ethical instructions to us, but not to consider the framework itself. We can consider the nature of the framework, and we have just been doing so, but we cannot wonder why it is as it is. It is God and his authority on which the ethical system rests.

But is this not just an example of *taqlid*, or blind obedience, the sort of attitude that even al-Ghazali criticized? He was very critical in his later work of any kind of imitation of anything except God. It does not have to be *taqlid*, though. It is rather the acknowledgement that in a world that has been created by God there are many things that God knows more about than we do. This is hardly a perplexing idea. After all, even in our ordinary lives we accept that there are many things which others know more about than we do. The person who creates and installs my central heating system knows more about it than I do, I hope; if this were not so, I should probably have installed it myself. If he gives me advice, then I am likely to be justified in taking it. This is the case even, or, one might say, especially, if I have no idea why what he says is as he says it is. When I look at the pipes and dials of the system, I am utterly ignorant of how they work, and must do as I am told by those who know. If I try to fiddle about with the system by turning things on and off without understanding what I am doing, as I often do, disaster may well result. There is the difference here that I could, at least in theory, understand all that there is to understand about the system, since there is nothing mysterious about it – it is essentially knowable by human beings. So we need to contrast this with the structure of reality and the nature of salvation.

To a certain extent these are also essentially knowable, but only up to a point. It is hardly surprising that at least part of the meaning of life should not be accessible to us, but accessible only to the creator of that life. When he tells us how we are to live, this is information that we can rationally accept as worth obeying because of its author (Leaman 1995b). We do not have to understand why it is worth obeying. Indeed, we should not expect to have that sort of under-standing, since a world which possessed no mystery would surely have no place for God. This is precisely the basis of al-Ghazali's critique of the *falasifa*. Although the latter constantly talk of God, they identify him more with the central heating engineer than with the creator of the meaning of the world, and thus place the meaning of the world within the world itself. As a result, he suggests, they exclude God from any meaningful role.

The need for guidance

We should recall how precarious our grasp of how to act may be. In the Qur'an there is a plea to God to 'Guide us to the straight path' (*al-sirat al-mustaqim*) (1: 5), and there is a *hadith* according to which that path is stretched over hell, and is thinner than a hair and sharper than a sword. Everyone has to take this path, and only those who succeed in getting to the other side reach salvation. We do not have to be committed to any particular faith to understand the truth of the idea that it is very difficult to be good. If we are committed to a faith, though, it is not improbable that our creator will have provided good advice as to how to remain on the straight path and avoid going awry. We might hope to work out for ourselves much of the neces-sary information about the correct route; but, given the difficulty of the enterprise and our essentially limited point of view, it would be foolish, to put it no more strongly, to rely entirely on what we can work out by ourselves. If we could work everything out by ourselves, there would be no need for a guide.

I would not want to argue that the Ash'arite line on ethics is the only line we could take here from an Islamic perspective, but the idea that the only respectable approach from a rational point of view is its contrary is clearly not going to work. The Mu'tazilites present their opponents as thinkers who are incapable of examining the rational credentials of their moral beliefs, but the position is rather that the Mu'tazilite position is simplistic. In insisting on a rather banal notion of justice it restricts moral truths to that notion. The Ash'arites accept that we may not understand as much about our moral duties as does our creator, not a ridiculous idea in a moral system with a deity playing what one might expect to be a leading role in helping us determine our moral responsibilities.

7

Politics

There has been a great deal of discussion since the Iranian revolution of 1979 about what an Islamic state is (El-Affendi 1991; Leaman 2000a). The overthrow of the Shah and the imposition of clerical government brought the impact of Islam on politics well to the fore, and shocked the largely secular West with its apparent fervour. But, of course, even in recent times there have been a number of states which have called themselves Islamic, and Pakistan is a perfect example of a state whose entire official rationale is Islam. One of the criticisms that are often levelled at such governments is that they are medieval in nature, the assumption being that there is something wrong with this. We shall examine this argument in due course, but at this stage it will be useful to comment on some of the links between religion and politics in Islam.

Plato vs Aristotle

In political philosophy Islam has far stronger links with Plato than with Aristotle, and this is a very important difference between it and the sorts of political thought which developed in Christian Europe in the Middle Ages. The enthusiasm for Plato is in some ways rather surprising, since many of the *falasifa* are less complimentary about Plato as compared with his pupil Aristotle, who glories in the name of the 'first master' (*al-shaykh al-ra'is*) and who is seen as the author of an especially rich logical system. In the rather developmental way in which they saw philosophy, a later thinker was likely to be superior to an earlier one (perhaps on a parallel with the later Islam supersed-ing the earlier monotheistic religions?), though Plato and Aristotle were often interpreted along Neoplatonic lines as essentially agree-ing on most things. In politics, Plato was the more widely discussed of the two, since his political works were more easily accessible; indeed, Aristotle's *Politics* is often referred to as a work which the *falasifa* tried to get hold of, but without success (Leaman 1997b). Given the eclectic tendency of Neoplatonism, which was not much concerned with political philosophy anyway, the *Republic* was seen as the political conclusion of Aristotle's *Nicomachean Ethics*. Of course, the former is ideally structured to be used in Islamic politi-cal theory from the point of view of the *falasifa*. It advocates rule by philosophers, surely a tempting prospect for many philosophers, and emphasizes the significance of control of both the individual and the state by reason. We should remember that many of the *falasifa* would have felt a special resonance reading Plato, since they were themselves intimately involved in the running of the machinery of their states. It is not difficult to see why this work was taken up with such alacrity by the *falasifa*.

There are other attractions in the text. Plato distinguishes between different sorts of state, ranging from the perfect state down to timoc-racy (rule based on honour), oligarchy (rule by the few), democracy and tyranny. The *falasifa* could find many contemporary parallels to all these forms of government, and in his *Commentary on Plato's Republic* Ibn Rushd delights in pointing to instances in al-Andalus of the putative forms of political organization that Plato described. But he sternly chides Plato with using too much figurative language in the text, which Ibn Rushd saw as inappropriate to technical philosophy, and which actually has the disadvantage of making that philosophy far too available to the wider public. Ibn Rushd was particularly scathing about the Myth of Er, which comes at the end of the book, and which gives Plato the opportunity to expound fantasies and stories about varieties of possible afterlife. For Ibn Rushd, this is most unsatisfactory; such a way of writing has no place in a philosophical work. We have to remember here that Ibn Rushd was an Aristotelian and not Aristotle. Aristotle himself had no difficulty in producing lists of possibilities, and the style of much of his writing is quite hesitant and speculative. For Ibn Rushd, by contrast, Aristotelian philoso-phy is properly decisive and final, and has no room for this sort of indeterminacy. Of course, if one were to remove the figurative and imaginative language in Plato, one would not be left with much that is originally Platonic; but Ibn Rushd is quite right as regards the nub of the argument, which is that society is best ruled when it is ruled by reason. There is no necessity for those who rule with reason to explain to the masses precisely what they are doing or why they are doing it, since the latter would neither be interested nor able to understand the principles of government. This stance is often criticized as being elitist, and it is very elitist, but we should remember that for Ibn Rushd government is just like any other sort of skill, one that is best carried out by those who are trained and competent in its practice. We should no more expect the expert watermelon salesperson to understand the principles of politics than we should expect the administrator to know how to sell watermelons. Both activities are useful, and the state is best managed if everyone sticks to his or her own speciality and does not stray outside it. It is this principle that Plato raises to a guiding political axiom in the *Republic*.

What is the role of religion in the state? One might think that the answer is to inform and inspire the rulers with the truths and principles that they can in turn inculcate in their subjects. For the *falasifa*, though, it is not easy to see what religion adds to the state, apart from its ability to organize and inspire the masses (Rosenthal 1968). We should remember that for them the only difference between philosophy and prophecy lies in the faculty that the active intellect affects. The philosopher is affected in his reason, while the prophet is able to develop his imagination; yet the information that they receive is identical. As Ibn Rushd puts it, the Prophet Muhammad is the seal of the prophets, since he is the seal of the ways of putting over the truth to the largest possible constituency. It is not that he knows something that the philosopher does not know; what he knows is how to get the information across to the public at large. The philosopher may actually know how to do this theoretically, but be unable to do it in practice. So, although all the *falasifa* emphasize the role of religion in the state, it is very much a practical role, not one which is going to supply the ruler with special kinds of theoretical information (Daiber 1996).

It is worth remarking on another aspect of the Platonic tradition, which is that practical life is very much a second best when compared with the life of theory. Plato's rulers work out of a motive of civic duty, but they would be far happier were they able to spend all their time on theoretical work, and that is what makes them ideal rulers. They are probably the only people in the state who do not want to rule, and so they are the best people to rule. (One is reminded of countries where strict measures of gun control are employed and only one question need be put to a prospective gun owner, and that is 'Do you want to own a gun?' Anyone who replied in the affirmative was not fit to have one; the only people who ought to own guns are those who do not want to own them. Similarly with the rulers in the Islamic state: they are fit to rule just because they would prefer to do something else.) Although philosophers have the roles and the skills of the thinker and the imam, they would much prefer to be thinkers. This conflict between the theoretical and the practical life also comes out nicely in Aristotle, who seems to argue that the social and ethical virtues are really secondary to the theoretical, and that the latter are superior since they represent us as most God-like. From a religious perspective, this could be interpreted in a rather negative way, since it implies that a life of prayer and ritual is inferior to a life of thought. If God made us all different, and if some find it easier to think theoretically than others, then it seems a bit unfair for the thinkers to have a higher form of existence available to them as compared with everyone else.

There are two ways of dealing with this apparent problem. One is to argue, as Ibn Rushd does, that there are a variety of routes to the truth, and that they are all equal to each other, in so far as they all get travellers to the same place in the end, albeit along different paths. It is difficult to avoid the impression, though, that some of these routes are far more direct than others, and surely it would then be unfair if some were unable to reach their goal with as much efficiency as others. It is as though the members of a motoring organization were to consult the organization for a map of how to get to their destination, and be given different maps on the basis of their differing capacities to drive. But this should not be thought of as unfair, since the organization would indeed provide such maps, based perhaps on the time which travellers have for their journey, whether they want the fastest or the prettiest route, whether they feel that they can cope with rush-hour traffic, how good they are at navigating and so on. Since people are different, we should expect them to have different ways of approaching the truth, and to accept different roles in the state. They can hardly complain if, as a result of these differences, a range of roles is made available to them in accordance with their varying skills and propensities. Of course, one might go on to ask the further question of why God did not make everyone the same; but that is a different question from how different people can have access to salvation. Once we discover that there are routes for everyone, the charge of unfairness is lifted, at least in so far as salvation is concerned. One might speculate that God created everyone differently in order to provide his creatures with a more interesting environment. After all, not only are we all different, but we do not know how different we are; we have to find this out, and our lives consist largely in a continual process of such discovery. Not only is this process interesting, but it also permits us to acquire merit, and God might be thought to have designed us and our lives precisely to make this possible.

The diversity of human beings

But should God not have made everyone the same? He could have done so, and he did not. This question is closely connected to the traditional question of God's responsibility for evil, and the difficulties of answering this question had a lot to do with intellectual dissatisfaction with the Mu'tazilite position. The trouble with the latter is its simplistic demand that virtues be rewarded and sins punished, if not in this life, then in a future life. This led to questions such as why God would allow someone to die before he could make any moral mark on the world, which then excludes him from paradise. This seems unfair. But even more unfair is the case of someone who is sent to hell because he sinned, when God could have brought his life to an end earlier, before he had sinned. It is the banality of the Mu'tazilite world, in which justice prevails totally, that gives us an insight into the emptiness of utopia.

The Ash'arites are in a much stronger position when they say that it is impossible to insist on some general adherence to a human notion of justice on the part of the deity. This position vindicates the inequalities and differences that exist in this world, in that we can ascribe them ultimately to God, who has a purpose in mind that is not visible to us. It also points to a world that is far more complex and variegated, and perhaps more interesting: one in which anything can happen, morally speaking. Individuals are capable of acts of extreme cruelty, and also of great tenderness, and it is possible for the best of us to perish suddenly through some accident. Given the differences that exist naturally, we should expect of a political philosophy that it represents these differences in some way. It does not matter if everyone has different attributes and skills, provided that they all have some route to achieve their aims.

Now it may be said that this is hardly satisfactory, since some will find it much easier to achieve their aims than others. For example, the philosopher will be able, through demonstrative reason, to understand the nature of happiness which leads to salvation, and the mystic may be able to attain a perfect link with God through his practices and preparations; yet the ordinary believer is obliged to continue with her prayers and rituals in such a way that she never really gets very close to understanding the truth as it is in itself. Is this fair? Why should some people be obliged to circle the palace, as it were, while others can walk in and go right up to the king, to use a popular philosophical example? The answer is that this is inevitable, given the differences that exist between people. For example, there is an opportunity for all sorts of people to participate in the marathons that are run in many cities, yet there are different events for different sorts of people. Competitors in wheelchairs have the opportunity to compete, but their event does not have the same prestige as does that of the main event. In the same event, it may be a tremendous thing for Mr Smith of 231 Chestnut Road to come in the first 20,000 runners, if Mr Smith is not a particularly good runner, and there is no need for Mr Smith to feel let down because he was not of the quality to come in the first 100, or even the first 10,000. Running just is not something at which Mr Smith is particularly good, and there is no need to think that he has been done an injustice because of this. As long as he has the opportunity to compete at a level that is appropriate to him, he has the opportunity to set off on a route to the destination that he can set realistically for himself. The skilled runner may smirk as his eye goes down the long list of other runners, but there is nothing unfair in the fact that we all have different abilities at different pursuits, and some of us have no skill at anything apparent. This is just how it is, and the state has to represent these inequalities and differences by ensuring, if it is well organized, that everyone has some opportunity to contribute to the general direction of society. There is no reason why this should involve everyone contributing at precisely the same level. The successful state will provide for each citizen a role in which that person feels competent and which makes a contribution to society as a whole. It is important that everyone is able to tap some source of self-esteem, but not important that this source should be the same for everyone (Alon 1990). This establishes yet again the close links between the state and religion, since the position is exactly the same for a religion. Each believer should be able to feel that he or she is able to approach God, albeit in their own way. Any successful religion will make appropriate arrangements for the vast variety of believers that exist. It is hardly surprising, then, that a close connection exists between religion and politics in Islam.

Islamic accounts of history

History is a crucial concept for religion, since the rationale for a particular religion may well be historical. For example, it is often argued by a religion that the truth of its doctrines lies in the facts of the past, and, were it not for those historical facts, that the religion would be unworthy of acceptance. This is certainly the case for the three Abrahamic religions, all of which assign great importance to the proper interpretation of the past. How has this affected the nature of Islamic political philosophy? There is, of course, no such thing as Islamic political philosophy, but just a lot of different philosophies, and most political theories found in the West have an echo in the Islamic world (Ayubi 1991). Yet there is an important trend in Islamic political thought, and that is to base the polity on the original Islamic rules of community. During the *Nahda* or Arab renaissance movement of the nineteenth century, the challenge to Islamic thought was clear. How can Muslims develop a view of society which incorporates the principles of modernity, yet at the same time remains Islamic? It would be easy to go overboard and follow a Western model of society, and this was done by Marxists and socialists, since on such a view religion is an obstacle to social improvement. According to this approach, the Islamic renaissance should follow the Western renaissance, and put religion in its place; only in this way can the Islamic world participate in the material and political successes of the West.

This has not been a popular strategy. The danger is that it leads to an ending of what is distinctive about the Islamic world, namely, its Muslim character, and makes everything subservient to the desire for economic and political progress. Such a line could not be attractive to anyone with a firm religious faith, since the most important aspect of life for such people is not the material aspect, but the spiritual side. Would it not be possible to combine the useful features of modernity with a strong religious belief and develop this into a political system? There clearly is no difficulty with a religious person also being modern, and there are plenty of scientists, for example, who have profound commitment to religion. So, is it not possible to use the technical aspects of modernity to improve the material aspects of life, while at the same time retaining Islam as the guide to the spiritual part of our lives? On a personal level, the answer is clearly that it is possible, and there are many pious modern Muslims, in whatever way one wants to interpret modernity.

When one looks at the sources of Islamic society in the relevant texts, problems on the political level quickly arise. Of course, it will depend upon what sort of Muslim one is: the sort of political system appropriate for an Isma'ili is probably very different from that for a Hanbali. Yet the sources for both will share an allegiance to the early years of the *umma*, to the time when the Islamic community was at its purest, when it was under the guidance of the Prophet himself and the righteous caliphs, and perhaps of an appropriate imam. To understand the nature of this sort of society one has to have a grasp of the early history of the Islamic world, and also a theory of how that world deteriorated and became corrupted, how it responded to challenges from without and within, and how we have reached the present political state of affairs. This is how we have reached the present nature of the discussion, in accordance with which political thinkers are obliged to present an analysis of the history of the Islamic world on the basis of which the way forward is to develop some aspects of the original position so as to prevent many of the present political problems from arising.

The notion of the 'medieval'

Western commentators frequently remark that the debate about the nature of the Islamic state appears to be 'medieval'. In medieval political theory the most important question is the relationship between the state and religion, and the latter has the leading role in organizing the former (Funkenstein 1974). That is, in the best sort of state the ruler is both imam and philosopher. His status as imam is a reflection of his ability to understand the religious nature of reality, without which he is incapable of producing a polity that can reproduce the spiritual nature of the community. He must also be a philosopher so as to be capable of understanding rationally why the polity should take the form it must if it is to be perfect. The imam shares the ability of the prophet to represent imaginatively and attractively to the greatest number of people the religious and rational truths that he can acquire through his personal abilities. The important thing to recognize about such a state is that it is organic; it is a unity that is directed to satisfying both the material and the spiritual aspects of human life, and the scope for individuality is severely restricted. Since there is only one genuine route to the truth, once this route has been clearly signposted, there is no point in ignoring it or rejecting it. Such behaviour would be perverse, and the individual who seeks to behave in such a way cannot be allowed to upset the harmony of the state; nor can he be permitted to draw others away from the truth.

This is very different from the varieties of liberalism that have become part and parcel of the modern Western state. It is of the very essence of liberalism that no one has privileged access to the truth, so diversity of opinion is not just to be tolerated, but to be encouraged. It is only if there is the greatest possible diversity of opinion that the true opinion, if there is such a thing, can be determined. Any attempt to limit the variety of intellectual goods on display is to restrict consumer choice, and if choice is restricted, then we will not be able to shop around as widely as we should like. The market in ideas has to be a free market, since, if it is restricted, we may be missing the very best product for our needs, and we can only determine what this is if we have the opportunity to experience a diversity. Society, on such a view, is not obviously organic; or, if it is, then it is a very limited notion of organicity, since the state is a balance of competing interests and opinions. The idea that there is a single, overreaching truth to which all else must be subsumed is very foreign to the notion of the modern Western state. It cannot even be said that the central organizing principle is that of liberalism itself, since there are many groups in the state who themselves reject liberalism and argue for restrictions on tolerance. The liberal state itself tolerates supporters of intolerant ideas, provided they do not become so powerful that they interfere with the workings of the state, because it advocates the widest possible diversity of view. In doing this, it is pursuing some of the leading principles of modernity, such as individualism and autonomy, principles that run right through the nature of Western society.

The ideal of Islamic politics is very different. There can certainly be tolerance and diversity of view, yet this should be quite strictly limited. It would be inappropriate to allow significant opposition to the truth to overwhelm the state, or even to be in the position of possibly overwhelming the state. The state bears a paternal relationship to its citizens, and the latter need to be informed how they should act. After all, if they could work out by themselves how they should behave, there would be no need for religion. Guidance would be superfluous. It is because guidance is so important that the state has to be brought under the domination of religion. To use one of the medical and legal analogies so beloved of the *falasifa*, it is like going to one's physician or lawyer for advice. If one were capable of finding out by oneself how to reach the solution, then there would be no need to go to such professionals. But if I am ill, or someone is suing me, then I require specialized advice, and I may not really understand that advice. After all, if I understood how the advice is supposed to bring success, I probably would not need to go to the professionals at all. I could take a leaf out of the liberals' book and treat myself, or defend myself, but the consequences of this are likely to be dire.

This is where Islam comes in, in the view of Muslim political thinkers (and, as we previously saw, in ethics also). It shows us how we are to behave, and even those too benighted to realize its virtues will do better living within the context of an Islamic state than in a secular society.

One major difference between liberal and Islamic political philosophy lies in attitudes towards history. For liberals, history is an important source of instruction, inspiration and caution, but the past represents a state of affairs from which we are, hopefully, moving away into a more positive future. For Muslims, the reverse is often the case. The object of political development is to move back into history, into the past when the *umma* lived harmoniously within the context in which it was set, or so we are told. The early period of Islam represents an ideal to which we should aspire to return. This might seem to be reactionary, and in a sense it is; it is a reaction to the idea that we are engaged in a historical process of development that constitutes a progressive improvement, albeit with bumps along the way. The liberal path is essentially away from God and towards humanity. Liberals have confidence in the ability of human beings to sort out their own affairs in generally acceptable ways, even if people differ radically as to the principles that should be followed. The Muslim way is to God, and has little confidence in the ability of humanity to organize its own affairs. In a sense, the political mood here is pessimistic, and the only really positive development is to go back to where one started, to the early years of Islam.

It might be thought that this is not really accurate of either Shi'i or Sunni Islam. The latter has features that bring it much closer to Western political systems than is immediately apparent. The former incorporates the idea of future imams whose influence will be progressively felt by future generations, and in the end salvation will be made available generally to those worthy of it (Sachedina 1980). It is true that Sunni Islam has some institutional features that look promising from a liberal point of view. For instance, the importance given to the concepts of *ijma'*, consensus, and *shura*, consultation, looks a bit like democracy, and the Qur'an is replete with a good many reasonable restrictions on the arbitrary behaviour of individuals towards each other. Islamic law provides scope for thinking that some attempt is made to preserve the rights of the individual and to defend personal autonomy. It certainly is true that Islam was often an improvement on the social system that preceded it, especially in the Hijaz. Yet there can be no real argument that the concepts of liberalism are prefigured in Islam. What is of overriding significance in Islam is the guidance that God offers humanity, and the precise political arrangements that humans make are largely irrelevant to the spiritual side of reality. Some political arrangements are more likely to be satisfactory in drawing the *umma* together in its approach to God, and these are to be followed; but there is no independent value in any other aspects of such arrangements, such as autonomy, democracy or individual rights. If these have value, it is purely instrumental.

The Shi'i school is even more distant from liberal ideas. The emphasis upon an imam reduces the significance of the notion of personal autonomy even further than is the case with the Sunnis. The concept of *velayet-i faqih* (guidance by the legal authority) in the Constitution of the Islamic Republic of Iran makes the legislature redundant once the person learned in the law has come to a decision. When Khomeini was interviewed on television, the topic of how an Islamic republic would operate was raised, and he was asked what role parliament had after the *faqih* has come to his ruling. He responded with a very puzzled look. What the look meant was that once the *faqih* had decided on the Islamic solution to a problem, nothing could make it more Islamic, so more legal, just by virtue of taking a vote. Whereas for liberals the constitutional process is itself a part of arriving at the correct decision, for some interpretations of Shi'i Islam it is largely irrelevant. The state is run best if it is organized by the person who is in contact, however remotely, with the imam, and whatever constitution prevails should be that determined by the imam. Whatever constitution emerges, the decisions of the imam will not be a result of the constitution. On the contrary, the only legitimacy that the constitution has is based on its source in the imam.

This appears to be an approach radically opposed to modernity, and it is. Is it, then, largely irrelevant today as a potential political system? One can see the electoral advantage of the slogan 'Islam is the answer' in areas of the world which are largely Muslim and which have tried a variety of secular political systems that have all turned out to be unsatisfactory. But is there any future in basing a political system on a religious system in a modern environment? If the historical period that Islamic political theory is trying to reconstitute is essentially very different from the present and the future, then clearly the answer is that any such attempt is doomed to failure. On the other hand, if we are entering a period that might be described as the 'New Middle Ages', then the attempt to go back in history for a political model takes on a new relevance.

What is meant by the 'New Middle Ages'? It is supposed to describe a state of affairs in which there is a break-up of a global notion of legitimate authority, which is replaced by the constant warring of separate groups. As Minc puts it:

> The New Middle Ages is made up of the absence of organized systems, the disappearance of all notions of centre, the rise of fluid and change-

able solidarities, indeterminacy, chance and flux. The New Middle Ages sees the development of 'grey zones' which grow outside of authority . . . the sinking of reason as a fundamental principle, to be replaced by primary ideologies and ancient superstitions. The New Middle Ages is the return of crises, of shocks and spasms as a feature of the everyday. It is the site of a progressively reduced 'ordered' universe, and of regions and societies which are more and more impermeable to our practical policies and even to our analytical capacities. (Minc 1993: 10–11)

If, indeed, the New Middle Ages represents the state of affairs which we are now entering, perhaps we should take another look at the leading ideas of Islamic political thought, since the accusation often thrown at it, that it is 'medieval', might well become something of an advantage rather than a criticism. When we see ships captured by pirates, and civilians and soldiers kidnapped by hostile groups in the Middle East and held to ransom, it is easy to think that we are not that distant from the Middle Ages. Random acts of violence carried out for reasons of religion, strenuous attempts to convert those of other faiths, bitter interreligious debate often misnamed as 'dialogue', these are all familiar to us from the Middle Ages. This is certainly not the place to enter into a discussion of how accurate the New Middle Ages thesis is as a description of the present and future political system in the world. What is worth holding on to is the idea that this is an interesting and feasible thesis, and that it places theories such as Islamic political philosophy in a much more sympathetic light.

Liberalism vs Islam

Liberalism does not get much of a grip in the New Middle Ages. Within such a state of affairs, its optimism, for one thing, is entirely misplaced. Its trust in reason is inappropriate, and its ability to understand how individuals group together to found communities is weak. What is required is a political theory, one which bases itself on the community, which sees authority as emanating from a powerful emotional idea, and which is not worried about opposition. Most importantly of all, it needs a political theory that bases itself solidly on a particular view of history, since the past represents basic truths about human beings and the nature of the world in which they live. Since the world is a divinely created place, there is going to be no dramatic change in human or any other sort of nature which does not originate with God, and we should be able to work out what God has created by examining the earlier stages of creation under the instruction of the relevant religious texts. The events of the past have a purpose, and that purpose is educative, and, if we are to improve the future, we must base our thinking on the past. This is not to suggest that we actually need to return to the past, but it does imply that we should extract the best from the past and build the present and future accordingly.

This approach has the great advantage of treating history with respect, of acknowledging the role that the past has played in constructing the present. Although each generation may think that it can throw off the traces of its predecessors, it cannot, and to pretend that it can is to deny the divine nature of the pattern that God has imposed on his creation.

Another advantage of the Islamic position in political theory is that it locates the decisions of the agent within some social or group setting. It is true that some thinkers emphasize the individual agent, especially those who are committed to some form of mysticism, but even for them, on the political level, it is vital that the agent sees himself within a social setting and addresses himself to God and to his fellow human beings within the context of that setting. One is reminded here yet again of the celebrated debate in Greek philosophy, which was taken up with alacrity by the *falasifa*, as to whether the highest form of human existence is intellectual or social. Some of the *falasifa* argued that the social virtues are a necessary condition for the realization of the intellectual, so that they are secondary on the level of perfection, and in themselves entirely instrumental. For others, though, the social virtues are themselves part and parcel of the best form of life available to us, so that whatever our intellectual achievements, these are of little value without an active, appropriate participation in the community. It is worth pointing to an important feature of this debate that is shared by both sides. Social life forms an essential aspect of our existence as human beings, as God's creatures, living as we can within a community that works according to divine laws. This is not to say that we are to be blind slaves to such laws. There is always going to be scope for the individual to work out for himself where his duty lies, and although he has the assistance of *fiqh*, it is always up to him to decide which school of *fiqh*, and which particular *fuqaha'* (jurisprudents) he is to follow. As we know from research on how actual legal decisions are arrived at in particular cases, there is even a large contribution on the basis of local custom and the desire to establish harmony within the community. A social setting is prescribed for our lives, and within that setting it is sensible to consider taking certain decisions and choices. Without that setting such individual choices appear to be arbitrary.

Many Muslims would argue that a culture which portrays itself as modern, or even post-modern, is precisely a culture in which decisions are arbitrary, and, if they are arbitrary, they are not even rational, let alone in the interests of the individual. If the individual sees the structure of the community as following from, rather than leading to, his choices, then those choices are so free as to be limitless. They betray our nature as essentially social creatures, and are a sign of a lack of freedom as opposed to pure freedom. Being free is not equivalent to acting randomly.

If we are in the New Middle Ages, then we are in a situation where there is a problem in knowing how to act. The world is awash with crises, and the rational solutions that we have to such problems no longer seem to get to grips with them. Not only is respect for reason under attack, but even traditional ways of thinking about how we are to live and what we are to believe are being replaced by a cacophony of strange alternatives. As G. K. Chesterton famously remarked, when people stop believing in God, they do not believe in nothing. Rather, they believe in anything. Of course, even in the new state of affairs, if it is a new state of affairs, many people continue to adhere to the traditional religions, and also obey what they regard as pretty objective moral rules. The point is that they do this despite what is happening in the world, as opposed to finding their personal and moral views vindicated by their experience. The breakdown of traditional ways of doing things means that those who still follow the traditions have to base their behaviour on their own convictions alone. They can discover no response in society to their beliefs, except in so far as they live in a community that is cut off from society. The history that led up to their traditions has been radically severed, and the future is no longer based on continuity with the past, with the result that they do not know what to expect. The future is open; the past can provide no key that will explain the future or even the present, so there is no point in looking to history as a source of understanding.

The final point is that for Islamic political philosophy, history is sacred history. That is, the world is the locus of religious meaning, and human beings are the representatives of God on earth. There is a pattern to what happens, and, to understand history, we must understand that pattern. The converse is also true, so that to grasp the meaning of the world, we must examine history. This is not to suggest that everything that happens was brought into being by God, but it does mean that there is divine influence on the general organization of events. History has to be taken very seriously, then, as a means of guidance through the confusing flux of facts. From a liberal point of view, this is problematic, since the suggestion is that unless one grasps the spiritual dimension of reality, one will not be able to understand the pattern that is produced in the world. The liberal will want to know what privileges one version of how the world is over any competing version, and one account of history over another.

This is certainly not the place to defend or attack Islamic views of the meaning of the world, but it is worth pointing out that from a religious perspective, the only difference between the past and the present is our attitudes towards these different times and events. From God's point of view, the world just exists, and he knows everything about it all at once. So the distinction between the past and the present and the future is a distinction that has meaning only from our limited point of view. The past cannot just be the past, for it has the same ontological reality as the present and the future, and clearly it can be accorded just the same significance. So there are strong reasons for looking to history for guidance as to how we are to proceed.

One of the comments which writers on Islamic political philosophy often make is that it is irremediably conservative. Even the so-called modernizers have in mind some sort of theocracy, a state in which religion plays a leading role. The historical account of when such a state, or, better, community, existed happily plays a vital part in its rationale. We might be critical of such an approach, thinking that it is hardly appropriate to life in modern society. Of course, if we believe that we are entering a New Middle Ages, we do not need a theory that will fit with modernity, since modernity has imploded. We are in a world that is no longer adequately described using the concepts of modernity. Even if this hypothesis is unsatisfactory, and the challenge remains to find a political theory which accords with modernity, there is no easy way to dismiss the Islamic approach. For it manages to capture within itself the attempt to reproduce politically the spiritual dimension of reality, something which alternative secular theories fail to grasp. There is nothing special about Islamic thought here, since any religious approach to politics will do this, but it is worth noting this spiritual aspect of Islamic political thought rather than simply remarking how reactionary it is. It is reactionary, because it is reacting to the view that history is unimportant. This kind of reaction is radical in its effects, and argues for a reorientation of our relationship with our past, with ourselves, and with our present and future.

The case of *jihad*

Let us take a particular ethical issue and see how it illustrates specific justificatory strategies in Islamic thought. One of the most discussed notions is that of *jihad*, which is often translated as 'just war'. The first point that needs to be made is that *jihad* is not the same as just war within the Western tradition, though there are important similarities. There are criteria within Islam which determine whether a war is just, and these relate both to the waging of war and the behaviour of Muslim participants (Peters 1977). A rather crude notion currently popular in the non-Islamic world is that the world can be divided up into two neat regions, a *dar al-Islam*, the land of Islam, and a *dar al-harb*, the land of war. It is taken to be incumbent upon Muslims to seek to expand the former at the expense of the latter. There is something in this, in that the *dar al-Islam* is identified with the *dar al-salam*, the region of peace, and it is only right that the peaceful part of the world should eventually come to increase at the expense of the rest of the world. This is just, since it results in benefits not only to Muslims but also to non-Muslims whose rights to worship and to property are protected under Islamic rule. Non-Muslims also benefit, of course, through proximity to Islam and the opportunity to become Muslims! Some Muslims do talk as though they were engaged in a constant struggle with the non-Islamic world, and any religion that sees itself as embodying the truth is going to be interested in communicating that truth to the widest possible audience. If that audience is prevented from hearing, or appreciating, the message through the activities of their infidel rulers or just through ignorance, then it might well be thought to be acceptable to intervene militarily to bring the truth more speedily before the minds of unbelievers.

There are certainly passages in the Qur'an that concur with this more aggressive aspect of Islam. For example:

O Prophet, struggle with the unbelievers and hypocrites, and be harsh with them. Their refuge is Hell. (9: 74)

Fight them until there is no persecution and the religion is entirely God's. (8: 40; see also 2: 193)

If we had wanted, we would have raised up a warner in every city. So do not obey the unbelievers, but struggle with them powerfully. (25: 34)

When you meet the unbelievers, smite their necks, then, when you have killed a lot of them, take them prisoner. When the war is over, you can set them free, either for ransom or grace. If God had wished he would have avenged himself against them. He may use them as a means of testing you. Those who are killed in the way of God he will not send awry. He will guide them and dispose their minds correctly, and will admit them to Paradise, which he has made known to them. (47: 48)

These passages do not exhaust the more warlike messages of at least part of the Qur'an. Indeed, the early years of Islam were frequently characterized by struggle, against considerable odds and with frequent reverses.

There are also passages in the Qur'an which emphasize self-defence:

And fight them in the way of God who fight with you, but aggress not: God loves not the aggressors. (2: 186)

There is no compulsion in religion. (2: 256)

Had God wished, he would have given them authority over you, and then they would certainly have fought you. If they leave you alone and do not fight you and offer peace, God does not allow you to go against them. (4: 91)

There are, then, a wide variety of types of advice about conflict in the Qur'an, some more aggressive than others, and we cannot talk about the Islamic view of conflict. Given also the doctrine of abrogation, according to which some passages abrogate others, some verses may be taken to abrogate or replace others; thus it may be entirely erroneous to try to find a general principle that can encompass them all.

Those commentators who emphasize the defensive nature of the Islamic theory of conflict point to aspects of the early history of the Prophet and his followers. The Prophet proceeded very cautiously in his dealings with non-Muslims, and certainly did not indulge in a policy of total, unremitting hostility. Some of his suggestions, especially those in relation to the al-Hudaybiyya, were so lenient that they were criticized by his followers. Muhammad is said to have insisted on the sanctity of agreements, regardless of the religious affiliation of the other parties involved, and a large number of different kinds of agreement were made during the early years of Islam. Between the extremes of the *dar al-islam* and the *dar al-harb* there existed a whole continuum of arrangements, from the *dar al-sulh*, the land of peace, to the *dar al-aman*, the land of safety, and the *dar al-ahd*, the land of agreement. Not only are all agreements to be taken seriously, but there are cases where agreements with unbelievers take precedence over those with fellow Muslims (Khadduri 1979, 1984).

War is to be avoided at all costs, and when it becomes necessary, it is supposed to be carried out in an open and direct manner, so that the enemy always has the opportunity to repent and come to a peaceful agreement with the Muslims. The purpose of war is to promote peace. So we are told:

> Fight them until persecution is ended and religion is for God. If they desist then let there be no hostility except against evildoers. (2: 193)

These evildoers are aggressors, and the implication is quite clearly that Muslims should certainly defend themselves, but should stop fighting once they have achieved the goal of being free from aggression. The only sort of war that Islam sanctions on this view is one of self-defence.

But this, of course, is not the whole story. There are a variety of verses which take a more aggressive line, and which perhaps stem from a period when Islam was more settled and successful in its political life. These verses imply that Muslims must constantly take up cudgels for their religion, since surrounding non-Muslims are intent on aggression, even if there is at any given time no direct evidence of such hostile intent. The more 'dovish' passages in the Book perhaps reflected policies that were prudent when Islam was relatively weak and in need of consolidation and protection; but once Islam was more secure, it was appropriate to go on the offensive and attack unbelievers. Historians suggest that this more aggressive tendency in the Qur'an is a reflection of Muhammad's disappointment at the lack of response among the Jewish and pagan tribes of Arabia to his initially rather tolerant, relaxed approach to conversion (Leaman 2006c). Whatever the truth of the matter, the rapid expansion of Islam after the death of the Prophet was supported conceptually by the more aggressive passages of the Book, while the more defensive passages came to the fore when the Islamic world started to contract politically and sought to establish itself as just one nation, or combination of nations, interested in peaceful coexistence with the rest of the world.

The religious authorities differ not only in when a *jihad* may be declared, but also regarding what sorts of behaviour during war are acceptable. Some argue that killing all polytheist enemies is permissible, even women and children, while others offer a range of options, including pardon, enslavement, ransom, or poll tax for the *dhimmi*s, protected people. Monks seem to get off lightly, both the Prophet and Abu Bakr being in favour of leaving them alone. There is a tradition that has it that the Prophet himself never killed prisoners, although Qur'anic passages go in different directions here (47: 4 versus 8:

67). How much general destruction may be carried out in war? The Prophet is said to have set fire to the palm trees of the Banu Nadir during a military engagement, yet Abu Bakr is said not to have advocated felling trees or demolishing buildings.

There are two Qur'anic terms for conflict, a more secular term, *qital*, which means 'fighting', and a more religious term, *jihad*, which comes from the more general verb *jahada*, which means 'striving'. This latter term is often used in a spiritual sense, with the implication that the Muslim should strive to live in an Islamic way, in accordance with God's law (Nasr 1982). Many commentators regard the remarks on *jihad* in the Qur'an as relating primarily to this *jihad al-nafs*, a spiritual striving against forces within us that seek to make us more like animals than human beings. This is also sometimes referred to as the greater *jihad*, the minor *jihad* being actually taking up arms against an enemy. One can see why this is so, since it is in a sense far easier to set out to vanquish an external, physical enemy on the battlefield than to transform the life of a believer in a manner which makes it amenable to the message of Islam. More is required here than merely following religious form; a real turning of the heart towards God is what is being described here, and such a change in the behaviour and thinking of the believer clearly calls for a major effort to change, one which goes against the lifestyle which has been adopted up to then. It calls for attention to every aspect of life and a thorough re-evaluation of that life, and this spiritual struggle is more demanding than the sorts of challenges that arise in physical and political warfare.

The distinction between Sunni and Shi'i Islam has only one important consequence for the laws of war, and that relates to the person who is authorized to declare war (Kohlberg 1976). For the Sunnis, any relevant de facto political authority can declare war, while for the Shi'i it must be an imam, a divinely appointed leader. The insistence by the latter that only an imam can initiate *jihad* is at least partially motivated by the argument that it is vital to be clear about the real nature of the conflict which it is proposed to enter. It is all too easy for political rulers to declare what they call *jihad* when all they are really doing is furthering their own political interests, or those of the state. A problem with war against unbelievers who do not actively challenge the Muslim community is that it goes against the frequent references in the Qur'an to the importance of free will in religious matters and the Book's apparent acceptance of large numbers of people who will not necessarily accept the message of Islam. Of course, it can always be argued that toleration of unbelievers is a threat to the community of faith, so needs to be challenged militarily in order to preserve the community. Yet one must beware the initiation of what is called *jihad* when what is really at stake is an opportunistic attempt at self-aggrandizement, rather than preservation of the Islamic community. One of the advantages of the Shi'i approach to the initiation of *jihad* is that it reflects the importance of the political leader being motivated by the appropriate religious and moral considerations.

Modern political consequences

If we look at contemporary practice in the Islamic world, we can observe a big gap between the rules of *jihad* and what is called a *jihad*. For example, the Ba'athist regimes in Iraq and Syria in the 1990s were outstandingly secular polities whose rationale was based on Arab nationalism, not religion. Both Syria and Iraq were ruled by elites who stem from a national minority. In the case of Syria, the 'Alawis are such a heterodox sect of Shi'ites that few other Shi'i groups would acknowledge them as part of the same movement within Islam. The Takritis in Iraq are part of the Sunni community, which makes up at most a third of the population of Iraq, and perhaps a lot less, and is more entitled to regard itself as part of the Islamic mainstream. In the past, both regimes have been unswervingly hostile to a role for Islam in politics, the Syrians massacring large numbers of their own citizens to bury the threat of the Islamic Brethren, and the Iraqis denying any role for religion in the state. When these regimes needed to borrow a rhetoric to establish a wider consensus than is available solely through Ba'athism, they generally went for traditional custom and history, rather than religion. So, for example, during the Iran–Iraq War the Iraqis represented themselves as engaged in a struggle of Arabs against Persians, and their propaganda frequently spoke of the battles as Saddam's Qadisiyya, harking back to the original defeat by the Arabs of the Persians. Legislation changed during the war to make it more traditional, but not more Islamic. So in 1989 crimes of honour were no longer treated as offences in Iraq, in order to preserve the morale of the troops at the front worried about the violation of their spouses. Before the war, Iraq had been one of the most progressive states in the region with respect to women's rights and employment, but, once the war started, it became necessary in the government's opinion for the population to increase in order to match that of Iran, so much of the more progressive legislation was jettisoned. These changes came about not because the regime had suddenly discovered new Islamic credentials, but rather due to the need to appeal to the broadest possible public.

The Ba'athist regimes in Syria and Iraq were on different sides in the war over Kuwait, but both described themselves as engaged on a *jihad*. The use of the word *jihad* does not mean only that it is a struggle that they are engaged in; it is intended to involve all the emotive meaning of a war fought for the benefit of Islam. What justification could there be for such a claim? As we have seen, the criteria for a *jihad* in Sunni Islam are quite loose, at least in so far as they concern the person who is able to initiate a *jihad*, and it might be argued that any conflict that the ruler thinks is in the interests of the state could count as a *jihad*. It might be claimed that the term is being used in a slightly different way here from its religious usage, and that this usage is not thereby illegitimate, just different. There are problems with both these suggestions. Not any conflict can be a *jihad*, even within Sunni Islam. There has to be some religious aspect to the struggle. It is not usually difficult to find such an aspect, and the Iraqis described their assault on Kuwait as part of the general struggle against Israel, which certainly could come under a religious label. It has to be said, though, that the justifications for the invasion of Kuwait varied wildly over the period of occupation, ranging from helping an internal struggle by progressive forces in Kuwait, resisting an initial Kuwaiti aggression perhaps represented by the Kuwaitis asking to be repaid the money they had given Iraq to fight Iran, keeping the price of oil high, helping the Palestinians, and seeking to overturn the corrupt royal regimes.

The Syrians were similarly in difficulties in representing what they were engaged upon as a *jihad*, although they could draw on the many years of support for Iran in the previous Gulf War and the varieties of rhetoric that they had employed then. The Syrians were in an awkward position in the second Gulf War, since they had previously represented themselves as standard-bearers of the cause of Arabism, only to end up supporting the traditional enemy of the Arabs, the Persians, in their war against the Iraqis. Asad's ruthless suppression of Islamic fundamentalism within Syria had made it unnecessary to appeal to fervent Muslim opinion within the country; yet it was still important to address the majority of Sunni citizens who might be wondering why their country was first of all supporting the Persians against the Arabs and later the Americans against the Arabs. In what we might call the third Gulf War, in which the Americans overturned the Saddam regime completely, the Syrians found it easier to establish some nationalist reasons for opposing the invasion, and often those reasons acquired a religious tinge.

Although the general propaganda line was based on nationalism, it also tried to import religious terms such as *jihad*, in order to bolster the Islamic basis of the struggle of both the Persians and the Syrians against the Iraqis. The Syrians paid a lot of attention to the support which the Persians had given to the Palestinians in the first Gulf War, and to the way in which the Iraqis had 'helped' the Israelis in the second Gulf War by forcing the Americans to enter the conflict against an Arab country, on this occasion directly, and not through its proxy in the region, Israel. The Syrians were appealing here to an important legal principle governing conflicts between Muslim states: namely, that such conflicts should be resolved within the Muslim community itself, and without outside intervention. Many Muslims were affronted by Western intervention, for the very reason that it seemed to go against the principle that Muslims should be allowed to sort out their own arguments by themselves. The Syrians argued, rather disingenuously, that the Iraqi regime had made such foreign intervention inevitable by its inability to accept compromise and the advice of neighbouring Arab states. Hence it was necessary to reverse the Iraqi aggression with the assistance of Western forces, in order to prevent even greater foreign intervention in the region. Whatever else can be said about such arguments, they hardly establish the Islamic basis of the conflict.

From a religious point of view, the Iranians were in a much stronger position in the first Gulf War against Iraq. First, they had been attacked, and a treaty that had been signed previously by the Shah and Saddam Hussein had been unilaterally renounced by the latter. Second, they had an imam to pronounce on the legality of the war. The latter was important from a Shi'i point of view, but had pragmatic significance too. As we have seen, it is all too easy for a ruler to set off a conflict and quite arbitrarily to label it a *jihad*. One of the advantages of having a leader in contact with the deity is that he will be able to decide which conflicts deserve the description of being the sort of event that can be called a *jihad*. As an avowedly Islamic state, the Iranians were also in a position to represent their conflict as in defence of Islam, rather than just of the state and its interests. Although they had difficulties with the famous *hadith* that 'If two Muslims meet with their swords, the killer and the killed go to Hell', they were able to argue quite persuasively that, since they were the victims of aggression, their conflict was justifiable. At the time of the first Gulf War an interesting propaganda battle took place. The Iranians stressed their Islamic universalism, and criticized the Arab nationalism of their Ba'athist opponents, while the Iraqis emphasized the national struggle of the Arabs against the Persians. The Iranians interpret Arabism as a snare and a delusion, since it concentrates on Islamic unity in only part of the Islamic world, and indeed the sort of unity which it has in mind is not primarily Islamic at all, but really Arab.

In the second Gulf War the Iranians were in the happy position of being able to criticize everyone concerned, and they were volubly suspicious of everyone's motives in the conflict. The important point to make, though, is that the use of the term *jihad* to describe any conflict whatsoever will not really do, since the whole point of using the term, as opposed to another term for conflict, is to import a religious tinge. It might be suggested that the way in which the term is used by secular states provides evidence of a change of use such that it is unacceptable to insist that only the religious use is legitimate. There certainly has been an attempt at changing the use of the term, but such a change only has a point if the religious use remains legitimate after the change. Were the term to be used to represent conflict as such, it would not be doing its job, which is to suggest that the conflict in which the participants are engaged is in some way one with religious backing, so that if one dies or suffers, one is doing it for more than just the interests of the state. There are great conceptual dangers in using religious terms in contexts that do not support them satisfactorily. For example, it could be argued that the frequency with which the Iranians have described a whole host of crimes as *fasad*, or corruption against God, suggests that they too are guilty of using a religious term so broadly that it loses its link with the original Qur'anic and Islamic sense. Even in an Islamic state, one might think that not all crimes can be called corruption against God without trivializing that notion. It is an error to insist that terms are used properly only when they are used in strict accordance with their original meaning, but one has to pay close attention to the context within which such terms are used before one can accept them as legitimate applications of the basic idea. Of course, this is not a problem for propagandists, who glory in the looseness with which words can be used; but it is a problem for anyone who is concerned about the exploitation of religious language in the interests of particular regimes in appropriate circumstances.

When we look at the notion of a just war in Islam, a number of features emerge. There is no clear doctrinal account of when a war is just, although what is clear is that for it to be just, it must have some religious basis. There is a tendency for rulers to throw around the description *jihad* in much the same, loose way that theologians throw around the description *kafir* (unbeliever), and this is unfortunate, for the term then loses its connection with religion and becomes the plaything of politicians. It was suggested that the Shi'i view of who can declare *jihad* is useful in that it places restrictions on this free and easy use of the term; however, there is no evidence that Shi'i imams are any less likely to declare *jihad* for secular reasons than their Sunni peers. The popular idea in the West that *jihad* constitutes the normal attitude of the Islamic world to the West is inappropriate, and there is no need to identify peace between the Islamic and the non-Islamic worlds as merely a temporary ceasefire. The rules of warfare in Islam, including the conduct of war and the initiation of conflict, are entirely on a par with those in liberal societies, apart from the fact that a *jihad* has to have a religious basis. There is, then, no distinctive theory of justice in Islamic thought; nor is there a view of what constitutes a just war which could not be found in any society in which religion is expected to play a significant role. Islam is in no different a position here than most other religions that have a doctrine of when violence is acceptable. They all are flexible enough to fit in with the wishes of the local rulers, or the leading ideas of the time that are shared by the majority of the community. Were this not to be the case, these religions would have had a much tougher time surviving through the vicissitudes of regime change and the typical turmoil of historical development.

8

The Question of Transmission

Philosophy and religion

One of the interesting features of Islamic philosophy is that it not only involved a number of radical theories about how to understand key philosophical concepts, but it also created a metatheory, a theory about theories, which is even more radical than the theories themselves. This metatheory is sometimes called the 'theory of double truth', and it argued that the truths of religion and philosophy are so distinct that there is no way that they can contradict each other. In that case it hardly matters if they appear to be in opposition to each other, since it is only an apparent opposition. In fact, the opposition is almost imaginary, since it has no real being. There has always been a good deal of controversy as to whether Ibn Rushd held this position, and in its crudest form he probably did not. The crude form is the suggestion that since religion and reason are different activities, they have no relevance to each other. But this is very crude indeed, since there needs to be some explanation as to why they do not affect each other. After all, both reason and religion are shorthand expressions for ubiquitous arrangements of ideas, and surely it would be very surprising if such ideas did not come into contact with each other.

Ibn Rushd did, of course, provide an explanation. He argued that if they do not come into opposition with each other, it was because they are entirely different ways of doing the same thing. That is, reason is the entirely demonstrative approach to the nature of reality, and is capable of analysing and expressing that nature in clear, complete terms. Religion presents a version of precisely the same reality, but it does so in very different ways, ways that make it acceptable to the ordinary member of the religious community. The truth is still the meaning and the message, but it is translated into language that resonates with everyone, not just with the philosopher or the scientist. So, when it is said that religion and reason do not come into conflict, what is meant is that they are really about the same truth, expressed in different ways. They cannot come into conflict, since there is nothing for them to be in conflict about. It is as if one wishes to go from the airport to downtown; one can go by bus or taxi, perhaps. These two means of transport are not in conflict with each other, although they may be in competition. It does not make sense to ask which is the right way and which is the wrong way; this is an entirely misguided question, unless we are provided with more context.

The idea that religion and reason are entirely different approaches, albeit to the same truth, was a revolutionary idea in a Europe which was accustomed to link these notions, and we should remember that the universities in the Middle Ages were essentially clerical and religious institutions. So the first effect of Islamic philosophy on Western thought was that it paved the way for the strict separation of religion and the secular, a division which was to have, and is still having, important repercussions for European thought. It was certainly experienced as the radical doctrine that it appeared to be when it became popular in Christian Europe, in the way that shocking ideas do rapidly become both fashionable and widespread.

After the first introduction of Islamic philosophy into the Christian world, it fell under something of a cloud, given the opposition of some of the ecclesiastical authorities, but, more importantly, because Greek texts which had previously been unavailable became widely known, so there was no longer any need to work with what were, after all, at best rather third-hand translations. At issue here are texts which were originally Greek, then translated into Syriac, from that to Arabic, then sometimes into Hebrew, and finally into Latin. The alternative of going to the original source was obviously very tempting! Yet the main Islamic thinkers, in particular Averroes (Ibn Rushd), Avempace (Ibn Bajja) and Avicenna (Ibn Sina), to give them their Latin names, remained much used, as did some of their Jewish counterparts such as Maimonides (Rabbi Moyses) and Ibn Gabirol (Avicebrol); this was due to their role as commentators. They represented a long tradition of commentary, and the works of the Greek philosophers, and in particular Aristotle, are hardly so straightforward that they do not benefit from commentary. So there was continuing use of the commentators who had emerged within the

Islamic tradition, since they had interesting and challenging things to say about the text.

There was a third, as yet little understood form of influence, via the ways in which thinkers such as Leibniz and Descartes had imbibed aspects of Islamic philosophy and transformed them into modern philosophy. There are, for example, many resemblances between Avicenna's flying man example, and the structure of Descartes's *cogito* argument. This example is of someone who has no contact with his physical properties, and has to rely on thought alone to work out who and what he is, an example that Ibn Sina used to good effect to prioritize knowledge acquired through reason alone. He also used it to emphasize the distinction between the body and the soul, and to argue for the priority and independence of the latter. Since the flying man example was well known in Latin and would have been available, we do not know whether he borrowed it from Avicenna. We do know, though, that both Spinoza and Leibniz made serious use of some of the *falasifa* since they actually mention them in their work (Wilson 1996). One should always beware of falling into the fallacy of *post hoc ergo propter hoc*, and there is certainly no room for confidence in the nature of this sort of connection.

A useful way of proceeding is to look at the sorts of issues that were taken up in Western philosophy, and to examine how close these are to the main principles of Islamic philosophy. We need to examine the main aspects of Averroism to get anywhere here, since the other leading theories of Islamic philosophy were undoubtedly important for the construction of the detail of Western philosophy, but perhaps not so much for the whole spirit of that form of thought. Where Averroism really had an impact was on the West's view of the relative significance of religion and philosophy. The arguments, about how orthodox an Averroist Averroes himself was, rather lose their point here, although they are worth pursuing. What is important is that once one accepts that religion and philosophy are two routes to the same truth, one has given up much of the purpose for arguing that one is superior to the other. We need to look here at two of the main theses of Averroism, which certainly were faithfully derived from Ibn Rushd himself, and these relate to the Aristotelian notion of there being varieties of precision in language and varieties of valuable lifestyle (Leaman 1996a, 2005a).

The approach to language here is very important, and there is a chapter in this book devoted entirely to the issue of language. Is one form of language superior to others? According to Aristotle, there is no such thing as a neutral concept of precision, for precision is itself dependent on the sort of language that is being used and the context within which it is used. This is a point which Ibn Rushd makes constantly in his work, responding to the attacks which al-Ghazali and others make on philosophy's use of language. The latter argue that philosophers do not use language correctly, since they have no room in their descriptions of how the world operates for the direct action or knowledge of God. They claim that what it means for God to be an agent is that he is entirely unconstrained, except by the laws of logic, in what he does. They accuse the philosophers of pretending to accept that God has a role, through the use of traditional language about that role, but without actually giving him anything to do. As we have seen, the arguments that they produce in defence of their thesis are strong, and they certainly do establish that a thinker such as Ibn Sina is using traditional theological language in novel ways. The point that Ibn Rushd makes, however, is that this is not really much of an objection. There is no one proper use of language; there are a variety of uses, and none of those uses can be privileged. So the ordinary believers' use of language is just as correct as that of the philosophers, and probably more correct than that of the theologians, given the context in which it is used. This is a very Renaissance kind of thought, the idea that it is we who determine levels of precision and meaning, not someone (God) or something (reality) itself. This idea is replete with the confidence and exuberance of the Renaissance, since it implies that nothing need constrain us in what we say, provided that we can find a context within which to say it to give our words a role and a sense.

Although much is often made of the absence of Aristotle's *Politics* in Islamic philosophy, the text on the whole not being available in Arabic, Ibn Rushd had few problems in using Plato's *Republic* to make the sorts of points which he thought Aristotle would have made (Leaman 1997b). Of interest to us here is the notion of how we should live. Should we concentrate on just one type of life in particular, the life of reason, or should we seek a diverse range of activities, including moral and social duties? This is a question which Aristotle never finally settles: we never really know what his final position is on this, though it is probably true that he leans more to the intellectualist conception of happiness. Ibn Rushd interpreted his position on this as undecided, and he argued that this is because there is no one way of life which is the only route to happiness, or even the best route. There are only different routes. Each may be acceptable in its own way, and provided they conform to the rules of acceptable behaviour, then there is no reason why a variety of human practices should not be part and parcel of the best form of life. It was often argued by the *falasifa* that the secondary virtues, the social and political virtues, are important because, unless they are made part of one's life, one will not be able to expend as much effort as otherwise on intellectual thought. But if one takes seriously the idea that there are varieties of ways of approaching the truth, each of which can be valid, then it follows that one might consider valuing different forms of life equally. Then the question of which is superior to which would no longer be significant; it is really for the individual to work out for himself or herself how to act. This again might be regarded as a very modern implication of Averroism.

The notion of cultural contact

There are a number of ways in which one can talk about the effect of one culture on another. Sometimes and perhaps most often the effect comes about through the shock that results from that contact. When we talk about impact, we often mean a form of contact that is unpleasant in some sense, as when someone makes an impact on someone else by hitting him over the head with a brick. This is the sort of impact which Islamic philosophy had on Christian and Jewish Europe; it presented Christian and Jewish thinkers with a range of propositions and arguments which it was difficult to refute, and which, if they are true, posed problems for some of the major theoretical positions of their systems of belief (Leaman 1996g). We can thus talk about an impact even when we do not mean that there was agreement and incorporation of the new view; the impact was brought about by the effort involved in addressing the new view. So the impact of Islamic philosophy on the medieval European world outside the Islamic realms often came about through the efforts of Aquinas, Albert the Great, Duns Scotus and others to understand and respond to the important arguments and interpretations which their Islamic predecessors had produced (Marenbon 1996).

The position in modern times is less easy to describe. Some philosophers, such as Spinoza and Leibniz, were thoroughly imbued with the main principles of Islamic philosophy, in the sense that they had a deep knowledge of what the important arguments were and how they could be addressed. But other modern philosophers, such as Descartes and Kant, for example, had a far less perspicuous relationship with Islamic philosophy. Kant does, it is true, present his antinomies of reason in a way which suggests some acquaintance with the traditional way of setting out the basic *kalam* arguments; but there is no reason to think that this is where he got them from. One might think that Descartes would have come across some aspects of the Averroist controversy through the training he had in early life; but there is no evidence that he did. What is perhaps of more importance than direct evidence of a connection here is the impact of the whole Averroist controversy – which after all lasted for around 300 years, from the thirteenth to the sixteenth century – a controversy which extended throughout Europe, from England to Poland. What the Averroist controversy established, despite all the denials and refutations, was that it is feasible to argue that philosophy and religion are entirely different areas of enquiry. Of course, what Averroes actually says is that they both refer to the same truth, and there is no reason to doubt that this is the main focus of his argument. But what is important about the argument is that for the first time it placed philosophy on at least an equal footing with religion. It was no longer feasible to argue that reason has to cut its cloth according to a pattern established by religion. This is very much part of the agenda of modern philosophy, and signals the break with medieval philosophy.

This is not to say that the philosophers of the Middle Ages subordinated their philosophical work to their religious principles, which is very far from the truth. On the other hand, they were often happy to assign religion a particularly high status with respect to philosophy, and, as a result, it was often acceptable to say something like *bi-la kayfa*, that one just has to accept that something is the case, even though one cannot see how it possibly could be. This is even quite common in thinkers such as Averroes, who prevaricates a good deal on certain sensitive issues: this has encouraged the idea that he is dissimulating. But, whatever the precise truth about his real views on issues like personal immortality, there is no doubt that his discussion of this is rather sparse, as though he realizes that what he is proposing runs against a common understanding of faith, and so needs to be restrained in what he says. This is not an acceptable strategy in modern philosophy; even committed believers in religion feel it appropriate, and indeed important, to interrogate and defend all aspects of basic religious principles. Ibn Rushd was able to place his thought in an entirely modern perspective by frankly assigning religion and philosophy equal status; and the Averroist movement explored this radical idea far more frankly than its originator either would or could (Leaman 1994, 1996a).

Another interesting feature of the transmission process occurs when one culture is affected by another, and the result is something rather different from the original idea which produced the change. This occurs because the local conditions and interests are different, and so the idea is, as it were, transformed to fit local conditions. Later on, though, this transformed idea returns in its new guise to the culture in which it originated. This is sometimes called the 'pizza effect', from the way in which the pizza went to the United States with immigrants from Naples, and now the sort of pizza on sale in Naples is often the American variety, not the original. This 'pizza effect' occurred particularly with the thought of Ibn Rushd, which was taken up in nineteenth-century Europe by anti-clerical thinkers such as Ernest Renan, who in turn used it to argue for the basic conflict between religion and philosophy. Ibn Rushd emerges as the defiant, courageous defender of reason in opposition to the reactionary forces of religious authority. During what came to be known as the *Nahda*, the Islamic renaissance, this version of Ibn Rushd became attractive, since modernizers in the Islamic world were looking for someone who was both a defender of Islam and an advocate of 'modern' ideas. The Ibn Rushd they invoked was very much a creation of the nineteenth-century European imagination, although it does have distinct resemblances to the views of the man himself, and it is hardly surprising that this should be the case. After all, the Islamic renaissance had as its leading motive the need to deal with the relationship to Europe in some radical and authentic manner, and who better than Ibn Rushd to illustrate the possibilities that exist here. Yet it is worth emphasizing that the renaissance thinkers were using a rather Eurocentric model of Ibn Rushd as compared with the thinker himself, a point to which we shall return later.

The Andalusi connection

Until quite recently it has been commonplace to value Islamic philosophy, if it is valued at all, as the source of transmission of predominantly Greek ideas to both Christian and Jewish Europe. From the twelfth century CE there was, as we have seen, a translation project that mimics what took place in Baghdad several centuries earlier, albeit the direction of the translations then went in the opposite direction. The high intellectual reputation of al-Andalus was well known throughout Europe, and naturally there was a demand for the products of that culture. Both Muslim and Christian thinkers were interested in Greek Peripatetic thought, and the former seemed to have far more of it, and of a superior provenance, than was the case in Christian Europe. But it was not only as transmitters of a tradition that thinkers like Ibn Sina, Ibn Bajja and Ibn Rushd were valued. It was also very much as interpreters, as people who could put the bare text of what was originally Greek philosophy in a form that would both throw light on it and also raise important issues.

It was because of this dual role that Islamic philosophy quickly came into conflict with the local Christian authorities. As al-Ghazali had pointed out, albeit from a different perspective, it is not easy to reconcile some of the leading theories of *falsafa* and religion. This became apparent to the Christian theologians, and the same sort of dispute arose between them and the philosophers as had existed earlier between the *mutakallimun* and the *falasifa*. Whereas earlier it was argued against the latter that there is no need for Muslims to go to pagan Greeks for their ideas, so now it was argued that there is no need for Christians to use the conceptual machinery of Islam to resolve theoretical problems. In particular, the sorts of solutions that became popular seemed to go entirely against the normal understanding of religion. This is particularly the case with the thought of Ibn Rushd, who in his Latin guise of Averroes came in for both adulation and great hostility in Christian Europe. The ideas which were particularly controversial were those which involved doubts as to the feasibility of an individual afterlife, those which argued for the eternity of the universe, and those which challenged the notion of God's knowledge of particulars, all staple features of al-Ghazali's attack on philosophy. Some of these ideas were directly banned from the University of Paris in the thirteenth century CE, which gives some idea of how prevalent they were. If these theories had not been popular among both teachers and students, there would presumably have been no need to ban them. There certainly seems to have been a lot of excitement over these new ways of looking at issues, which provided their users with far more powerful conceptual tools than had existed previously; and it seems that the boldness and breadth of the new learning had a thoroughly exhilarating effect on European cultural life.

Yet it might be argued that we should be interested not only in the transmission of Greek philosophy to the Islamic world, and then back to the Christian and Jewish world. We should also take note of the process of transmission of philosophy from the east of the Islamic world to the west, from the earliest repositories of Islamic knowledge to the newer territories on the edge of the Islamic world. This is an important matter, because it cannot be overemphasized that the main source of Islamic philosophy for the non-Islamic world was Andalusi philosophy, philosophy from the Iberian Peninsula (Jayyusi 1992; Urvoy 2006). Andalusi philosophy had a flavour of its own, and it might be argued that it differed from the philosophy of the East not only in degree but also in kind. One of the superficial differences between Andalusi philosophy and the philosophy from the East is that the former, not the latter, was what was directly transmitted to Europe. Even the philosophy of the eastern part of the Islamic

world which was translated into Latin and Hebrew, and which then
became part of the Western curriculum, was often transmitted via
Andalus. After all, al-Andalus was the closest region of the Islamic
world to the main centres of Christian culture, at least in the Western
Christian world, and it also incorporated a blend of cultures, which
made it feasible for different cultures to understand each other's cultural products. As long as Islam was the leading culture, it became
important for both Christians and Jews to understand Arabic, and of
course they did, in the same way that ethnic minorities in any culture
work within the language (and indeed the culture) of the most influential group. Moreover, al-Andalus was in many ways the cultural
capital of Europe for several centuries, in that it had the most civilized
approach to medicine, engineering, astronomy and of course philosophy, so there was a great deal of interest in the West in the cultural
products of this region. Not only was there this interest, but there
were also on hand plenty of potential translators, often Jews who
translated from Arabic into Hebrew, and then a translation would
be made into Latin. It is worth remarking on how this paralleled the
early transmission of Greek texts into Arabic, which often took place
initially via Christian translators, who first translated the Greek into
Syriac. This is surely more than a metaphor for the deep cultural links
between the three monotheistic religions.

Andalusi philosophy is clearly based on the philosophy of the
East, but it took the latter and passed it on to Europe in a radically
changed form, in much the same way as Christian and Jewish Europe
changed radically the nature of the Islamic philosophy that was
passed on to it. This is something which has to be constantly borne
in mind; when we talk about transmission, we tend to think of a
body of thought merely changing hands, as it were, by becoming the
cultural property of another group. But intellectual property is very
different from other kinds of property, whatever lawyers may tell us.
With ordinary property, once it leaves the original owner, that person
loses it. The original owner has transferred his right to it in passing it
on to someone else. With knowledge, by contrast, however much is
transmitted, it remains the property of the original owner. Intellectual
property increases in value as it is disseminated more widely; knowledge that remains private and restricted, by contrast, has limited
value. Moreover, when it passes from one owner to another, it tends
to change, so that it is not precisely the same property that is transmitted. This was certainly what happened when Greek philosophy
was transmitted to the Islamic world, and the physical traces of this
change can be seen in the languages that were used in the process. The
same thing happened when Islamic philosophy entered the West, via

al-Andalus, in the transformation from Arabic to Latin, sometimes via Hebrew (Leaman 1996g). Yet what is at issue here is not only, or mainly, the difficulty of expressing a set of arguments and ideas, formulated in one language, in a different language. What happens is that a creative and critical consciousness transposes such arguments and ideas from one context to another, and what results is a new and original product. It is certainly true that this product has important links with what preceded it. But that is very different from claiming that it is the same thing, or more or less the same thing.

There is a traditional way of understanding the movement of ideas from Greece to the Middle East and then back to Europe that is far too simplistic. It assumes that Europe, the original home of reason, lent it to the Islamic world, and then took it back many centuries later, through that part of the Islamic world which most dramatically impinged on Europe, al-Andalus. It is important to challenge this picture, since it is based on a number of misleading ideas. The first point which ought to be challenged is that there is just one notion of reason, the sort of reason embodied in *falsafa*, the sort of philosophy which in Greece was called Peripatetic and in Arabic *mashsha'i*. This is the type of philosophy which was transmitted to Europe and which flourished for so long in al-Andalus. Yet the spirit of Andalusi *falsafa* was often quite different from that of the *falsafa* from the East.

Getting back to basics

There are two main features which mark this difference. One is that Andalusi philosophy generally tried to get back to the origins of the thought with which it was operating. The sort of philosophy which had arrived in the Islamic world was certainly built around the works of Aristotle, and to a lesser extent Plato, but was heavily influenced by the commentaries and works of many of the Neoplatonic thinkers, some of whose works were even confused with those of Aristotle himself. It was this corruption of the real Aristotelian texts which led thinkers like Ibn Rushd to try to sort out which ideas were genuinely Aristotelian and which were later accretions. From the point of view of the philosophy of the East, the commentaries and works of the Neoplatonists were important aids to understanding Aristotle himself, and were to be welcomed as providing interesting arguments along the lines which *falsafa* investigated. From the point of view of al-Andalus, by contrast, it tended to be held important to try to work out which opinions were genuinely Aristotle's, and which were those of his successors or predecessors, since the untidy accumulation of theories and ideas was thought to weigh down *falsafa* and to make it less easy to see precisely what its import is.

Let us take two examples here. In many of his commentaries on Aristotle's works, Ibn Rushd suspects that much of what was supposed to be Aristotelian was in fact something else. In the original commission – which we are told (although how reliably is unclear) he received from Abu Ya'qub – to summarize (*yulakhkhisuha*) the works of Aristotle, it is obvious from the language used that what was wanted was a clear demarcation of the aims of Aristotle, as compared with those of the other philosophers whose views often came to be confused with those of the 'first master'. This is not to suggest that Ibn Rushd was able to abandon the Neoplatonic curriculum and embrace a pure Aristotelianism, if there is such a thing. He certainly could not do that, since Neoplatonism was very much the philosophical curriculum of the time. But he was able, remarkably given the state of the editions with which he was working, to suggest time and time again that a particular point apparently made by Aristotle could not really be as it was supposed to be. He did all that he could to preserve the purity of the organon, the basic Aristotelian idea of the logical, not defending Ibn Sina, whom he criticizes for his lack of adherence to basic Aristotelian ideas. This makes his defence of *falsafa* rather problematic. When he defends *falsafa* from the attacks of al-Ghazali, he makes it clear that he is defending not the form of *falsafa* which was created in the East, but a new, purified form of Aristotelianism which he sought to create in the west of the Islamic world.

Another example might be taken from the thought of Moses Maimonides, a Jewish defender of *falsafa* well within the tradition of Islamic philosophy (Leaman 1997f). A problem for religious philosophy at the time was the view that Aristotle had defended the idea of the eternity of the world. Aristotle seemed to argue that the world must be eternal, at least in so far as time is a function of change, and before the world was created (if there was such a time) there could have been no change; so the world could not have been created in time, at a particular time. This implies that God could not have created the world out of nothing, *ex nihilo*, at a certain time, which appears to limit the power of God. God and the world, then, are co-eternal, which is certainly very different from the usual religious idea of the dependence of the world on God for its existence and nature. Maimonides argues that Aristotle could not have argued in this way for the eternity of the world, since this is not something for which evidence could exist. That is, the sorts of analyses which, Aristotle argued, are appropriate for understanding aspects of the world are different from the analysis which we would need to understand the world as a whole, since the logic of how a system operates is very different from that of how part of that system operates. This is buttressed by the Aristotelian argument that different levels of precision apply to different forms of language. We can be quite precise, using science, as to how a particular phenomenon came about, but we should not expect the same precision to obtain when we contemplate the causes of the system as a whole.

Let us examine another example of this attitude of getting back to basics. In his *Hayy ibn Yaqzan*, Ibn Sina presents a model of a mystical journey across different levels of reality, using the familiar imagery and language of Eastern mythology. By contrast, in his *Hayy ibn Yaqzan*, Ibn Tufayl presents an analysis of what it might be like to have to build up a language and a conceptual scheme from the ground upwards. In this philosophical *Robinson Crusoe* we read of the way in which an infant is brought up on an island with only animals as companions, and is then obliged in complete isolation from other human beings to construct an understanding of the universe around him. He is able to do this by means of reason alone, and his intellectual construction is adequate to the task. When he is visited on the island by a Muslim, Hayy already knows everything except the details which the visitor has to impart. When they both visit the 'civilized' world, they are brought up immediately against the hypocrisy and the artificiality of that world, and return quickly to the island, where they can continue to live as human beings should, in line with the quiet contemplation of reality. This confidence in the use of independent reason is very much in the spirit of al-Andalus, the spirit that urges the individual to throw off the accretions of past knowledge and step out afresh into the realm of science and true knowledge (Goodman 1996c).

Andalusi thought is in essence radical thought, in that it examines the roots of a problem and applies new solutions. Ibn Bajja, like many of the *falasifa*, uses Plato's *Republic* in the development of his thought on political philosophy, with one very interesting, novel, feature. He argues that there are states that are so imperfect that philosophers will find themselves treated as weeds (*nawabit*) there. It is as though they find themselves surrounded by wild beasts, and the best they can do is to take steps to withdraw from society until the situation improves. This is a very radical move, since it suggests, unusually, that it is permissible to abandon society to its fate, as it were, in particularly unpropitious circumstances. This is a step which few of Ibn Bajja's predecessors were prepared to contemplate, since the assumption was, on the whole, that whatever the state of the *umma*, the philosopher, like other Muslims, must remain a member of it and participate in its activities. Ibn Bajja was prepared to argue that there are situations in which this is impossible, where the state and the individual are so opposed to each other that the only move the individual can make is to leave the state.

Perhaps the most radical of the Andalusi *falasifa* was Ibn Rushd. In his *Fasl al-maqal* he defended the compatibility of religion and philosophy, but he did not take the line that there is no essential contradiction between them. He might have been expected to argue that they are each appropriate to different sorts of reasoning, and that the theologian should stick to theological issues, and the philosopher to philosophical ones. He might have been expected to argue that theology and philosophy represent different forms of life, different sorts of language, each useful in its own sphere, and that each should be respected and allowed to operate within that sphere. But no, he took the aggressive line that theology is really unable to deal satisfactorily with theological issues. Where there is some doubt about the meaning of a religious term, for example, there is no point in looking to theology to resolve the doubt, since the technical machinery which theology has at its disposal is inadequate for the task. All that theology can do is operate dialectically, using premises which are generally accepted as true within its own realm of discourse. Only philosophy can really resolve such problems; only philosophy has the demonstrative force to end the debate once and for all. Only philosophy works with premises that it can establish as true, so only philosophy can reach a conclusion that is both valid and true.

This is a radical response to the claim that philosophy needs to be justified from a religious point of view. It resembles nothing so much as Socrates in the *Apology*, when he is on trial for his life, antagonizing the jury not just by arguing that he is innocent of the charge, but by further arguing that he is carrying out a public duty and ought to be rewarded by the city of Athens for his philosophical work! Ibn Rushd does not argue that the theologians should tolerate the philosophers; rather, he suggests a little grudgingly that the philosophers should tolerate the theologians, provided that the latter are restricted in what they say about the texts they examine. If anyone is to be accused of *kufr*, unbelief, Ibn Rushd argues, it is the *mutakallimun*, since it is only they who broadcast widely the difficulties in understanding problematic passages. They are the only people who encourage believers to question and doubt the meaning of religion. The philosophers, by contrast, do not write in such a way that the public can follow their arguments; but in so far as they do write about such issues, they resolve them once and for all in an entirely satisfactory way. The theologians, by contrast, argue constantly about what sort of answer would be appropriate, and surely nothing is more likely to weaken the faith of the community than such behaviour by those who state, to anyone who is prepared to listen, that they know the real meaning of the text.

Falsafa and *hikma*: philosophy and wisdom

There is of course another type of reason in philosophy, apart from this sort of *'aql* which we find in *falsafa*. Islamic philosophy, like many systems of philosophy, makes a basic distinction between *falsafa* and *hikma*, between Peripatetic and mystical thought. One way in which to make the distinction is to describe the former type of reason as linear, the latter as circular. Peripatetic reason is linear, since it operates via syllogisms, through the analysis of premises and the working out of the implications of those premises. If one sees the world as conforming to a logical pattern, then in principle it would be possible to work out exactly what features the world would have if one had the basic axioms of the system and then followed their logical consequences. Mystical thought, by contrast, is not analytic but synthetic. It brings elements of reality together into a whole, rather than taking them apart, and it is circular in nature, in this way representing the circularity of reality. Of course, to claim that a reasoning is circular is to criticize it from a Peripatetic point of view, since it means that there is a hidden premise which illegitimately includes the conclusion. From the point of view of mysticism, however, such hidden premises accurately describe an aspect of reality that the end is in the beginning, as it were, or that events follow a particular pattern that is constant.

Although we tend to distinguish between *falsafa* and *hikma*, we must not take the language of this distinction too seriously. Most of the *falasifa* referred to what they did as *hikma*, and to themselves and their colleagues as *hukama'*. Nevertheless, they were on the whole quite clear on the distinction, which was perhaps made most succinctly by Ibn Sina in his original remarks on the distinction between *hikma mashraqiyya* and *mashsha'i* thought. Al-Andalus was the region in which great progress was made in what I am here calling *hikma*. There were many important thinkers, among whom the most important are Ibn Masarra, Ibn Sab'in and, perhaps the most notable, Ibn al-'Arabi. They all shared the Andalusi tendency to return to the origins of their form of thought, to rethink it, and to come up with radical conclusions as a result. Ibn Sab'in, for example, criticized the entire Aristotelian project for requiring a categorial analysis of reality which misunderstands the radical unity of that reality, and the supreme oneness of the deity. This is very much a theme among the Andalusi *hukama'*. Ordinary language and the philosophy that is built on it misrepresent the omnipresence of the deity in the world, and the world in the deity; whereas what is required is an entirely different way of conceptualizing reality, a way that is in line with the pervasive spirituality of that reality (Taftazani and Leaman 1996).

It might be thought that it would be difficult to argue that the Andalusi form of mysticism is different from that produced in the East, since the main principles of *tasawwuf* surely come from the East anyway. Yet there are distinctions which can be made here. The sort of mystical reason that was developed in the East has a very personal, private character. Take a thinker like al-Ghazali and his *Ihya' 'ulum al-din*, a work in which he defends a mystical approach to reason as compared with other approaches. It quickly becomes evident to the reader that al-Ghazali is describing a private spiritual journey. In fact, he is a representative Eastern thinker, in that his writings are all very personal, and they represent what seemed to him to be the way forward, and why. Others might choose to follow his path, in so far as they can, but it is really up to them what conclusions they draw from their experience. Contrast this with the arguments of the Andalusi defenders of mystical reason. They sought to represent their private thoughts and experiences in political action, in establishing ways of living that would embody that form of thought. Indeed, Ibn al-ʿArabi sought in his celebrated (but fictional) debate with Ibn Rushd to destroy publicly the sort of approach to philosophy advocated by the latter. The point of the debate was to show that this form of *falsafa* was no longer viable, and the accompanying of the body back to Cordoba was taken to symbolize the burying not only of one philosopher by another philosopher, but of one philosophy by a new philosophy, in a very public, demonstrative sort of way. Again, this is typical of the political spirit of Andalusi thought, the fact that it tried to embed itself in the practical structure of its time, even when it was aligned with *tasawwuf* with what might be considered to be the most private, asocial aspect of philosophy.

The concept of religious reason

Another type of reason which was defended in al-Andalus was religious reason. This was designed to defuse the apparent conflict between religion and reason, the conflict between faith and philosophy. If it could be shown that religion embodied a form of reason, then there would be no conflict between religion and reason, since they would both be forms of reason and could hardly come into conflict (Leaman 2006a). Ibn Rushd argued that religion was just as rational as philosophy, in that they both embody logical processes of thought. In fact, Ibn Rushd argued that every kind of human thought is built on a form of reasoning, since the only way in which statements can have meaning is if they are analysable into propositions that adopt some logical structure. Religion is no different here from anything else, and religion represents the social, emotional and practical side of rationality. There are many people in the *umma* who would find it difficult to know how to behave unless they had the assistance of religion, since their rational faculties are not independent enough, or they do not have either the time or the inclination to spend much time developing their independent reason. It is for such people that religion has been constructed, so that they will know how to live and what to believe. The propositions which religion urges people to accept are not false; nor are they misleading. They are simply versions of the philosophical truth appropriate to a public which is unable, or unwilling, to grapple with philosophy.

Does this suggest that the public is at a disadvantage as compared with the philosopher in acquiring the truth? In a sense it seems to, and the public appear to be fobbed off with a pale imitation of the truth, a truth that only the philosophers can really appreciate. This would indeed suggest that the notion of religious reason is rather misleading, since the sort of reason that is being described here does not look like any sort of reason at all. Rather, it looks like something that one is obliged to adopt because one cannot really understand what the truth is. Yet we do not have to accept this. Take this example. I know very little about how the stars and planets operate, so when I look at the sky on a dark night I see lots of twinkling lights and different hues, without really understanding what it is all about. I know vaguely that bodies in space move around each other in some way, but that is about the limit of my knowledge of astronomy. Now, when an astronomer looks at the sky, she knows far more than I do; she can name the constellations and the individual bodies, and she knows what principles lie behind their appearance. She would know, perhaps, that some of the bodies which we observe no longer exist at the time we apparently see them, since in the interval it took for the light to travel to Earth, the star was destroyed! Does this mean that I know nothing about the heavens, though? I do not think so. I may know all that I need to know, or want to know. I may be vaguely aware how to acquire more information, but I have no interest in doing so. Or I may want to find out more about the sky, but cannot really understand the books I consult, not, perhaps, because I am stupid, but because I am not good at understanding scientific theories and facts. My ignorance of the nature of the sky does not mean that I cannot admire the moon and the stars; nor does it mean that I cannot know something about the sky. It is just that what I know is necessarily incomplete and limited as compared with the astronomer. Yet what I know has a logic to it, and a rationale which is perfectly adequate to my needs and interests; so it is not a misleading version of the truth which the astronomer possesses.

The concept of inclusive reason

Finally, it is worth pointing to yet another feature of the Andalusi use of the idea of reason, and that is as something inclusive. The Greeks used the notion of reason to distinguish between themselves and others, and in this sense it was an exclusive notion. Plato did not think that reason constituted a basic difference between men and women, but he did think that its possession or absence led to radical differences between the various strata in society. Aristotle thought that reason was limited to men and to those who were not slaves; thus one was entitled to treat people differently on the basis of their differences. The account of reason that Ibn Rushd, for example, provides is of an inclusive reason; it includes the whole of humanity. This is surely as it should be, since God could not have justly created people with different intellectual capacities and then limited the possibility of salvation to those with well-developed intellectual powers. God provided all his human creatures with some rational ability, and then left them with a choice as to how they would use that ability, how they would react to the guidance that in some form or another he supplied (16: 36; 4: 164). Some would improve on what they started off with, while others would let their natural talents lapse and get by with only a minimal use of their reason.

It is surely the same with our physical skills; some of us may exercise and strive to improve our repertoire of physical abilities, while others of us may do very little and fail to improve on what we started with. It would be unfair if those who were not interested in, or good at, physical activities were to find that their bodies started to collapse. Similarly, it would be unfair were those uninterested in perfecting themselves intellectually not to have available to them a form of salvation, since they can use their limited reason perfectly adequately in their social, emotional and political lives to exist in harmony with their neighbours and their environment.

Some commentators point out that what made Averroism such a potent mixture intellectually in Western Europe was that when it moved to the West, it abandoned its restrictiveness. That is, the limitations which Ibn Rushd and the other *falasifa* had placed on public dissemination of philosophy to all and sundry did not travel with the philosophical doctrines themselves. To a degree this is true, but it should not be taken to hide the fact that Averroism itself embodies an inclusive form of reason. Just as reason underlies the whole of human activity and thought, so it is a common feature of all human beings.

In this way the development of Averroism may rightly be seen as a harbinger of the Renaissance and the Enlightenment, and it is this use of reason as a notion which brings people together and assures them of their equal role in the understanding of reality which caused such an intellectual storm when it became part of Western intellectual property. It was no longer acceptable for people to hide behind the certainties of religion or philosophy, since those certainties could no longer hide them from their peers who decided on following a different approach to the truth.

There are useful ways of comparing different philosophers in Greece to each other, and likewise in thinking about how they might be linked to thinkers in the Islamic world. The sophists might well be linked to the *mutakallimun*, since they both adhered to the value of following a reasoning from particular premises which are held to be true within the context of a form of life. For the sophists, the axioms constituted the system of morality that was important for the community, while for the *mutakallimun* they are the principles of religion, of a particular religion. The latter are linked to a notion of particularism, to the significance of working out the implications of a particular way of living, an individual form of thought and life that throws up problems and dilemmas that then need to be resolved. The Greek philosophers in the style of Plato and Aristotle and the Islamic philosophers, by contrast, were universalists; they sought to establish as axioms principles which could be justified in any possible system of life and belief. When we think of the Islamic philosophers, we often say that they could not be as independent in their conclusions as could the Greeks, since the Islamic philosophers were, after all, Muslims, and were constrained in their conclusions by their religion. But in fact the reverse is the case. Islam was a liberating force in philosophy, in that it supported the hypothesis that every human being was created by a God who could not allow natural differences among people to affect their ultimate fate. For those natural differences are, from a religious point of view, supernatural differences, and since they stem from God, they cannot be the basis for discriminatory behaviour. The restricted universalism of the Greek philosophers became a far freer universalism when practised by the Islamic philosophers, and when that form of thought 'returned' to the West, it returned in a very different guise.

Robinson Crusoe and Hayy ibn Yaqzan

In conclusion, let us return to that archetypal Andalusi figure, Hayy ibn Yaqzan. In *Robinson Crusoe* the arrival of a stranger on the island provides someone whom Robinson Crusoe can tame and train to obey his wishes. His attitude to his environment and to the person he finds in it is one of exploitation and domination. In the philosophical novel by Ibn Tufayl, by contrast, the stranger on the island is greeted enthusiastically by Hayy, and theirs is a genuine dialogue of views and forms of knowledge. Hayy has the confidence of someone who has gone to the source of knowledge, the principles of reason alone, and when someone comes, he is eager to share his knowledge and also to learn from him. When both are disappointed by life in 'civilization', they return to the island and seek to resume their simple yet perfect lives there. One wonders how Hayy has the ability to act so differently from Robinson Crusoe, why he is prepared to take such risks in his trust of the stranger, and how he can just leave the environment in which he feels secure and then return to it again. Robinson Crusoe has no doubt about the sort of society in which people ought to live, and if someone like Friday is unaware of the principles of that society, then he must be forced to obey the commands of the person who does understand those particular principles. Hayy, by contrast, believes that his life and thought are in line with the universal principles of reality, and so he is relaxed in his relationships with those who are less able to grasp such entirely general truths. It is this kind of universalism which had such a radical effect on the West, and which transformed philosophy into a dynamic and revolutionary doctrine. And it is this kind of universalism which produced such a strong reaction, an attempt to throw back the challenging principles of Andalusi thought.

If, as has been argued here, the sorts of reason that were championed in al-Andalus were so various, the question obviously arises as to why only some of them were transmitted to the West. The answer is surely that the West had no need of Andalusi mysticism, since it already had a perfectly adequate system of mysticism of its own. Every culture with a philosophy also has a mystical tradition, and it is interesting how similar those traditions usually are. It is only in recent years that the West has shown an interest in Andalusi mystical philosophy, and in particular in the thought of Ibn al-ʿArabi, perhaps as a result of the progressive weakening of the indigenous mystical traditions in the face of the progress of scientific forms of thought. It is also worth pointing out that Averroism influenced not only the West in the Middle Ages, but also the growth of modernity in the Islamic world from the nineteenth century onwards. The *Nahda* movement in particular was marked by a renewed interest in Ibn Rushd as a thinker who confronted the issues of modernity and religion head on, and so Ibn Rushd comes over as being a very modern thinker, someone who has a good deal to say about present problems and future possibilities. This is, of course, the mark of a considerable thinker, that he created and was part of a system of thought which maintains its relevance in very different social and cultural conditions. Andalusi philosophy is essentially modern philosophy, in that it reaches into the future in its attempt to understand the past. We cannot consign this type of philosophy to a footnote in the history of philosophy. We have to acknowledge that it is part of the continuing debate over how to reason and, as such, part of the mainstream of philosophy itself.

9

Language

Philosophy in the contemporary Islamic world is rather like philosophy everywhere. Particular thinkers work on the theories and traditions of philosophy that interest them, and frequently today these come from the Anglo-American tradition of philosophy, or the continental traditions. The major thinkers within Islamic philosophy are often discussed as well, of course; their thought is sometimes treated as of historical interest only, but occasionally it is discussed in relation to modern developments in philosophy. If any of the arguments that have been presented so far are successful, they will have demonstrated that Islamic philosophy is primarily philosophy, and relates to the pervasive theoretical issues that have been considered by philosophers down through the ages. Of course, it takes place within a particular religious and cultural background that strongly determines its style, but no more than that. If Islamic philosophers were to say that certain conclusions could not be drawn from a reasoning process because they contravened the principles of religion, then they would be failing as philosophers. It might be that their motive for rejecting a conclusion was religious, but it would behove them to come up with an argument as to why it is reasonable to reject the conclusion. As we have seen, even those who are intent on countering the main arguments of Peripatetic philosophy provide arguments against those arguments, which is why it is appropriate to dignify the debate as philosophy.

But even though it may be accepted that Islamic philosophy is philosophy, just as Indian philosophy and Chinese philosophy are also philosophy, it is sometimes claimed that the leading ideas of

Islamic philosophy are primarily of historical rather than general significance. To a degree this is due to the common misapprehension that Islamic philosophy died with Ibn Rushd in 595/1198, and when one looks at the medieval curriculum it appears to be rather dated, to put it mildly. The sorts of ideas and theories of that period often fail to connect obviously with modern ideas, and the reader may conclude that interesting though these ideas are, they are not really part of the continuing philosophical debate which links modern thought with the Greeks. This seems especially the case when we think about the detailed categories of philosophical psychology for instance, the precise distinctions between the active, acquired and passive intellects, not to mention the speculative and material intellects, topics in a debate that was abandoned long ago (and rightly so!). Yet we have seen that these notions are entirely appropriate in the analysis of the nature of human thought and knowledge, even if they require some translating into more modern ideas, and the fact that the language of the philosophy of the past is sometimes obscure is no reason to regard such philosophy as no longer relevant today. The fact that philosophy in the past may have been written within a religious context is also no reason to think that it is relevant only within that context.

Is there any point in talking of such a broad category as 'Islamic' philosophy, given the vast variety of ideas and arguments that fall under this heading? This is itself the focus of an often heated debate, and one that applies to any general label and its accuracy in describing an area of investigation. There is a tendency in philosophy to look for an essence which can be used as the central principle of a particular school or area of philosophy, and which does something which no other area does to quite the same extent. Of course, there is a tendency to do the same with religion, so that one thinks of particular religions having specific principles that characterize them and differentiate them from other religions. No doubt there are such principles, but it is very difficult to say what they are, since they either become so general that they cover a number of religions or they are so specific that they rule out some aspects of the religion itself. There has been no attempt here to try to organize neatly the main 'conclusions' or 'axioms' of either Islam or Islamic philosophy. But it is interesting to look again at some of the most important arguments within Islamic philosophy and reflect on how relevant they are as aspects of philosophy itself.

Within both the Anglo-American and the continental systems of philosophy, little attention is paid to what is sometimes called 'medieval philosophy'. In both traditions there is often a rapid move from Aristotle right up to Descartes, with a rare pause to consider some aspects of Thomism on courses with a Catholic slant. The whole agenda of post-Aristotelian thought seems very distant from us today. Neoplatonism, with its proliferation of metaphysical and ontological entities, seems wedded to a view of the world which really does not make contact with most of the theoretical problems which have been of interest in Europe since the seventeenth century. We tend to think of medieval Islamic and Christian philosophy as irremediably part of the Greek tradition, and Jewish philosophy is also closely tied to the forms of thought of its monotheistic partners. Yet we have seen that there are many debates in Islamic philosophy that are clearly of continuing relevance and interest, despite, or perhaps because of, their use of ideas first produced in the heyday of medieval thought.

The case of Ibn Rushd

Ibn Rushd (Averroes) seems to be just as irrelevant to us today as he was to his contemporaries. Indeed, his position has become worse, given his general antipathy to mysticism. One important aspect of Islamic philosophy is its general interest in mysticism; so it might be argued that even though the Peripatetic *mashsha'i* tradition does not make any real advance on the general line of Neoplatonism, the mystical tradition – which reaches its height in the work of Suhrawardi, Ibn al-'Arabi and Mulla Sadra – does do something very different from its Greek predecessors. The distinction between *falsafa* and *hikma*, between analytical thought and mystical philosophy, is a rather artificial distinction in most Islamic philosophy, since thinkers like Ibn Sina and, of course, Ibn Rushd's compatriots Ibn Bajja and Ibn Tufayl, worked on both levels simultaneously. Yet Ibn Rushd is particularly unusual, as compared with his Andalusi peers, in his hostility to mysticism and his adherence to a view of reality according to which everything can be understood using the processes of rational and organized thought (Leaman 1992).

There are certain aspects of Ibn Rushd's thought that are particularly important and deal with issues that are, and have been, of constant philosophical interest. This is not the place to present a detailed account of his views, but it is worth making some remarks on their leading characteristics with reference to the philosophy of language. According to Ibn Rushd, the paradigmatic meaning of predicates is represented by their association with God. For example, knowledge itself is the activity carried out by God that involves the knower actually creating not just the act of knowledge, but its object as well. This is perfect knowledge, since God knows every aspect of an object he has, after all, created and he knows how that object relates to every other object in the universe. We, by contrast, have to make do with an etiolated concept of knowledge, since we do not create our own objects of knowledge, except in the very limited cases where the object is something internal to us as a sensation or a report on how the world appears to us to be (A 71–81).

What is important about this point is where Ibn Rushd takes it. He could argue that only God really knows, and that we only know in the sense that what we experience is a pale reflection of real knowledge. This is very much the line that the mystics adopt, arguing that what we take to be knowledge is not knowledge at all when compared with the perfect and perspicuous grasp of reality that God possesses. Ibn Rushd could have used the principle of negative theology that was so popular in Neoplatonism to suggest that really there is no link between our understanding of knowledge and God's knowledge, where the latter represents knowledge itself, or the essence of knowledge. On this view we would have to work out what knowledge is by linking together the examples of knowledge that make sense of our experience of knowledge and then deny that these are really constitutive of the concept of knowledge itself. He could even have taken the contrary position, and argued that there must be a close link between the paradigmatic sense of knowledge and our notion of knowledge if these are both instances of the same concept. This is very much the position adopted by al-Ghazali, for instance, in his assault on the philosophers in his *Tahafut al-falasifa*. Although this theory is used to challenge the philosophers' use of language to describe God, it could be turned against al-Ghazali by arguing that God really does know in much the same way as we know, albeit with certain essential differences. For example, Ibn Sina talks of God having knowledge of particulars, but of rather different particulars from those that occur to us (unique particulars such as planetary events and so on). God's knowledge can be regarded as existing on a different scale from our knowledge, in the same way as an elephant exists on a different scale from an ant, though the only difference between them lies in the matter of scale. We can still basically talk of even such different beings knowing and experiencing the world.

Ibn Rushd on meaning

Now, there is nothing wrong with any of these competing theories, and there are corresponding modern theories that are constructed on the same principles. All I wish to do here is to point out how interesting and relevant Ibn Rushd's account of language is. What he is arguing is that we can relate different uses of the same term even though the uses are quite different. That is, there is a paradigmatic application of the term, and then there are less clear applications of the term; but the less clear applications of the term are nonetheless applications too. They are not instances of another term; nor are they mistaken attempts to link different terms. They are also not examples of the same term being used in slightly different ways. On his theory of meaning, there is a clear application of a term as defined in a particular way, and once it has been defined in this way, we have what might be thought of as the perfect example of its use. Then there exists a range of other uses which do not display the clear criteria of its definition, but which preserve enough of its basic meaning to be acceptable applications of the same concept (*A* 179–96; Leaman 1997c).

We might, to adapt an idea produced by Frege, see the basic meaning of a term as the point at the centre of a circle, around the periphery of which exist applications of the term that are not perfect examples of it, but are nevertheless applications. If I draw a perfect circle, and then draw a much rougher representation of a circle, what is the relationship between them? For Ibn Rushd, the relationship consists in a loose link, there being enough similarity to the perfect circle for the rough circle still to be called a circle. But the important additional point that he makes is that there is nothing wrong with the rough circle, in the sense that if I was explaining to someone what a circle is, it would, in most contexts, be good enough to draw the rough circle. Yet what makes the rough circle a representation of a circle at all is its link with the perfect circle, and of course what I have called the perfect circle here is not really a perfect circle, since if one examined it closely, one would observe all sorts of imperfections that interfere with complete roundness and regularity. It is because we know what a perfect circle is, in the sense of knowing what the principle of circularity is, that we can talk about a wide range of slightly, or very, deviant circles as being circles.

This is a crucial aspect of Ibn Rushd's theory of meaning, stemming perhaps from Aristotle's observation that the degree of precision which we should employ in language is a function of the context within which we are working. The implications that Ibn Rushd draws from this theory are radical. First, it means that there is no privileged access to the nature of reality that represents how things really are. The ordinary person has just as valid a grasp of how things really are as does the philosopher or the religious thinker, provided that the ordinary person is able to use concepts that connect with that reality in a loose way. Let us take as an example here the notion of an afterlife. For the philosopher, this should not be understood, Ibn Rushd argues, as the individual survival of the person after his or her death in an environment rather like the environment of the world of generation and corruption. Once our body perishes, there is no sense in thinking of the continuing existence of the individual soul, since the soul is just the form of the material body, and, once the latter disintegrates, there is no longer any matter to be informed by the soul.

Yet the descriptions of the next life that we find in the Qur'an are very different from this. They are full of vivid descriptions of events similar to events in this life, and one might wonder at the difficulties of reconciling these two apparently different versions of the same thing. Ibn Rushd argues that the philosophical understanding of the next life is the most perfect understanding of it; this is what the next life really is. This is how it can be understood from an investigation of the appropriate concepts. The religious understanding is less perfect, since it involves a lot of elaboration and description which, strictly speaking, do not represent the next life as it is in itself, but rather as it is for us, or for those of us who find the purely conceptual understanding of it unsatisfactory or difficult to grasp (A 82–116).

But is this not a bit disingenuous? After all, either there is an individual afterlife or there is not an individual afterlife and, if the ordinary believer thinks there is, he is just plain wrong. We should be mistaken if we feel we have to insist on the Law of Excluded Middle, though; since if we take seriously the notion that the link between the ordinary and the philosophical use of language is one of metaphor, ambiguity and looseness, then the question 'Is it true or false?' of the corporeal notion of the afterlife does not apply. Take the example of someone who understands the logic of numbers, so that she appreciates precisely why $2 + 2 = 4$. Compare this with someone else who has learned the multiplication tables by rote, and when he hears the combination '2 and 2', he just says, or thinks, '4'. It is automatic; it is done unthinkingly, since he has learned his tables automatically, and does not even think of what the numbers represent, or why they work out in the ways they do. Is he wrong in his way of working out the sums? No; he just does it in a different way from the more sophisticated mathematician. Am I wrong to think that I can use the computer on which I am typing this given I have no idea how it actually works, what makes it possible for it to operate in the ways in which it normally does? I 'know how the computer works' in the sense that I know how to switch it on and what generally happens, but when my knowledge is compared with that of someone who understands how computers actually work in the sense of why they work, it can hardly be dignified with the term 'knowledge' at all. Yet of course it can. In philosophy we no longer prioritize one particular form of expression as the right way of describing a state of affairs. The scientific view of the world is better than the magical view in some senses and with particular ends in mind, but, as alternative views of the same phenomenon, they are just different ways of describing the same state of affairs.

As we know, this principle became highly controversial in Christian and Jewish Europe when it was generalized into what came to be known as the 'doctrine of double truth'. According to this doctrine, a proposition could be both true philosophically and true theologically, even though the philosophical understanding of it is contrary to the theological one. This is sometimes seen as far too radical a notion to be identified with Ibn Rushd, but I have come to think that this is probably wrong. Certainly no proposition could be both true and false at the same time, but it is clearly possible for a proposition to be true when taken in one way, and false when taken in another. This is surely what the doctrine of double truth came to mean in medieval Europe, and this also explains how radical it is. Some commentators have spoken of a thirteenth-century European renaissance, and if there was one, then the principles of Averroism played a large part in it. According to those principles, neither religion nor philosophy has the last word to say on the issue of truth (Leaman 1991). Both are equally valid views of the same truth, so neither the philosopher nor the theologian is in a superior position when it comes to determining the nature of reality. We tend to see this as the view that religion does not have priority over reason, but we could equally well take it that reason has no priority over religion. Both are valid and have appropriate uses; the problems arise only when one tries to mix them up and insist that one has priority over the other or that one form of argument may be assessed according to the criteria appropriate to the other.

Now this is a very modern notion, one might even say post-modern, which is of course not to say that it is right. It is hardly surprising that this notion had such an enormous impact on medieval Europe, from where it was re-imported into the Islamic world during the *Nahda* and became a force for modernity there also. We need to link Ibn Rushd's theory of meaning with his philosophy of mind to bring out its really radical implications. Again, when one examines the sort of conceptual vocabulary that Ibn Rushd uses when discussing the mind, it seems that this is a very dated, obscure area. But in fact he makes some points which are not only very interesting, but which are also highly intriguing from a philosophical point of view.

The Averroists held certain positions on the philosophy of mind that proved to be controversial. There was, for example, the idea that not only the active intellect, but also the passive intellect, is just one thing. This means that the basis of human thought is the same in everyone, and the only ways in which we can distinguish between ourselves as thinking things is through the nature of our differing thoughts. There seems to be an inconsistency in this theory, since, as we progressively make our thoughts more and more abstract, as we move further away from imagination and closer to demonstration, so the individuality of our thoughts might seem to become dissipated in the unity of the active intellect. This latter, the productive capacity of abstract thought to connect up both with us and with abstract thought itself, is taken to be one thing, and is the source of our ability to use abstract thought itself. As we perfect ourselves, as we come closer to the active intellect, we become more like the abstract ideas themselves and less like individuals. This is an aspect of the theory of the afterlife that makes the Averroistic argument so apparently threatening to traditional faith. It presents as a picture of the afterlife a model that is so refined it could hardly be of interest to the ordinary believer.

Ibn Rushd and elitism

Before we get into the faith versus reason debate again, we need to recall how the theory of meaning makes sense of this variety of approach to the concept of the afterlife. The ordinary believer finds it difficult to think of the afterlife as something that does not have any reference to his individuality. Similarly, he thinks of the afterlife as a state to which one is elevated as a result of moral and religious actions. Yet the philosopher, or at least the Averroist philosopher, knows that this cannot really be ultimate perfection, since our social duties embed us in individuality. Our afterlife cannot really be a matter of whether we have done our duty and prayed regularly, since these actions and the principles on which they are based are far from theoretical. This might seem a bit harsh, since surely the principles on which our actions are based can be just as pure and theoretical as the principles of science. Perhaps they can; but what is in question with the ordinary conception of the afterlife is the preservation of something like this life on the basis of actions that have taken place during this life. Suppose that I give regularly of my meagre resources to a charitable cause, entirely anonymously, and without expectation of temporal or even divine reward. Here is a good action, an action for which we might expect that I should be rewarded in the next life. Yet, on the account of the afterlife that Ibn Rushd presents as the most perfect view, this is not possible. I shall have missed the best form of afterlife which is available, the one attained through linking my thought with the active intellect. This appears to cut off the vast majority of the human population from the most perfect form of immortality, the intellectual and non-individual form.

This is only a problem, though, if we fail to take seriously the theory of meaning which goes with the theory of the afterlife and other similar accounts of important religious and political concepts (Leaman 1995a). Most people, with their individual notion of immortality, have a notion of the afterlife to which they can relate and which makes sense to them. It specifies what are appropriate forms of behaviour, and provides them with a range of activities in which they can engage and a set of ends which they can seek to attain. It does not matter that they cannot reach the heights that are achievable by others, in exactly the same way that it does not matter if I cannot draw a perfect circle. What is important is that everyone should be able to do something which bears some resemblance to the ways things really are. Then they are all, in a sense, doing the same thing, and justice is preserved in that there is for everyone a route to the truth, albeit some routes are more direct than others.

This comes out nicely in Ibn Rushd's political philosophy. His use of Plato's *Republic* as the main guide to political theory is appropriate, given the hierarchical nature of the teaching of that text. To use a term that is currently popular in politics, Plato's account of the just state is highly inclusive. It has a role for everyone, whatever their capacities and interests, and women, too, have a contribution to make to society (a shocking claim for an Athenian to make). This is not the place to re-examine the principles of Ibn Rushd's political theory, but it is worth noting how well it fits with the theory of meaning. The argument goes something like this. People are different. They have different capacities for intellectual achievement; they are able to control themselves to varying degrees; some are warlike and aggressive; others are passive and reflective. A just society is one in which people with these varied characteristics are brought under the aegis of a leading intellectual principle which will organize everyone in the most efficient and rational way. But the various members of society will not necessarily understand what role they are playing in the just society; they will simply perform the roles that are appropriate to them. There is nothing wrong with this, since if most people are unable to understand the principles underlying the organization of society, they are much better off leaving this to those who can (Leaman 1997b; Rosenthal 1968).

A suspicion arises here that this is all terribly elitist. Is it not wildly undemocratic to suggest that most people cannot, or do not want to, know how the best form of society is structured? Is it not highly objectionable to suggest that the political role is something best left to those who can cope with it, those who are skilled at it? This is not a problem for Plato, of course: for him, democracy was almost, but not quite, the worst form of government. But it is a problem for us, and it was also a problem for Ibn Rushd, working within the context of a religious philosophy according to which each individual deserves an equal hearing at the Day of Judgement. 'We have been sent to the red and black,' the Prophet is taken to have said, and this means that everyone is equal in the eyes of God, that the divine message of the Qur'an is for everyone and that no one is excluded from salvation as a result of his or her natural or intellectual differences. There are various ways of interpreting the elitism of Plato and Ibn Rushd. One is to approve of it, a strategy that became very popular among the conservative followers of Leo Strauss in the West. Another is to disapprove of it, but to relate it to the times within which both thinkers were working, and indeed to blame it on the times.

We do not need to adopt either position, though. The problem with the hierarchical nature of society as described by Plato and Ibn Rushd is that it seems to be based on the premise that everyone is completely different from everyone else, so there is no point in giving everyone an equal say in how the state is to be run, or an equal role in deciding what the nature of the state will be. As we have seen, this is a problem from the Islamic point of view, or might seem to be, in that the state is the sphere in which the spiritual as well as the material growth of the individual is to take place, and one would imagine that there should be some form of equality between members of the community. In particular, the devout, upright citizen should not be at a disadvantage by comparison with the intellectual; yet, according to Ibn Rushd, it is those with the right theoretical background who are the appropriate people to rule. It is true that they require a well-developed moral, religious and physical character as well; but these are only necessary conditions, which become sufficient once combined with the right intellectual skills. There is no doubt that whatever positive comments are made about what Aristotle called the 'secondary virtues' (our social and moral obligations), it is the intellectual virtues which rank highest in the value system for Ibn Rushd.

I do not think that this is objectionably elitist. What it points to is the fact that in a society with very different individuals and groups of people, there needs to be some demarcation of tasks for justice to prevail. Not everyone wishes to organize society; many people are happy to do what they feel is within their capacity and leave it at that. For example, when I have finished writing this chapter, I shall do some gardening, and this will consist in a fairly unskilled hacking away at some of the shrubs in my garden. I do not know precisely where to cut them, or even which shrubs I should be cutting, but this does not trouble me. I could find out what it is exactly that I ought to be doing, but I have no interest in doing so. I enjoy gardening in a haphazard manner, and if the result is a relatively untidy, disorganized garden, that is fine with me also. There is no need for me to know everything there is to know about the garden, and I have no interest in finding out everything I could find out about it. If I were a professional gardener, I could not adopt such a laissez-faire approach; but it is appropriate for me to be ignorant about a lot of things that I do not need to know. Indeed, if I require advice about the garden, I might go to someone who I think does know, without actually finding out why she advises me in a certain way. After all, she is the expert, and I should be happy to go along with what she says.

The important thing about my gardening conduct is that it is linked with the way things ought to be, given the desirability of a particular end. This link has to be stronger than a tenuous relationship, since if all that was involved in being part of the same activity was to do something a bit like the perfect example of the activity, then we should even call the four imperfect states of Plato's *Republic* a bit perfect. And of course they are a bit perfect, but not in the sense that we can call them all a bit just, as though they were only slightly off the principle of perfection. All these states are unjust, even if some are more unjust than others. They are not entirely unjust, in that even in the worst of them there is some principle of organization. So they are better than a chaotic state of affairs. One might think that this sort of analogy would show what is wrong with the idea of different routes to the same truth, since it could be argued that the imperfect states are different routes to the same notion of justice, which clearly would not be appropriate. They represent not different and weaker notions of justice, but notions of injustice. We might use this analogy to criticize the principle of different routes to one truth, as an argument that seeks incorrectly to connect mistaken concepts to the perfect concepts of which they are mistaken concepts. After all, it seems far too easy to assert that just about anything can be a loose form of something else, which is what the Averroists might well be accused of.

What is important is that there is an appropriate logical link between the perfect example of the concept, and the vaguer and looser instances of it. If I am playing a game in a casual and unskilful manner, then we would normally be happy to agree that I am still playing the game, albeit inexpertly; this is because there is a logical link between the throwing and hitting of a ball on a beach, say, and the complete activity when carried out by a fixed number of participants on an appropriate pitch. Does this apply, though, to some of the debates that we have discussed concerning the nature of the afterlife? Is there a logical link between the philosophical understanding of this as an entirely impersonal and spiritual state and the ordinary belief of it as a personal, corporeal state? Or is the link like that between Plato's unjust states and the just state itself? We need some argument to establish the link, and Ibn Rushd does supply such an argument.

He suggests that ordinary believers need to extract the practical essence from a theoretical argument so as to be able to act in appropriate ways, and that, as long as their behaviour expresses their way of understanding the argument, it is entirely acceptable. It is worth remembering the gardening example, for when in my ignorant and ill-informed way I hack inexpertly at the undergrowth, I am perhaps trying to follow the prescriptions of the experts, but can only do this at the level of my basic competence. What I call 'pruning the roses' bears very little relationship to what the professional gardener does; but it does bear some resemblance, and so it can quite properly be called the same sort of activity. A theory of society that acknowledges these differences between people and also combines them in such a way as to bring about a harmonious and spiritually progressive society presupposes a theory of meaning that makes sense of respecting such differences.

The Enlightenment Project

There is currently a good deal of criticism of what came to be known by its detractors as the 'Enlightenment Project'. This, basically, is the idea that the solution to all the problems that exist in the world rests in the appropriate use and understanding of reason. There is a lot of evidence that the creators of the *Nahda* tended to accept that what the Islamic world needed was more or less the same sort of passionate involvement with the Enlightenment Project as occurred, in some ways, in Europe and the United States. Critics of the Enlightenment point to the fact that the Enlightenment did not itself provide grounds for believing that reason is the principle of thought to be followed, so that its adherence to reason is itself unreasonable and uncritical.

Critics also discuss the terrible things that came into existence as a result of an unthinking adherence to a principle of rationality that is not in itself rich enough to constitute a sufficiently thorough guide to how we should live. Some critics of the Project and of Ibn Rushd's place in it comment on the low status which mysticism has in his thought, suggesting that the glorification of rationality as a form of thought ignores and misrepresents the spiritual aspects of humanity and our links with God.

Now this is not the place to enter into an analysis of the Enlightenment Project and its supporters and enemies, but it is the place to point out that Ibn Rushd does present an argument for adhering to what he calls reason; in fact, throughout his work he not only defends reason but gives arguments for adhering to it (Benmakhlouf 1997; al-Jabri 1985). Of course, these arguments suffer from the fact that there is nothing outside reason, as it were, which would serve as a justification of reason; but then nothing could. Muslims often point to Qur'anic verses and passages in the *hadith* which may be taken to vindicate the use of reason; but these do not clearly refer to any particular form of thinking which we can characterize as what Ibn Rushd advocates. He does argue that Islam directly vindicates the attitude to reason that he advocates, and does manage to produce some appropriate statements; but he really goes too far when he alleges in the *Fasl al-maqal* that there can be no conflict between religion and reason at all.

It might be thought that the argument so far has been too simple, since surely Ibn Rushd does not only argue that there is no real conflict between religion and reason, but also presents the thesis that the way to the truth reposes with reason. For example, he claims in the *Fasl* (p. 5) that '*wa-huwa bab al-nazar al-mu'addan ila ma'rifat-hi haqqa al-ma'rifati*' ('it is the door of reason which leads to the most genuine knowledge of Him [i.e. God]'). In the *Tahafut* he suggests (pp. 427–8) that '*min ahl al-sa'ada al-tamma mawadi'a ha min kutub al-burhan*' ('the people of perfect happiness are those who enquire into the books of demonstration'). Does this not suggest that he is seeking to prioritize reason over every other approach to knowledge, precisely the arrogance which the critics of the Enlightenment Project accused the rationalists of displaying? In a sense he is, in so far as reason presents the truth in the clearest, best-defined, most explicit manner. Where Ibn Rushd's adherence to reason looks most ungrounded, perhaps, is in his apparent opposition to mysticism. He does not actually say anything explicitly about mysticism, but his silence here serves to distinguish him from the long line of *mashsha'i* thinkers who indulged in Sufi or mystical techniques.

This was particularly the case with the Andalusi philosophers, and one of the remarkable features of philosophy in that part of the world was how well developed it became as regards both analytical thought and mysticism. It is a little misleading to make a sharp distinction between the two, however, since at the time, unlike nowadays, the roles of the *faylasuf* and the *hakim* were not closely distinguished. Many thinkers from al-Andalus, like Ibn Bajja and Ibn Tufayl, had no difficulty in combining the two, and this enabled their work to survive even after the general demise of *falsafa* in the western part of the Islamic world. As far as we know, though, Ibn Rushd did not join in this general adherence to mysticism as a valid form of thought, and his few references to it are either noncommittal or rather scathing. The motive for this apparent antagonism is not difficult to find, and rests on his general view that the meaning of the world is not difficult to determine, since it is in the world itself. That is, once we understand the nature of the world, using philosophy to grasp the general principles on which the world rests, there is nothing more mysterious to know; if there is, it is just a way in which religion provides a route for those who want to think of the world as mysterious to find a satisfactory way to view the abstract principles which govern the world. Yet Ibn Rushd nowhere produces a solid argument against mysticism, or for the thesis that the world is a place without secrets or mysteries; he just assumes that once one grasps certain principles, one has grasped everything important that there is to grasp. Is this not an uncritical approach to the role of reason in the understanding of the world?

Ibn Rushd as a critic of mysticism

Here we have to provide some arguments for Ibn Rushd. I suppose he might well argue that the trouble with mysticism is its inherent subjectivity, a problem with which the Sufis were themselves very familiar. Anyone could point to a particular experience or vision and claim some important role for it; but there are no objective criteria as to which experiences are valid and which are not. Compare this with the processes of Aristotelian logic. Here there are such objective criteria, albeit objective only in so far as one accepts that logic as valid; but, to be fair to that kind of reasoning, it does offer a proof of its validity. It does not just claim that it is valid and then look for support as a result of that claim; the claim to validity is based on proof. Admittedly, such proof itself presupposes trust in reason, since it is rational proof, not anything else; but it does set out objective criteria in accordance with which it may be assessed. Doubting the independence of such criteria is equivalent to doubting the results of opening our eyes and looking at something, merely because it implies that we trust what we see when we open our eyes and look at the world. If I am told that I am unreasonable to believe that I can see words in front of me while I type this, because the only vindication of my belief lies in the reports of other people's eyesight, which, after all, are only more reports of eyesight, then I do not know what more can be said. I am tempted to say that certain processes are justifications for our ways of doing things, whereas some ambitions that we have seem to have no objective criteria at all, hence Ibn Rushd's failure to be impressed with mysticism. The celebrated debate which, apocryphally, took place between Ibn Rushd and Ibn al-'Arabi really represents a controversy as to the appropriate range of views on objectivity as opposed to subjectivity, and one very much doubts whether the real Ibn Rushd would have thought that Sufism represented the way forward in philosophy.

The implications for language

Ibn Rushd's adherence to reason is not as uncritical as it looks. It is based on an analysis of the language, or rather languages, which we use when describing a variety of subject matters. These subject matters all display some connection with demonstrative reason, since every subject matter has as its basis the communication of a piece of information. Even poetry is an evocative and loose way of getting over a message, albeit using a very different method from the methods followed in philosophy. If one sees language as having as its basis the communication of information – not, one might think, a wildly implausible idea – then clearly it is the manner in which the information is transmitted that is crucial to understanding the nature of the language. What follows, according to Ibn Rushd, is that if we are to understand different kinds of speaking, we must understand the logic underlying the ways in which the information is delivered. This is explained in terms of the organization of different forms of reason, where the very best and purest kind of reason, demonstrative reason, is present in differing ways in everything else which can be dignified by the name of an assertion, albeit often loosely and ambiguously.

Now there is a lot that can be said about this approach to meaning, and it clearly is not the only plausible account of meaning that has been devised. On the other hand, it is also clearly one of the important, constant strands in discussions of the nature of meaning over the centuries in which philosophy has existed, and it is replete with observations which are no less relevant today than they were in the past.

Ibn Rushd's clear demarcation of tasks as between the philosopher, the theologian, the lawyer, the ordinary believer, the politician and so on is very interesting. We tend no longer to make these sorts of exact discriminations between different ways of speaking, especially if we are impressed with Wittgenstein's arguments for the family resemblance nature of what links different forms of discourse. One of the problems that Ibn Rushd had to address was that of identifying the appropriate person to deal with theoretical questions. Was it the theologian or the philosopher who had the last word to say on the nature of the creation of the world, for instance? The problem could be solved, he argued, if there were a clear demarcation of spheres of influence, so that the theologian is the right person to ask for answers to theological questions, but the philosopher is the right person to ask for information about the most difficult and general issues. One might expect that the theologians were not happy with the idea that they were not necessarily the best people to sort out theoretical issues, or even the best people to interpret difficult passages in the Qur'an! Even this, according to Ibn Rushd, was to be the prerogative of the philosophers.

What lies behind this notion of the demarcation of roles is the idea that language as used by different people to perform different tasks is different, and that it is only by respecting and understanding those differences that we can come to understand what the precise rules of the various forms of language are. This was perhaps a more popular notion in the early decades of the twentieth century than it is now, since at that time a belief very much on the agenda was that if we could only grasp the appropriate analysis of language, we could sort out long-standing theoretical problems. But, of course, it is still very much on the agenda, and Ibn Rushd's theory of meaning, with its emphasis on the significance of looseness and ambiguity, fits nicely with current concerns about understanding the different kinds of language, yet also recognizing that there are often only vague boundaries between one kind and another. I am not sure that Ibn Rushd would really have appreciated our drawing out the full implications of his theory of meaning, since he seemed to want to hold it along with a theory of strict demarcation according to the universe of discourse. This is acceptable provided the argument goes that each realm of discourse is linked with every other along loose, ambiguous lines; but he did not wish to accept this. He argued for indeterminacy connecting each realm of discourse and the paradigm of truth that serves as the perfect principle of truth, and at the same time for a strict, determinate definition of each realm of discourse. This conflict between the practical notion of language as loosely connecting terms with meanings and an 'ideal' notion which identifies meaning with determinate criteria continues to bedevil modern philosophy.

It should now be clear that whatever one thinks of the specific arguments of Ibn Rushd, he is very much within the tradition of philosophy itself. In the previous sections of this book I have argued that similar claims may be made of many other Islamic philosophers, whether they worked in the *falsafa* (Peripatetic), *ishraqi* or Sufi traditions, and this suggests that we view their arguments from the perspective of philosophy itself, not from that of the history of ideas. Unless we do this, we fail to give credit to an important strand of the history of philosophy that represents the cultural heritage of a significant proportion of humanity (Smart 2008). Islamic philosophy is not the only type of philosophy that requires rehabilitation as philosophy, of course, but it is the focus of my argument here. In the future it will be less easy to disregard the philosophical achievements of cultures that are seen as foreign to the West, and that is a state of affairs heartily to be welcomed.

10

Islamic Philosophy Today

There are a number of themes that occur again and again in modern Islamic philosophy which differentiate it from other kinds of philosophical thought. In addition, there are the familiar issues of philosophy that arise within the Islamic academic sphere just as they do elsewhere, and these are carried out exactly as they are elsewhere. The only difference is that they take place within the Islamic world as opposed to elsewhere, although this notion of the Islamic world is becoming increasingly irrelevant, since there is almost nowhere that can be contrasted with the Islamic world. Muslims now live everywhere and even in places where they are small minorities have the ability to consider theoretical issues, and in particular how they are to relate to the non-Muslim community. We should not overemphasize the significance of religion or ethnicity here, since we should not assume that just because someone is a Muslim the religious affiliation is going to affect their thinking in any way at all outside their religious commitments, and often not even then.

Nonetheless, a topic that is frequently discussed is how distinct Islamic philosophy ought to be from other types of world philosophy, in particular, systems of thought not related to religion. Another and related issue is what relationship Islamic philosophy should have with Western thought, itself a huge oversimplification as a general term. Some thinkers in the Islamic world have used general philosophical ideas and have applied them to what they see as the leading issues of the day within their cultural and political environment. And, of course, traditional ways of doing philosophy have continued.

An issue that philosophers have considered with some enthusiasm is the relationship that the Islamic world should have with the West, and more broadly with other civilizations. This issue is of course one that has existed for some time, but arose with particular force from the nineteenth century onwards, with the success of colonialism, imperialism and Zionism in apparently gaining supremacy over the Islamic world and bending it to its will. In earlier periods the Islamic world had represented a powerful and often superior cultural and material force in the world, but over the last few centuries it was perceived to have radically declined, and the reasons for this apparent decadence were and continue to be much discussed by philosophers. In political terms, some argue that the source of decline is a lack of interest in religion. Others argue that, on the contrary, the main source of the problem is the reliance on religion and the lack of commitment to modernity and technology.

The *Nahda* or Islamic renaissance that started in the nineteenth century and really took root in Egypt was based on philosophical ideas that have continued to be significant. The leading issue is how to preserve a distinctive Islamic identity and yet at the same time incorporate modern scientific and cultural values, where these are compatible with Islam. The two leading thinkers were Jamal al-Din al-Afghani (1838–97) and Muhammad ʿAbduh (1849–1905), who both argued that Islam is perfectly rational and in no way opposed by Western scientific and cultural ideas. The Egyptian philosopher Mustafa ʿAbd al-Raziq extended their ideas and suggested that all the main Islamic schools of thought, even the mystical schools of Sufism which were much suspected by the *Nahda* thinkers, are inherently rational and in no way opposed to the science and rationality which are such an important feature of Western culture. In fact, they throw the accusation of science against the Christian world by arguing that it was the latter that had a problem with science, not Islam. Indeed, there were events in the Christian world in the past that demonstrate a grave lack of confidence in the ability of religion to cope with science. Much reliance is placed on the thought of Ibn Rushd here, since he seems to have argued for the compatibility of Islam and reason, between religion and science, and to have shown that there is no problem in linking these two diverse approaches to the truth. It is worth saying, though, that if it is really true that Islam, unlike Christianity, did not have a problem in reconciling religion with reason, then it is surprising that so many of the Islamic philosophers should have spent so much time talking about the issue.

Many Islamic thinkers have been critical of the large role that religion, and especially the tradition that goes along with it, has in the Islamic and particularly the Arab world. Muhammad ʿAbd al-Jabri, for instance, takes up this point when he argues that the tendency in the Arab world to value tradition and imitation was very damaging, although he also suggests not accepting uncritically a hostile approach to tradition. This point has been taken up by many Arab thinkers, the appropriate attitude that should be adopted to tradition. It seems difficult to establish what position works here. A critical attitude to tradition can be made to look very much like an uncritical enthusiasm for another tradition. Supporting the original tradition looks like an uncritical acceptance of the culture in which one is living, and seems problematic also. It is on the horns of this dilemma that so much of the discussion in Islamic thought on this topic has taken place.

As one might expect, there is no general line that is adopted on this issue, and a whole variety of opinions and arguments have emerged. An interesting line has developed, of thinkers like Fazlur Rahman and Fuad Zakariyya who have suggested that Islam itself was originally critical of tradition, and that there should be no problem in Muslims today following this approach. When the Prophet came to present the message, part of it dealt with the importance of his audience taking seriously what they were hearing and not rejecting it just because it differed from what they had been traditionally brought up to believe.

This line is worth pursuing a bit further, since it is quite plausible. Many Islamic reformers have argued for the significance of rejecting innovations in Islam even if they have become part of what has become traditional. In particular, Ibn Taymiyya (661/1263–728/1328) and Ibn ʿAbd al-Wahhab (1703–92), very much the intellectual founders of the present regime in Saudi Arabia, robustly attacked the worship of things that are other than God, as they saw it, in the Islamic world. So they criticized the practice of praying at graves or special places, and of venerating particular individuals, yet what they were attacking had become the tradition, indeed the leading tradition in much of Arabia. Even today, one cannot but feel a twinge of regret that people frequently gather at the tomb of Ibn Taymiyya in Damascus to pray! Of course, they were criticizing what had become the tradition because it was different, they suggest, from the real tradition, and it is the latter that needs to be re-established. In some ways, one could point to Islam itself, which sees previous religions as having corrupted the original tradition of monotheism, which was represented once again accurately by the message revealed through the Prophet Muhammad.

Abandoning one's tradition is a very radical sign of disenchantment with the culture, and suggests a need for a new culture. This is highly problematic from any background, let alone an Islamic standpoint, since there is no obvious reason to disapprove of Islamic tradition by comparison with any other tradition. The fact that many predominantly

Muslim countries are poorer than many other countries has nothing to do with their religion, but other factors are significant, and there are of course many wealthy and successful Muslim countries, and Muslims. It cannot be anything in the religion or the culture then that condemns its practitioners to poverty and backwardness.

There is another approach to Islamic tradition that argues, on the contrary, that it should not be rejected since it is particularly benign and progressive. This works from the principle that Islam is far superior in its treatment of minorities and dissidents compared with Christian countries, that it had a far more progressive attitude to science and rationality, and ultimately that it is wrong to treat Islam as just another religion. It is superior to that sort of treatment since it has a far more positive history than other religions. Now, this is not the place to investigate the details of Islamic history, but it is widely believed by Muslims that this is entirely different from the experiences of other religions. The treaties made by the Prophet Muhammad were models of intercultural cooperation, the early Muslim civilization represented a remarkable degree of tolerance of other communities and support for science, and Islam is based on the idea of there being no compulsion in religion (2: 256). There is no doubt that one can find these features at certain points of Islamic history, but there are also plenty of negative events, when Muslims destroyed any religious opposition, murdered and enslaved those of other faiths, and forced people to choose between conversion and death. A very selective attitude to history can represent such events as the norm, or as never occurring, and as usual the truth is somewhere in the middle. Christians and Jews have become rather adept at confronting the negative aspects of their histories and coping in a variety of ways with them, while Muslims are not perhaps so experienced at this sort of activity. There is a feeling in modern times that Islam is under attack and this breeds a desire to circle the wagons, becoming defensive and not being prepared to be frank about the questionable things that have been perpetrated in the name of all religions at one time or another.

The West as decadent

A number of thinkers have linked the West with decadence, and identify Islam as the solution. The growing secularization of Europe, and gradually of the United States, has led to a situation in many countries where the small Muslim minority has more people going to worship in the mosque on Friday compared to Christians going to church on Sunday. In a perceptive comment on European society about a hundred years ago, Said Nursi contrasts what he calls the real Christianity that persisted in the past with the sort of lukewarm attitude to spirituality that was becoming the norm, and that has led to an increasingly materialistic ethos in much of the industrialized world. This was something that Said Nursi saw as very destructive of social cohesion and, of course, of religion.

Both Hasan Hanafi and Seyyed Hossein Nasr refer to the success of the West as resting on weak foundations, since material power is seen as without much ability to persist unless it is linked with spiritual power. A large number of social ills are linked with the decline of religion, and the fact that people still seem to want some spiritual support without knowing where to find it suggests that materialism is not enough in itself to construct a whole social philosophy. Religion, by contrast, has played this role for a long time, and Islam in particular is ready and willing to take on a greater share of influencing and inspiring the private and social lives of the people in the West.

This is a problematic argument, although quite often heard. One might think that what is important about religion is its truth, and this is what would make it effective in producing a stable society based on general acceptance. That is, it is because people follow God's law that society is improved, not because people act as though something was God's law. There are many positive features in Islamic societies and families, and it is certainly worth pursuing these, but it should also be acknowledged that there are also many problems. Some people have difficulties accepting the demarcation of roles between men and women, for instance, which are often rather important in the stability of the Muslim family. It is certainly true that if everyone accepts traditional roles, then this will lead to far less conflict than in families where many participants are unsure of their roles and how far they should cooperate with others. But that does not show that this sort of stability is worth pursuing at the cost of restricting the freedom of family members, or that the laws within Islam have a divine basis. Perhaps there is something in modern societies that demands a new kind of family, the kind that looks from a traditional perspective to be damaged yet might be more functional in a contemporary social context.

Confronting tradition

Al-Jabri argues in many of his works that the ways in which the Arabs confront their culture is very different from the practice in the West.

For one thing, the whole notion of that confrontation is very much a reflection of the Western challenge to Arab intellectuals. This led many of them into a traditionalist retreat, and he correctly identifies many of the leading figures of the *Nahda* as in fact staunch supporters of tradition and its religious interpretation. He calls for what he terms the deconstruction of the Arab mind, by which he means that the tradition should be examined critically and in particular without the methods of the Islamic sciences that restrict where such a deconstruction could go. Al-Jabri reserves his scorn for what he calls the Arab love of language, and its tendency to replace facts with words. Added to this is the subjection to authority, both human and divine, and the idea that the world is really at the total disposal of higher forces, so that even ordinary causal agency does not really exist except through divine fiat. In the past, the development of philosophy was unable to carry out this reforming programme since it was fascinated with the theories and arguments of the Greeks, who became yet another authority to be obeyed. By contrast, the West has managed to use aspects of its heritage to criticize that heritage and move on, while the Arab world remains stultified due to the desire to maintain the existence of a stable and ancient tradition that must continue to be venerated and obeyed.

The dream of al-Farabi, according to al-Jabri, was to present a model of religion and philosophy in accordance with which they were reconciled to each other, and in this al-Jabri sees the desire of the ʿAbbasid empire to receive intellectual support for its perilous position. By contrast, the second phase of philosophy is represented by the more radical thinkers of al-Andalus, such as Ibn Bajja an Ibn Tufayl, who were prepared to ask serious questions about how scripture is to be understood and how religion and philosophy can be understood so that they both continue to enjoy some autonomy. Ibn Rushd rejected the dream of al-Farabi, al-Jabri suggests, by rejecting the whole Sufi approach that exists to a degree in Ibn Sina and his followers, and by insisting on a naturalistic understanding of the world. It is a historical fact that the Europeans took on Ibn Rushd's rationalism and used it to develop new ways of thinking, while the Arab world remained stuck in the world of Ibn Sina.

Fuad Zakariyya is critical of those who ascribe science to previous Islamic thinkers and their discoveries. He acknowledges the value of what was done in the past and refuses to accept that it has a role in present-day problems in the Arab world. The modern period consists of *inhitat* and *takhalluf*, decadence and retardation, because of a lack of will to be critical about religion. The West is prepared to undertake this, and modern science developed from that attitude. Muslims often are suspicious of science and its compatibility with Islam, seeing in it a challenge to their faith and the authority of their leaders. The attempt by the Islamic authorities to control all aspects of daily life contrasts with the ways in which the Christian churches tend to restrict themselves to the spiritual needs of their congregations. The language of religion changed and provided room for science to develop relatively undisturbed. While Muslims are in awe of a tradition they cannot change, Arab society needs a *tajdid*, renewal, since otherwise it will stultify.

Muhammad Arkoun is unusual in not being very interested in the clash between West and East, perhaps because he was acculturated within French culture. He very much follows the approach of Foucault on the contrast between Islam, on the one hand, and the other monotheistic religions, on the other, in that the latter can calmly consider the context of revelation, while Islam sees religious language as useful only for legitimizing the search for power by the various contesting leaders of the community. Arkoun favours a deconstructive approach to religious texts, which is based on a changing form of rationality that refuses to see the Qur'an as something frozen in time, as a well-reserved tablet or Mother of the Book, as it is by contrast traditionally regarded. This leads him to the notion of what he calls Islamic reason, and is rather similar to the other religions where the desire to foster the impression of a stable and unchanging reality beneath the text tends to predominate. Yet Islam should escape from this, especially given the dialectical relationship between the Meccan and the Medinan *surahs*, and the whole process of *asbab al-nuzul*. Revelation occurs at the nexus of the sacred and the profane, the temporal and the eternal, and yet becomes frozen at the hands of the commentators and transformed into something entirely different.

Arkoun is interested in the idea of what is unthought in religion, which he acutely thinks defines the differences between religions. So, for example, modernity often involves some degree of gender equality, religious freedom, human rights and toleration, which Muslims might not regard with equanimity, and leads them not to think about these issues at all, or at least not in a similar way to that occurring in other cultures. For one thing, the account that the Qur'an and associated authoritative documents provide of Islamic history is highly suspect from a factual point of view, as is the case with all sacred history, and the refusal of Muslims to reflect on the nature of that history represents part of what is unthought in Islam. A good example of what happens when Muslims try to present a critical analysis of basic texts can be seen in the cases of Nasr Abu Zayd and Muhammad Khalafallah, who thought about what is unthinkable in public consciousness about Islam and suffered the consequences by being spurned by their communities and threatened when they refused to recant.

While Arkoun follows a post-modern and hermeneutic approach to the text, Hasan Hanafi pursues a phenomenological line. He develops the concept of occidentalism (*isti'ghrab*) This enables him to study the presuppositions of Western thought, and be critical of them, rather like the common attitudes to the East, and the critical perceptions of it. Hanafi attacks the copying of the West in the Arab world and ascribes many of the major modern trends to the impact of the West and its ideas on Arab thinkers. He seeks to redress the imbalance that exists culturally between the East and the West, and in this way bring more objectivity into the relationship between the cultures.

However, he does not in any way advocate just sticking to traditional methods of intellectual enquiry in studying the Qur'an. He suggests a system of following some of the main Western approaches to the text, combining it with the medieval Islamic tradition of commentary and philosophy, and finally bringing in how we experience the social reality mirrored by these texts in both Islamic and Western traditions. On the other hand, like so many Muslim commentators, he cannot prevent himself from asserting the superiority of the Qur'an as compared with the Jewish and Christian texts, since the latter were put together over a considerable period, while the Qur'an was directly revealed to the Prophet over twenty-two years. However, he advocates that Islam, like other religions, should be studied in terms of the experiences of the present and how this changes over time, and relates to previous sets of experiences, so he puts right in the forefront of how we should do philosophy the study of experience. This seems to come down to the study of a variety of sources, in line with much Western scholarship, including social and political principles, our views of the past, the production of the verses of the Qur'an over time and in particular contexts, its link with earlier revelations, and so on. A principle that he frequently repeats is that human practice is the embodiment of truth, and religious truth has to make sense in terms of how people receive that truth, and over history can be studied in a variety of ways.

Islamic exceptionalism

The idea that there is something special about Islam, and its civilization, is a common line in Islamic thought. This might be called Islamic exceptionalism, borrowing the expression from American exceptionalism, which also argued that there is something special about the United States that makes it different in important ways from other countries. Islamic civilization is essentially seen as more spiritual, more permanent and more perfect than other civilizations, and this can be seen in Islamic comparisons of the different systems. For example, Seyyed Hossein Nasr is highly critical of Western science, praising some of its achievements but regretting the ecological consequences of a world-view that does not acknowledge the presence of God and so treats the world as merely a site to be exploited. Science without spirituality accepts no limitations to its actions, since there is nothing that it holds sacred, and it bases itself entirely on measurements of quantities, rather than on the quality of existence. Islam and other more spiritual philosophies are by contrast harmonious and integrative; they place spiritual values on the technological agenda and so make more responsible decisions about the world. For him, the issue is not what the East should take from the West, but vice versa. Along with this view, he has discussed in detail the theoretical context of Sufism, and his historical accounts of this doctrine have played a large role in its naturalization outside the traditional Islamic world, in what is perceived as the spiritually deprived West.

Whatever one's views of Sufism, it has to be said that there are serious problems with this account of Islamic science. For one thing, there is no evidence at all that when Islamic science played a significant role in the past it was any different from any other kind of science, then or now. Muslims are, of course, just as interested in using natural resources as anyone else, and this sometimes involves using them up. It might even be argued that there is nothing wrong with this from a religious point of view, since if one believes that God is in charge of the world, then one might have faith in God solving ecological problems eventually, if that is his will, or bringing the world to an end a bit earlier if it falls into a bad way. According to Nasr, Islam instructs us to act as the representatives of God in nature, and so we must look after the world. We cannot do just anything with the world since we have to regard it as something created by God and which he has instructed us to nurture. Even if we accept this, it does not tell us anything about how we should behave. For example, what level of risk in what we do is acceptable to us as nurturers of the world? We can see how futile this question is when we compare it with the levels of risk that it is appropriate to adopt as a parent towards the children in our care. If we have a very young infant, should we check them periodically to see if they are all right? Certainly, but how often, and how far should we risk that they just come to harm without our being aware of it? A court will ask the question of what it is reasonable to expect, and religion is no guide at all to what is reasonable. To take another example, suppose I am worried that since God has put us in charge of the universe, we need to safeguard its resources. Does this mean I should cycle to work, or is it all right to drive when it is raining and cold? Is it never all right to drive if I can cycle? Or should I drive if I think that cycling is unsafe and would result in damage to the environment by killing a creature, i.e., me? Or would it be an appropriate religious gesture to drive because God had provided us with the resources to make this possible and it would therefore be ungrateful not to accept such a table, laden with divinely provided goods? We can see here that how we resolve this issue is far from obvious, and the link with religion does not really help. So the idea of basing science on religion is problematic, and Islam is no different here from any other religion.

Nasr is a passionate supporter of what he calls perennial philosophy, and this is supposedly a long tradition of thought that has at its basis a spiritual dimension. Islamic philosophy is not the only exemplar of this tradition, but it is a particularly distinguished representative. Around this idea a group of interesting thinkers has arisen, including Shuon and Coomaraswamy, although the thesis has been comprehensively disproved by Walbridge when applied to particular philosophers such as al-Suhrawardi. Nasr's enthusiasm for Sufism does encourage him to see mysticism everywhere, and this too has often been attacked by Ziai. On the other hand, he is surely to a degree responsible for the considerable enthusiasm for Sufism in the West today, although whether this will prove to be more than a fad only time will tell. It has certainly encouraged the development of a great deal of solid work on mysticism in Islam (Baldick 1989; Chittick 1998; Lewisohn 1999a, b; Morris 2005; Schimmel 1975) and on a range of approaches to this phenomenon in Islamic thought.

Did al-Ghazali destroy Islamic philosophy?

Al-Ghazali is often blamed, or credited, depending on one's point of view, with having dispatched philosophy in the Islamic world. Although Ibn Rushd came to offer a stout defence, he may have won the argument but certainly not the battle, since after his death he almost entirely disappears from the Islamic world, with even his students apparently denying all awareness of him. Of course, when al-Ghazali was attacking philosophy he was targeting Neoplatonic thought, and has no difficulties with Sufism, for example, the sort of philosophy that he himself promotes. Yet it is not even true that he dispatched Peripatetic thought, since it continued to be practised in the Persian cultural world, and continues to this day. That form of philosophy also came very much into its own with the modern thinkers of the Islamic renaissance, the *Nahda*.

In the Islamic world today philosophy is pursued in much the same way as it is anywhere else. One of the differences that did occur in the past is that the assault on philosophy by the intellectual forces unleashed by al-Ghazali encouraged philosophy to go underground, taking the form of theology rather than the sort of philosophy that grew up in the West. Philosophy continued very vigorously in the Persian cultural world, especially the philosophy of Ibn Sina and the *ishraqi* (illuminationist) thinkers who developed and commented on al-Suhrawardi and Mulla Sadra, using their work to develop new and interesting approaches to philosophy. It is impossible to overemphasize the role of philosophy in Persian culture, or indeed the role of Persian culture in philosophy. In Iran, philosophy has now moved away from the theological school, the *madrasa*, into the university, but throughout the preceding centuries philosophy was alive and well in the Persian world while being under some suspicion in the Arab world. Two significant thinkers are Mehdi Ha'iri Yazdi and 'Ali Shariati. The former develops a complex theory of knowledge by presence, a form of knowledge which is incorrigible and which grounds our other knowledge claims. This is an important concept in *ishraqi* thought, and he combines the thought of al-Suhrawardi and the modern thinker Wittgenstein. 'Ali Shariati uses the *ishraqi* school's intermediary position between mysticism and Peripateticism to create a concept of the human being as having God at its essence while preserving its freedom to determine its own form of existence. The notion of unity (*tawhid*) is seen as therapeutic; it is designed to establish both personal and political justice and harmony. He interprets the main figures of Shi'ite Islam as models for us, not only in a personal sense but also to bring about more progressive social ideals; he sees them as fulfilling archetypes which are universally desirable. Over time the archetypes themselves have not changed essentially, but they have changed in appearance, to make them more suitable for the local audiences to whom they are directed.

The founder of the Iranian Islamic state, Ayatollah Khomeini, who overthrew the Shah and became both the spiritual and the temporal ruler of the Islamic Republic of Iran, was himself an energetic philosopher. He argued that religion should not just regulate private morality but should also be applied to the state as a whole, and the religious authorities are the natural leaders of the state, since only then will the community be rightly guided. The school of Qom, of which he was a member, contained Muhammad Hossein Tabataba'i, Murtaza Mutahheri and Muhammad Taqi Misbah Yazdi, all important religious Shi'ite thinkers who were interested in the forms of intellectual thought coming from the West. They argued that traditional Islamic philosophy could only gain by opening up and using some of the important philosophical achievements created outside the Islamic world. A more challenging philosophical voice is represented by Abdul Soroush, who took a rather critical view of religion when he applied what he took to be the arguments of Popper, Moore and Wittgenstein to provide a critique of religious belief. Soroush was opposed by Sadiq Larijani, the chief representative of the School of Qom, who suggested that Soroush had misapplied the theories of Popper, Stalnaker, Watkins and Hempel. It is interesting that the debate took the form not of religion as opposed to reason, but of what the correct philosophical view should be, and then how it should be applied to religion. This might remind us of the arguments between Ibn Rushd and al-Ghazali, where the latter criticizes philosophy not for being irreligious, although in his view it was, but for being rationally invalid when pursued by Ibn Sina and his school. Soroush not only upset the school of Qom, but also the supporters of Heidegger, who has many adherents in Iran, so he was inevitably isolated intellectually. Whatever the particular outcome of this clash of ideas, it is clear that Iran remains a very lively centre of philosophical debate, and is likely to remain so.

11

Does Islam Need an Enlightenment?

Let us take seriously the idea that al-Ghazali is supposed to have fostered, that philosophy in its Peripatetic form is not worth pursuing, but logic is valuable when applied to religion, in particular, to theology. There are thinkers like Ibn Taymiyya, very much the intellectual father of the present *salafi* ideology that prevails in Saudi Arabia and in many of the contemporary radical Islamist movements, who argue that logic is not independent of metaphysics. That is, he argued that it is impossible to use logic without also importing philosophical concepts, and so if one is suspicious of philosophy one ought to be suspicious of logic also (Leaman 2000b). We have seen that Ibn Sab'in also disapproved of logic for its metaphysical implications, in particular, the way in which it sought through analysis to treat the world as though it could be broken up into smaller parts. Yet most thinkers in the Islamic world accepted with al-Ghazali that logic is a tool or instrument for thought, not a part of an objectionable system of philosophical work. That means that Islamic theology should be pursued rationally and with arguments that are sound and can be rationally assessed. On the whole, this is how the discipline has been carried out, and different thinkers have argued with each other, seeking to produce more satisfactory arguments and hence advance our understanding of the basic principles of Islam, and, even more importantly, their implications.

The site for much of the debate was the Qur'an, and it is worth spending some time looking at how philosophical ideas have indeed entered into the understanding of the Qur'an in the modern Islamic world. The first thing that should be said is that there is now really no such thing as the Islamic world, but everywhere is the Islamic world in the sense that everywhere today there are Muslims. This means that Muslims are aware increasingly of different ways of looking at texts, in particular holy texts, and can consider which of these techniques they can take on board and which should be rejected as inappropriate for the Qur'an.

A revolution occurred in Christian and Jewish theology when Spinoza suggested that we have real problems understanding the Bible, since it was written so long ago and the religious account of its construction seems to be unlikely given what we know of the times and about the text. This has resulted in a critical industry of commentary on the Bible and New Testament that rather implies that its account of itself cannot be taken literally. That is not to argue, necessarily, that the Bible is not divinely inspired but it is to argue that the idea that it was straightforwardly given to the Jews by God on Mount Sinai, for example, cannot be literally taken to be true.

This is often regarded by Muslims as setting off on a slippery slope. Once you question the precise nature of the divine origins of a holy text, it is argued, then the text as a whole becomes less holy, since it is seen as an amalgamation of diverse ideas and writings, and loses much of its aura. The Qur'an, by contrast, sees itself very much as having come directly from God to the Prophet Muhammad, albeit via Jibril, and the question of whether this account of the text is feasible or whether there were earlier and various versions of the text is seen as questioning the sacred nature of the Qur'an as such. Muslims do not want to repeat the approaches of thinkers from the other monotheist religions since they see that as often having more to do with undermining the text than with explaining it. Hence the deep suspicion that greets anyone who looks at the Qur'an from the point of view of secular style, since that might seem to treat the Book as just a book. Added to this is the desire, of course, to resist what is regarded as a long campaign by the enemies of Islam in the West to argue for some secular understanding of the nature and origins of the Qur'an. Examining the links between the Book and pre-Islamic literature, for instance, might be taken to imply that the former grew out of the latter in more than just a chronological sense. Indeed, the whole idea that Islam grew out of earlier revelations can be part of the broader argument that it is not very different from them, and has a very different history from that accepted by most Muslims (Crone and Cook 1977; Wansborough 1977).

The significance of being prepared to contemplate the nature of the holy book without preconceptions cannot be overemphasized. If one is able to do this, then the implication is that everything is up for grabs, and one is prepared for a radical revaluation of the leading principles of life. In the Christian and Jewish worlds hundreds of years ago, this was also dangerous, and Spinoza was excommunicated by the Jewish community while Christian scholars were punished for even translating the Bible into the local language at one stage. This is very much the situation in many Islamic communities, where a willingness to challenge or even just examine some of the main accounts of the source and structure of the Qur'an can result in death, exile or problems in one's career.

There is a danger here that one will get into the state of mind of describing the Islamic world as mired in an inability to examine its holy book, while by contrast the Christian and Jewish worlds have been doing this for some time. We should not be so confident any more in the universal significance of the Enlightenment Project, and there are no doubt many things that are not considered appropriate for criticism among non-Muslim groups. It is also worth adding, something that Muslims have certainly noticed, that recently enthusiasm for religion seems to have suffered greatly in the Jewish and Christian worlds, in marked contrast with the situation of Muslims. Perhaps the critique of religious texts has something to do with this, since once the mystique that lies behind a text is dissipated, it is difficult to see it in quite the same way ever again. On the other hand, it is difficult not to want any religion to seek to understand itself critically, since any system of thought must surely ask the question whether the things it urges its followers to accept are worth accepting, and why. We also need to know why the words of a particular individual are significant and should affect us. All religions have accounts that address these issues on their own terms, and the sorts of questions that go further than these are surely also worth asking. So much of the discussion of Islam by Muslims just accepts the sacred history of Islam as it is understood by Muslims, and, even if that history is true, we need some reason for believing it beyond what we find in the religious texts themselves.

This brings us to the question of whether Islam needs an enlightenment, or perhaps it would be better expressed as Enlightenment, to make a connection directly with the European Enlightenment of the eighteenth century. One of the questionable aspects of this debate is that it rather assumes that the Muslim world today is where Europe was some time in the past. Yet it is a question that is often raised. In the nineteenth century two non-Christian communities were belatedly affected by the idea of enlightenment that had such a strong effect on Europe in the eighteenth century. Indeed, it might even be said that many Jews and Muslims became acquainted for the first time in a meaningful sense with the principles and policies of the much earlier European Renaissance during the Enlightenment. Jews and Muslims had certainly to a degree played a role in the Renaissance. Jews like Judah Abravanel (Leo Ebreo) were clearly part and parcel of the Renaissance (Frank and Leaman 1997), and during this period Muslims were enthusiastic traders with Europe and imported many of the Renaissance artefacts that were so popular in Europe. It has also been argued that the work of Muslim thinkers such as Ibn Rushd (Averroes) had a marked effect on the development of the European Renaissance, and it is certainly true that his works were much translated into Latin over an extensive period, and were received in Europe as radical products, as evidenced by the fact they were banned in Paris in the thirteenth century. Despite – or perhaps because of – the ban, Averroes continued to have many admirers in Europe who drew the conclusion that religion and reason are two entirely different activities, and that neither is superior to the other.

Another Andalusi thinker, this time in the Jewish community, Moses Maimonides, also threw out a challenge to the religious traditionalists in Judaism (Leaman 1997f). He presented in his *Guide for the Perplexed* an even more perplexing analysis of how to reconcile philosophy with Judaism, which at the very least treats the former with respect and argues for its significance within a Jewish view of the world. In his most famous legal text he sought to cut through the centuries of commentary and indecision by presenting clear and final conclusions on legal controversies, thus sidelining implicitly the Talmud and Mishnah, then as now the apogee of Jewish thought. It is ironic that today his *Mishneh Torah*, his *halakhic* (legal) summary of the law should be regarded as orthodox and kosher, while the *Guide* is seen as suspect, since really it is his legal work that is the more radical in import. It undermines by seeking to replace and summarize what came before it, and what makes this plausible is the depth of Maimonides' grasp of the law and the strength of his argumentation (Leaman 2005c).

The controversial nature of Maimonides' work was recognized early on, and often vigorously criticized, but in the end it became acceptable, and his *Mishneh Torah* entered the canon of commentary. His philosophical work did not so easily enter into the list of acceptable texts, and in any case its difficult and obscure style ensures its unavailability to the Jewish community as a whole. This is not to suggest that he deliberately wrote it in an obscure manner, but rather that he was dealing with difficult ideas that required some training and ability to grasp in the first place. What is clear, though, is that Maimonides was only able to survive within Jewish culture with restrictions, and these involved the deliberate de-fanging of his major radical theses. At least he did better than Ibn Rushd who largely disappears in the Islamic world after his death, and the sort of philosophy of which he was such a forceful representative also falls into a kind of limbo. The varieties of movements that flourished in the pre-modern Jewish and Islamic worlds after Maimonides and Ibn Rushd were kabbalah and Sufism. For Jews, forms of pietism flourished, and for many Muslims some versions of Salafism or traditionalism – whether of the Hanbali flavor or the more moderate but still revivalist nature of traditionalism that periodically swept the Islamic world when allowed to do so by its rulers. The Islamic renaissance is often labeled Salafi, since it represented for many of the thinkers a way of presenting Islam in modern times as having been modern all the time, if we return to its original nature and reject the more recent accretions that obscure its real message. This approach can obviously be given either a radical or a conservative slant.

Jewish and Muslim reactions to modernity

Two important political events led to a change in this situation. In the eighteenth century, Jews in Europe were for the first time treated more as citizens than as a minority whose only function previously was to be exploited or even killed at will. Muslims were confronted with a Europe that was starting to colonize the Middle East and other parts of the Islamic world, and also with a Europe that was obviously superior scientifically. Not only was science greatly advanced in Europe, but also many other developments were impressive, and it was difficult to escape from the feeling that the Islamic world had slipped a long way behind what had become a serious contender for imperial superiority – Christian Europe. What made this even harder for Muslims to bear were two widely accepted facts: in the past, the Islamic world had been superior in a whole range of material and intellectual ways to Europe, and also that Islam is the true religion.

Jews and Muslims had a variety of responses available to them, and they remain available today. They could turn their backs on much of what was vaunted as the social and technological success of Christian Europe, and insist on preserving their former style of existence and belief. They could accept the material aspects of modernity while rejecting its ideological basis, thus again preserving largely the traditional ways of acting and belief, albeit now with some adjustments for modern society. They could argue that there was no difficulty in accepting both modernity and religion, since both are true, in different ways, and both are therefore worthy of respect and allegiance. Finally, they could argue that the old ways should be abandoned and Jews and Muslims should become Christians, or the same as Christians in their behavior. This debate raged within the two communities for many years, continuing in one form or another to this day, and some Jews and Muslims followed each of these strategies. It is important to recognize that there was available to them a variety of responses, since concentrating on the history of just one response is unlikely to be very illuminating unless one puts it within the context of the alternatives. So, in the following discussion of the Jewish *Haskala* and the Islamic *Nahda*, we need to bear in mind the alternatives that the participants saw as possibilities for them, and then we will be in a better position to decide why they may have rejected them and chosen a certain way forward. There is no reason to think that everyone saw the way to make progress as the same, although from the perspective of later history we can often link what they saw as the problems that needed to be resolved.

Moses Mendelssohn and Muhammad ʿAbduh

Perhaps the most passionate Jewish enlightener was Moses Mendelssohn (1729–86). Mendelssohn defended the significance of applying reason to everything, including religion, and argued that Judaism emerges as a very rational faith, and so is worthy of support, at least for those who happened to be Jews, and tolerance and respect from others. It is not relevant at this stage to examine the details of the argument, but the form is interesting and is shared by many of those who saw themselves as part of the Enlightenment. The first stage is to say something positive about reason and the need to base our actions and beliefs on it, and not on tradition alone. The second stage is to refer to some of the central beliefs of a faith and to point out that they can be seen, at least to a degree, as rational, and so are not ruled out a priori by reason. The third stage is to suggest that religion and reason are not then in opposition to each other, but may be seen rather as complementing each other. The fourth stage that many take is to argue, like Mendelssohn, that not only is their religion not contrary to reason, it is rather particularly rational, so especially worthy of acceptance or at least respect by those of a rational disposition. He used this argument against those within the Jewish community who suggested that Christianity was the main religion of Europe, and so if Jews were to enter into the mainstream of European life they ought to become Christians, in just the same way that they ought to speak German or French and so on. He also used it against those Christians who criticized Judaism as an outdated and irrational faith, which ought to be abandoned in favour of modernity.

Mendelssohn stakes a claim to religion as rational, and so to modernity as compatible with religions, including his own, Judaism. Muhammad 'Abduh (1848–1905) was very much a disciple of al-Afghani but less directly interested in politics. He was mainly involved in religious, legal and educational reform. He had no qualms in accepting the significance of reason, and argued that Islam is perfectly compatible with both modernity and reason. Indeed, 'Abduh suggests that it was Christianity, not Islam, that had real theological problems with science. He also argued in favour of tradition and going back to the thinking of the forefathers of Islam. 'Abduh intriguingly suggests that it was the Islamic philosophers who did not respect reason since they upheld their opinions on the basis of the tradition of their Greek predecessors, whom they followed uncritically. They are the people who should be blamed for the Islamic world's eventual intellectual and scientific decay, since they failed to follow the original Islamic thinkers in their enthusiasm for reason and enquiry.

Like Mendelssohn, he argued for the compatibility of religion with modernity, and for the superiority of his own religion's rational credentials. Yet, as we know, the effects of these doctrines were very different in the Jewish and the Islamic worlds. The Jewish Enlightenment really came to dominate Jewish culture, and continues to do so today. In the Islamic world it had a far weaker grip on the polity, and certainly did not succeed in broadcasting widely fundamental doubts about the role of religion within the Islamic community. It is interesting to speculate on why that is.

Islamic exceptionalism again

One of the features of the Enlightenment that is worth noticing is its attraction to those on the margin. The Jews are an excellent example, of course, given their very problematic status in Europe as then the largest non-Christian minority, in a Europe that linked religion and civil status for much of the time. It extends to the non-Muslim minorities in the Islamic world, again the Jews but also the Christians, Baha'i and so on, who were enthused both by the Enlightenment and its ideas, but often also by the colonial powers who came to promote it in the countries they controlled. For the majority of Muslims, however, the Enlightenment could easily be represented as a threat, since it privileged non-Muslims, at least to the extent of relieving them of their *dhimmi* status, and it gave their faith a new and rather worrying status, that of one faith among many others. Yet this is not how Muslims tend to see Islam, neither in the past nor today. One of the disturbing aspects of the Enlightenment is that it demotes Islam to equality with other faiths, a status seen as far from reality given that Islam represents in its view the very acme of monotheism itself.

At this stage there is a familiar step in the argument that will not be taken. It seeks to argue that there is a difference in how individual religious groups reacted to the Enlightenment, based on the differences between the religions themselves. That is, there is taken to be something in the essence of Judaism that makes Jews likely to have welcomed the Enlightenment, while Muslims were not enthusiastic to the same degree because of something in Islam. It is tempting to ascribe this difference to a difference in the religions. Looking at Islam, this position could be called that of Islamic exceptionalism, playing on the comparison with American exceptionalism, the apparent difference between American and other political history based on the exceptional nature of the United States. This strategy is tempting, and has been followed by such diverse thinkers as Bernard Lewis, Ernest Gellner, Hamilton Gibb and a wide range of Muslim thinkers. It is often accepted by Muslim thinkers of the *Nahda* who point approvingly to the warm welcome that natural science received in the Islamic world, by contrast with its reception in much of the Christian world. This is because, they argued, Islam, unlike other faiths, is on the side of reason and so the question of how to make it more in line with reason is an inappropriate question. So, really, for the *Nahda*, the point was not to align modern Islam with modern science, but rather for modern Islam to get back to original Islam and rediscover its earlier enthusiasm for rationality and science.

Islamic exceptionalism argues that there is something unique about Islam. Only Islam takes religion seriously, some would say, and so it is an error to think of a secular sphere existing for Muslims. But this secular sphere appears to many to be precisely the sphere of science and technology, of rationality and democracy, and if Islam has no such sphere then it is very different indeed from other cultural forms (Leaman 2000a). It is certainly true that within Islamic culture a great deal of controversy takes a religious form, although it is not always clear that it is in itself specifically religious. There is nothing unique to Islam about this, for there are many contexts where religion plays a major role without our regarding the issue as really being religious.

We need to be more sophisticated in how we see religion as impacting on wider cultural issues, since otherwise we are going to be stuck with theories such as Islamic exceptionalism, where we say that there is something unique about Islam that makes the normal categories of social analysis lose their grip. Both the supporters and enemies of Islam believe in Islamic exceptionalism, and that gives us additional reason for being suspicious of it.

But is there not something different about religions that would explain the differences between how they react to enlightenment? One way of distinguishing Jewish and Islamic views would be to look for something essential in the religions that pointed their followers in different directions here. It is not difficult to identify candidates for such differences. In an argument often repeated by Islamicists, we are told that Muhammad was both a prophet – indeed, the Prophet – and a statesman, and that in Islam there is no contrast between religion and state. Christianity and Judaism, by contrast, do allow for a secular realm where religion does not really operate, and so it is hardly surprising that the *maskilim* (the Jewish enlighteners) and the *'ulama* (Islamic scholars) who embraced the *Nahda* nonetheless went in different directions on this point.

Neat though this answer is, the main problem is that it is false. No religion says that they want their followers to behave in one way in their religious lives, but they can do whatever they like in their private or secular lives. Judaism certainly does express views on how Jews should act in every aspect of their lives, in what the *maskilim* often saw as petty and overbearing ways, and so it is quite wrong to distinguish between Islam and Judaism here. It also has to be said that some Muslim thinkers are as disapproving of the traditional approaches attributed to Islam as are their Jewish peers to Judaism, and they do seem to be operating from within Islam. They might argue against the religious necessity of women covering themselves, for instance, or for the equality of women and men, the possibility of not legally punishing apostasy from Islam, and equal treatment of non-Muslims in any Islamic state. Muslims, like other religious people, do link religion and the state, but for some this does not in itself imply any particular sort of link. It could be a very different link from that made by other Muslims, and often is. Given the variety of interpretations of even a small religion such as Judaism, it is impossible to boil any faith down to a few basic principles and use those to distinguish it from other religions. For a long time, this issue was itself a very controversial issue in Judaism, with uncertainty whether it could be reduced to some crucial presuppositions that defined it. As we know from experience, religious practitioners often end up doing things that seem to be far at variance from anything that the religion might be expected to sanction, and surely it is this flexibility of religions that has helped them survive and indeed flourish over time.

The Enlightenment and theology

Many factors have been cited to show why Jews reacted more favourably to the Enlightenment, in general, than Muslims. It is said that Judaism, unlike Islam, is not a religion out to win new adherents, and so lacks Islam's sense of the need to expand. Yet Christianity is also a religion that seeks converts, and seems to have had little difficulty on the whole in aligning itself with the Enlightenment. It is also argued that Muslims were in a position of colonial subjugation for much of the time. But then so were Jews, with their position in much of Europe into the start of the nineteenth century being slave-like.

One of the features of the European Enlightenment that really did not extend to the *Nahda* was the former's antagonism to theology. The separation of Church and state, designed to protect and foster a variety of beliefs, ended up privatizing belief and abstracting it from central cultural concerns. Hence Faust's remark, when asked what he had studied, 'Leider auch Theologie' – hardly complimentary to the theological enterprise. The Enlightenment's hostility to theology was enthusiastically taken up by the *Haskala*, but not by the *Nahda*. For the latter, the point is not to reject theology but to replace one theology with another, more modern, theological approach. Many *maskilim* were fiercely opposed to religion, their own religion included, and their denunciations of Judaism are often quite violent. Of course, there is a range of views here among the Jewish thinkers, but a large number of them identified traditional Judaism as a significant enemy, and seemed very eager to exchange any vestige of allegiance to Judaism for the offer of equality as citizens in a modern Western state, or, in the case of Russia, something that looked as though it could become modern eventually.

Of course, Jews were a minority in Europe, while Muslims were a majority in the countries they inhabited in the nineteenth century, and this has significant consequences. The major thinkers of the *Nahda* were far more establishment figures in the Islamic world than were their Jewish peers. Muhammad 'Abduh became the mufti of Egypt and from such a position of influence was able to spread his views widely around the Sunni world. Al-Tahtawi was an important Egyptian civil servant deeply involved in organizing education in the country, while

Jamal al-Din al-Afghani spent much time with rulers in the Islamic world advocating a particular approach to preserving Islam in the face of what he saw as an aggressive modernizing Christian world encroaching on the land of Islam (Leaman 2003d). This is not to say that these were staid establishment figures. Al-Afghani, for instance, may well have been poisoned by the Turkish authorities, and the intellectual efforts of the modernizers were often the subject of sharp criticism by other Islamic religious figures. By the time we reach the second half of the twentieth century, a thoroughgoing rejection of modernity is introduced into Islamic thought very much in response to the modernizers, who were then regarded as the establishment. The *maskilim* would have loved to be in such positions of influence, and by contrast they inhabited a far more shadowy world. Hence, perhaps, the more enthusiastic timbre of their approach to modernity. Modernity, for them, meant being accepted – being ordinary members of society, being citizens. What this suggests is that the Islamic and Jewish Enlightenments took place in very distinct contexts, and so not unnaturally took different forms. The Jewish Enlightenment in particular really established deep roots in the Jewish world, and in one form or another gained the adherence of the majority of that world. The Islamic Enlightenment was more elitist and so ephemeral.

An explanation for this might be that there was less intellectual depth in the Islamic world at that time as compared with Europe, and so only a few people were really capable of getting on board the Enlightenment express. That does not seem to be true, though, since throughout much of the Islamic world there was a large intellectual class, especially in Turkey and the urban centres of the Ottoman Empire. There existed a large, perhaps even excessive, bureaucracy of literate and educated Muslims who could easily have acquired the same sorts of views as the *maskilim*. Perhaps they were prevented from adopting such views due to the possibility of persecution, or at least career problems, and this is certainly a reasonable claim. But, of course, the *maskilim* also would have often been nervous of the reaction by the Jewish community, who paid them for whatever their occupation might be, and they were far from confident of a warm reception in the non-Jewish world were they to abandon entirely their Jewish roots.

The antagonism of the *maskilim* towards orthodox Judaism is very extreme on occasion. For example, David Friedländer in Germany and Naphtali Herz Homberg in Austria were scathing in their accounts of Judaism. The latter was in favour of the closing of the Jewish schools in Galicia and forcing Jewish children to go to the state schools, and also argued for the censorship of Hebrew texts. It is worth pointing out also the rather anti-Semitic tendency of some Jewish socialist thinkers of the time, such as Karl Marx, Karl Kautsky and Otto Bauer, for whom Jews seemed to be the only minority not worthy of respect and consideration. Some have commented on modern Jewish anti-Zionists, that they seem keen on everyone having a homeland except for the Jews. In some ways this hostility of Jews to Judaism is a reflection of the Enlightenment and its tentative acceptance of the role of Jews in civil society. Many Jews were so delighted to be part of the new club, as it were, that they felt they had to trash the old club, and that seems easy to understand. If for a long time one had been limited to being in a restricted role in society and then the door was opened to allow one into wider society, it is quite natural to turn one's back on the previous lifestyle that was perhaps based on the earlier restrictions. Jews embraced the Enlightenment with enthusiasm and often took it as their escape route from Judaism as a whole. Those Jews who saw themselves as *maskilim* but still attached firmly to Judaism were often nonetheless in a position of difficulty with the religious establishment. One way this manifested itself was through the reinvention of the Hebrew language as a lingua franca. This was heartily supported by many *maskilim*, while vigorously opposed by the religious authorities who perhaps saw their control of the Hebrew language as helpful in their control over their congregations and communities (Parush 2004).

Christianity as the symbol of modernity

The enlighteners in the Islamic world were in a very different position. Already, they were the majority religion and in the most favoured positions in society, and, for them, the Enlightenment only meant working out ways of increasing the links between Islam and modernity. It was not a choice between Islam and something else, in which the something else was the belief system of the majority and privileged group. One might argue that Christianity should have been a temptation for those in the Islamic world, since scientific advances and modernity were entirely clustered in the Christian world at that time. But this was in many ways a distant civilization and religion. In any case, the examples of Christianity that were to be found in the Islamic world were not on the whole the same kinds of Christianity that prevailed in most of Europe and the United States (something that Middle Eastern Christians discovered to their cost at the time of the Crusades), and many of their adherents were just as distant from Western modernity as their Muslim peers. The efforts of the missionaries were hopelessly compromised by their connections with imperialism. They were also, it has to be said, rather half-hearted since many of the imperial powers saw themselves as allies of Islam rather than intent on its destruction, despite the widespread suspicion in which countries like Britain were held in this respect. The British wished to foster close links with the Muslims in India, for instance, in order to counter the opposition to their rule that they identified mainly with the Hindu population, and had no wish to antagonize the Muslim populations of those countries in the Middle East which they controlled in one way or another. The British were certainly happy to confront Muslims in their attempts at converting those in the rest of Africa, for instance, where the population was largely uncommitted to anything that looked like a respectable religion to a Westerner, but those parts of the world that had been Muslim for a long time were generally regarded as inappropriate targets for large-scale conversion campaigns (Karsh 2008). Ruling a large empire with a tiny army does entail many compromises with people whose views and customs might be found repugnant yet not unacceptable from a practical point of view.

Becoming a Christian, like becoming modern, was a constant temptation for Jews. Becoming a Christian *was* becoming modern, in a sense, since it represented the religion of Europe in just the same way that the secular languages were to replace Hebrew and Yiddish as the ordinary languages of the Jews. The most impressive argument in favour of Christianity was that presented by Hegel who argued plausibly that religions follow some principle of development through history, and that Judaism had been superseded by the new faith (Leaman 2006c). It is worth saying that if Moses Mendelssohn, the acme of the *Haskala*, was correct in arguing that the different religions were in agreement on basic issues, then why not choose the least problematic religion if one was to live in Europe, i.e., Christianity? Many Jews followed his advice and became both modern and Christian. There is not a lot of evidence that the motivation here was generally an enthusiasm to acknowledge Jesus Christ as their saviour. It was more that Jesus Christ seemed to play some role as the harbinger of modernity, and that was something that the Jews of Germany, in particular, and of the Austro-Hungarian Empire, were very interested in.

Recent work on this issue has pointed out, very appropriately, that there is more than just one account of what constitutes enlightenment, and that the Western paradigm, whatever that might be, is not the only candidate in the field. Indeed, a recent book on Buddhism in

Brazil by Cristina Rocha argues that a century ago many Brazilians were impressed by Japanese economic success, which led them to an interest in what they saw as the religion of Japan, Zen Buddhism (Rocha 2006). Today, in China, it is said that many are interested in Christianity since it is seen as the religion of the West and progress. Whatever we say about these interesting phenomena, it is clearly nothing about Christianity or Zen Buddhism in themselves that attracts people from China and Brazil. It is the connections that these systems of thought have – or are held to have – with something wider, such as a desirable form of modernity.

If, for Jews, becoming a Christian was equivalent in many cases to emerging from seclusion, there was no parallel in the Islamic world. Muslim thinkers had no seclusion from which to emerge. Although there was often much about contemporary Islam which they wished to alter, since they saw modern accretions as taking away from the original message of the Book, they were already very much part of the political mainstream. It certainly is the case that many of them had rather rocky careers, especially given their antagonistic relationships with the various imperialist powers of the time. They sought to upset the status quo and so often offended those with a vested interest in things staying the same. But they certainly were not emerging from seclusion or from living in separate and isolated enclaves within a wider and largely alien society. They were essentially comfortable within the tradition that they inhabited and merely sought more appropriate ways to live that tradition, as they would see it. Hence it is not surprising that there was a distinct lack of enthusiasm for the more radical and anti-religious features of the Enlightenment.

The need for an Enlightenment

It is often said that Islam needs an Enlightenment and has never had one. Putting aside the rather objectionable political implications that might be involved here in downgrading Islamic civilization with respect to 'the West', the feature of enlightenment worth noting, as Kant pointed out very cleverly in his 1784 essay on the topic, is that it is more of a process than an event. It is not as though the Islamic world is still waiting for enlightenment, while 'the West' has already gone through this stage. There have been many reformers in Islam, and even a *hadith* that refers to the necessity of a reviver of religion to appear every century. That is the main difference between the Jewish Enlightenment and the Islamic forms of enlightenment. The latter is much more an *ihya*, a revival of religion, while the former is often an attack on religion. There were, of course, many Jewish enlighteners who also were intent on reviving Judaism, and the creation of new forms of worship in Germany in the nineteenth century is evidence of this phenomenon. But there were also Jewish enlighteners who sought to challenge religion, and Judaism in particular, using the full force of what they saw as reason and the requirements of modernity. In an intellectual sense, this challenge was very useful since it obliged Judaism to examine itself thoroughly and consider what if anything should remain of past practice, and what should go.

We might seem a long way from Mendelssohn here and his argument that Judaism was just as, indeed more, rational than any other religion, and was perfectly compatible with modernity. This is, in fact, precisely the sort of argument that many of the Islamic enlighteners produced about Islam. They often contrasted Islam's attitude to science with that of the early Roman Catholic Church, and suggested that it was Christianity that had a problem with science, not Islam. The Qur'an stresses reason and the importance of argument, and also of course talks a lot about the natural world. Some commentators have suggested that the Qur'an even mentions future scientific developments, although the argumentation here is not usually very compelling. Details aside, the point in identifying the role of reason in religion is to show that if you value reason, then you can combine that with a positive attitude to religion, which was precisely Mendelssohn's position. He went further and argued that Judaism in particular was not irretrievably lost in tradition and ritual, but was just as rational a faith as any other, if not more so. He opened the door, and that door was subsequently pushed far more ajar by the increasingly radical thinkers that came after him, and who changed Judaism profoundly, or even abandoned it for other religions or no religion at all.

Why did this not happen in Islam? It is sometimes said that it was because the door of interpretation in Islam remained shut, as it had been for many centuries. From fairly early in Islamic history, a decision was taken by some theologians to limit the range of theological directions that could be taken, but we should resist the temptation of relying too much on this suggestion. In practice, the door of interpretation has always been wide open in Islam, whatever the formal situation may have been. A diverse range of thinkers has appeared at every time to propose changes and developments, often under the rubric of restoring Islam to its origins under the forefathers, the *salaf*.

In both Judaism and Islam, the enlighteners contrasted decadence (*inhitat*) with the need for renaissance (*nahda*), and the main battlefield was not philosophy or theology, as one would imagine, but really language. The revolutionary principle of both the *Haskala* and the *Nahda* was that ordinary people should be able to understand and discuss their basic religious texts. This meant that texts might need to be properly translated into the secular language, or, where this was not an issue, as in the Arab Middle East, that they should be explained in ways that made them accessible to believers as a whole. We often note that Mendelssohn produced an important translation of the Jewish Bible into German in order to improve understanding of the text by Jews who spoke that language, and also to advocate the value of German for those who did not yet know it. But we should note also the many works he wrote in Hebrew, and his argument on behalf of Hebrew as a living Jewish language, something it really was not to become until the twentieth century. Why Hebrew and not Yiddish? One reason is because Hebrew is the original language of the Jewish Bible and so mastering it helps us understand the Bible. It frees us from the previous and current schools of theological thought and commentary, and literally puts power in the hands, or rather the mouths, of the readers of the Bible. One of the intriguing aspects of the struggles between the *maskilim* and their enemies in the Jewish world was the argument over Hebrew, with the latter trying to restrict its use to religious contexts where its use would be passive and its users not fully aware of how the language operated outside its immediate religious context. This argument over the nature of Hebrew was essentially an argument about who within the Jewish community has the right to interpret texts, and ultimately became an argument about the new Jewish state, its rationale and character. Like so much of the *Haskala*, it struck at the foundations of Judaism and obliged Jews to undertake a radical investigation of their faith. In many ways the unity of the Jewish world has never recovered from this controversy, and the divisions that arose between different denominations of Jews is certainly linked to these persistent intellectual debates with respect to *Haskala*.

To understand the different history of the Enlightenment in the Islamic world, we should not compare Islam with Judaism, but rather the position in society of the Jewish *Aufklärer* (enlighteners) with their Muslim equivalents. The latter saw themselves as at the heart of Islam, and often eventually became authority figures within the Islamic world. For example, the man often regarded as the leader of the Enlightenment movement (*harakat al-tanwir*) in Egypt, Rifa'a al-Tahtawi (1801–73), was appointed by Muhammad 'Ali to be the imam on a study mission to Paris, and returned to Egypt to help construct and direct the education system. They were either part of the establishment within the Islamic world, or sought to become such a part, and so they tempered their radicalism with this sort of end in mind. You do not upset the apple cart if you have aspirations one day to operate it. The Jewish *Aufklärer*, by contrast, were outsiders both in their own society and in the Christian world as a whole.

The lack of radicalism in Islamic Qur'an commentary

It is wrong to say that there is no radical or critical scholarship on the Qur'an because it does exist, and of course there is the hostile commentary by authors who should perhaps be described as ex-Muslims (Ibn Warraq, Irshad Manji, Ayan Hirsi Ali). But compared with Christian and Jewish scholarship there is very little radical re-examination of Islam from within Islam. This could be seen as a sign of the greater faith of most Muslims, or the generally more satisfactory nature of the texts they deal with. In the Jewish world, Spinoza rocked the intellectual world of Bible criticism in the seventeenth century when he suggested that the Hebrew of the Bible was so far from us today that we often have significant difficulties understanding what the text means. Christians have a variety of Gospels to deal with, and have divided up into groups with very different interpretations of those texts and what their implications are for the understanding of how Christianity should be interpreted. At the time of writing, the Christian world is debating the appropriate role of previously excluded groups in the Church, such as gay people, and the contribution that women have to make to priesthood, if there is any such role. On these issues, Christians take up very different positions, and they interpret the basic texts of their faith in alternative ways. There are glimmerings of such debates in the Islamic world also, but only glimmerings, and they are very much restricted to the environment of Western academia, far from the everyday concerns of the Muslim community. This reinforces the stereotype of the forward-looking Christian and Jewish theological worlds, and the backward Islamic world that seems to require the sort of enlightenment that has occurred elsewhere, if it is to be brought out of its medieval gloom. And yet that gloom might seem rather attractive to many Muslims, if it is gloom, since within that cultural environment the sort of rapid retreat from faith that has taken place elsewhere does not seem to be occurring within Islam.

What I have tried to establish in this chapter is that whatever the reason for the different trajectory of the Islamic world from the Jewish and Christian worlds as far as theology is concerned, it has nothing to do with basic differences between the religions, but everything to do with basic differences between the social and political environments in which those religions have operated. It is important to grasp this for any understanding of Islamic philosophy, since otherwise one ends up speculating on how the essential differences between faiths change the nature of the philosophies associated with those faiths, and this is really not a helpful way of looking at them. For many centuries, Jewish and Islamic philosophy shared very much the same methodology and even language, and there was no obvious difference in philosophy stemming from what are obviously distinct religions. And why should there have been? Philosophers ask much the same questions wherever they are and whatever their religious beliefs, and their inclination to use philosophy to examine their own religions is based on what is plausible in their culture, not in their religion.

Certainly, it is true that the sorts of questions which Jews and Christians ask have not on the whole been raised in the same way or to the same extent by Muslims. Jews and Christians seem to relish the opportunity to challenge what many see as the basic principles of their faiths, to reformulate them or even abandon them, and the response from their communities is often grudging acceptance of their right to do so, if not enthusiastic applause for their efforts. Exactly the same theoretical resources exist within Islam for this sort of enterprise. For example, there is plenty of scope to discuss the precise context in which the revelations of the various *surah*s (chapters) and their *ayat* (verses) of the Qur'an were produced and how that context affects their interpretation. In fact, there is a whole system of interpretation called *asbab al-nuzul* that indicates how this can be undertaken. There is a rich system of legal schools that often suggest varying solutions for problems in jurisprudence, and also a science of *hadith*, the Traditions, which again give rise to a considerable debate about their reliability, and, even more importantly, how they are to be understood. Finally, and crucially, we see in Islamic philosophy a range of ideas and arguments that are capable of taking as critical a view of Islam as any other tradition and its philosophers, and, just as in the case of many other religions, these philosophers often seek to establish their faith on proper intellectual foundations, while possibly challenging some of the ordinary ways of understanding that faith. The process of enlightenment has been working for a long time in Islamic philosophy, and there is nothing about Islam itself to prevent its wider use. Whether Islam needs an enlightenment is really a strange question, despite its ubiquity. It is not really a question about Islam but about the Islamic world, and the more we appreciate the truth of this the further along we shall be in getting a grip on the issue.

So, if we rephrase the question, and ask whether the Islamic world requires an enlightenment, we are on surer ground. The first thing that has to be said is that there is no longer an Islamic world in a distinct part of the world, for the Islamic world is everywhere now, since Muslims live in most countries and there are few if any restrictions on their practice of Islam. Enlightenment does involve values that can be destructive, especially of tradition, and it is entirely proper to be concerned about it when looking warily at the prospect of a radical change in thinking, from within what might be experienced as a warm and secure community. We might also wonder whether this is an appropriate topic on which to have a view, since one is either more or less part of the enlightenment way of thinking, or one is not, and there is no apparently neutral point from which to consider the alternatives as alternatives. Clearly, most of the philosophers we have considered in this book are on the side of what came to be the Enlightenment, but people do not have to prioritize reasoning in their thinking. There are alternatives like passion, emotion, tradition and so on, and, although these will also include reasoning, they may not include it to any great extent. It is ironic that the very same people who are in favour of diversity in their own society often argue that groups such as Muslims should adopt Enlightenment values, so that they will resemble more closely most people in their society. But most societies now, like the world as a whole, are resplendent with a wide variety of views on how to live, what is important or how to decide issues in life, and we might prefer to value this sort of diversity rather than regret that more people do not adopt Enlightenment values. Rather than concentrating on what is lacked by those who are different in significant ways, we might want to celebrate those differences and see whether they have anything of value that we can learn from, since it is unlikely that those who are similar to us have achieved some greater perfection in knowledge of how to live or what to believe. If this is true, then it works for whichever groups we fit into the categories of 'us' and 'the other'. If there is to be no compulsion in religion, then perhaps there should be no compulsion in lack of religion either.

It certainly would not be true to say that the issues and arguments of Islamic philosophy are close to the hearts of most Muslims, but this is equally true of philosophy in the world as a whole. On the other hand, it has been argued in this book that many of the rather abstract ideas that are part of Islamic philosophy do touch on significant issues in the lives of believers, and provide a way of understanding what is behind religious and other ideals of how to live and what to believe.

By this stage of the book, I hope readers will share my interest in many of these ideas and arguments, and so will be encouraged to follow up the further references that immediately follow on, to guide them through much of the detail of Islamic philosophy as a whole.

References and Bibliography

HIP = Nasr and Leaman (eds) (1996) *History of Islamic Philosophy*, London: Routledge.

Abdel Haleem, M. (1996) 'Early Kalam', *HIP*, 71–88.
'Abduh, M. (1966) *The Theology of Unity (risalat al-tawhid)*, trans. I. Masaʿad and K. Cragg, London: Allen & Unwin.
Abed, S. (1991) *Aristotelian Logic and the Arabic Language in Alfarabi*, Albany, NY: State University of New York Press.
—— (1996) 'Language', *HIP*, 898–925.
Abrahamov, B. (1995) 'The *bi-la kayfa* Doctrine and its Foundation in Islamic Theory', *Arabica* 43(3): 365–79.
—— (1998) *Islamic Theology: Traditionalism and Rationalism*, Edinburgh: Edinburgh University Press.
Abu Rabiʿ, I. (1996) 'The Arab World', *HIP*, 1082–1114.
Abu Zayd, N. (1992) *Naqd al-khitab al-dini* [Critique of Religious Discourse], Cairo: Dar al-thaqafa al-jadida.
Acıkgenç, A. (1993) *Being and Existence in Sadra and Heidegger: A Comparative Ontology*, Kuala Lumpur: International Institute of Islamic Thought and Civilization.
Adamson, P. (2007) *Al-Kindi*, New York: Oxford University Press.
El-Affendi, A. (1991) *Who Needs an Islamic State?*, London: Grey Seal.
Ahmed, A. (1989) *Discovering Islam: Making Sense of Muslim History and Society*, London: Routledge.
Alon, I. (1990) 'Farabi's Funny Flora; al-nawabit as "Opposition"', *Arabica* 37: 56–90.
—— (1991) *Socrates in Medieval Islamic Literature*, Leiden: Brill.
Amin Razavi, M. (1996) 'Persia', *HIP*, 1037–50.

—— (1997) *Suhrawardi and the School of Illumination*, Richmond: Curzon.

Arberry, A. (1964) *The Koran Interpreted*, London: Oxford University Press.

Arkoun, M. (1985) *La pensée arabe [Arab Thought]*, Paris: Presses Universitaires de France.

—— (2002) *The Unthought in Contemporary Islamic Thought*. London: Saqi Books.

al-Ash'ari (1953) *The Theology of al-Ash'ari: The Arabic Texts of al-Ash'ari's Kitab al-Luma' and Risalat Istihsan al-Khawd fi 'ilm at kalam*, ed. R. McCarthy, Beirut: Imprimerie Catholique.

Aslan, A. (1998) *Religious Pluralism in Christian and Islamic Philosophy: The Thought of John Hick and Seyyed Hossein Nasr*, Richmond: Curzon.

Ayubi, N. (1991) *Political Islam*, London: Routledge.

Bakar, O. (1996) 'Science', *HIP*, 926–46.

Baldick, J. (1989) *Mystical Islam: An Introduction to Sufism*, New York: New York University Press.

Bello, I. (1989) *The Medieval Islamic Controversy between Philosophy and Orthodoxy: Ijma' and Ta'wil in the Conflict between al-Ghazali and Ibn Rushd*, Leiden: Brill.

Benmakhlouf, A. (ed.) (1997) *Al-'aql wa masala al-hudud* [Reason and the Question of Limits], Casablanca: Nashar al-fenek.

Black, D. (1990) *Logic and Aristotle's Rhetoric and Poetics in Medieval Arabic Philosophy*, Leiden: Brill.

—— (1996) 'Al-Farabi', *HIP*, 178–97.

Black, T. (2001) *The History of Islamic Political Thought from the Prophet to the Present*, Edinburgh: Edinburgh University Press.

Butterworth, C. and Kessel, B. (eds) (1993) *The Introduction of Arabic Philosophy into Europe*, Leiden: Brill.

Campanini, M. (1996) 'Al-Ghazzali', *HIP*, 258–76.

—— (2008) *An Introduction to Islamic Philosophy*, trans. C. Higgitt, Edinburgh: Edinburgh University Press.

Chittick, W. (1989) *The Sufi Path of Knowledge: Ibn al-'Arabi's Metaphysics of Imagination*, Albany, NY: State of University of New York Press.

—— (1994) *Imaginal Worlds: Ibn al-'Arabi and the Problem of Religious Diversity*, Albany, NY: State University of New York Press.

—— (1996a) 'Ibn 'Arabi', *HIP*, 497–509.

—— (1996b) 'The School of ibn 'Arabi', *HIP*, 510–26.

—— (1998) *The Self-Disclosure of God: Principles of Ibn al-'Arabi's Cosmology*, Albany, NY: State University of New York Press.

—— (2001) *The Heart of Islamic Philosophy: The Quest for Self-Knowledge in the Teachings of Afdal al-Din Kashani*, Oxford: Oxford University Press.

Conrad, L. (ed.) (1996) *The World of Ibn Tufayl: Interdisciplinary Perspectives on Hayy ibn Yaqzan*, Leiden: Brill.

Cook, M. (2000) *Commanding Right and Forbidding Wrong in Islamic Thought*, Cambridge: Cambridge University Press.

Corbin, H. (1993) *History of Islamic Philosophy*, trans. L. Sherrard, London: Kegan Paul International.

Crone, P. and M. Cook (1977) *Hagarism*, Cambridge: Cambridge University Press.

Dabashi, H. (1996a) 'Khwajah Nasir al-Tusi: The Philosopher/Vizier and the Intellectual Climate of the Times', *HIP*, 527–84.

—— (1996b) 'Mir Damad and the Founding of the "School of Isfahan"', *HIP*, 597–634.

Daiber, H. (1996) 'Political Philosophy', *HIP*, 841–85.

Davidson, H. (1992) *Alfarabi, Avicenna, and Averroës on Intellect: Their Cosmologies, Theories of Active Intellect and Theories of the Human Intellect*, New York: Oxford University Press.

Djait, H. (1986) *Europe and Islam: Cultures and Modernity*, Berkeley, CA: University of California Press.

Enayat, H. (1982) *Modern Islamic Political Thought*, London: Macmillan.

Fakhry, M. (1958) *Islamic Occasionalism and its Critique by Averroës and Aquinas*, London: Allen & Unwin.

—— (1991) *Ethical Theories in Islam*, Leiden: Brill.

—— (1997) *A Short Introduction to Islamic Philosophy, Theology and Mysticism*, Oxford: Oneworld.

—— (2002a) *Averroes (Ibn Rushd): His Life, Works and Influence*, Oxford: Oneworld.

—— (2002b) *Al-Farabi: Founder of Islamic Neoplatonism*, Oxford: Oneworld.

—— (2004) *A History of Islamic Philosophy*, New York: Columbia University Press.

al-Farabi (1969), *Alfarabi's Philosophy of Plato and Aristotle*, trans. M. Mahdi, Ithaca, NY: Cornell University Press.

—— (1985) *On the Perfect State: Abu Nasr al-Farabi's 'The Principles of the Views of the Citizens of the Best State'*, trans. R. Walzer, Oxford: Oxford University Press.

—— (1996) *La Città Virtuosa*, intro. and trans. M. Campanini, Milan: Biblioteca Universale Rizzoli.

Fenton, P. (1996) 'Judaism and Sufism', *HIP*, 755–68.

Frank, D. (1996) 'Ethics', *HIP*, 959–68.

Frank, D. and Leaman, O. (eds) (1997) *History of Jewish Philosophy*, London: Routledge.

Frank, R. (1994) *Al-Ghazali and the Ash'arite School*, Durham, NC: Duke University Press.

Funkenstein, A. (1974) 'Periodization and Self-Understanding in the Middle Ages and Early Modern Times', *Medievalia et Humanistica* 5: 3–23.

Gellner, E. (1982) *Muslim Society*, Cambridge: Cambridge University Press.

al-Ghazali (1953) *The Faith and Practice of al-Ghazali*, trans. W. Watt, London: Allen & Unwin.
—— (1973) *Ghazali on Prayer*, trans. K. Nakamura, Tokyo: Institute of Oriental Culture, University of Tokyo.
—— (1980) *Freedom and Fulfillment: An Annotated Translation of al-Munqidh min al-Dalal and Other Relevant Works of al-Ghazali*, trans. R. McCarthy, Boston: Twayne.
—— (1989) *The Remembrance of Death and the Afterlife*, trans. and intro. T. Winter, Cambridge: Islamic Texts Society.
—— (1992) *The Ninety-Nine Beautiful Names of God*, trans. D. Burrell and N. Daher, Cambridge: Islamic Texts Society.
—— (1997) *The Incoherence of the Philosophers*, trans. M. Marmura, Provo, UT: Brigham Young University Press.
Goodman, L. (1992) *Avicenna*, London: Routledge.
—— (1996a) 'Ibn Bajjah', *HIP*, 294–312.
—— (1996b) 'Ibn Masarrah', *HIP*, 277–93.
—— (1996c) 'Ibn Tufayl', *HIP*, 313–29.
Groff, P. (2007) *Islamic Philosophy A–Z*, Edinburgh: Edinburgh University Press.
Gutas, D. (1988) *Avicenna and the Aristotelian Tradition: Introduction to the Reading of Avicenna's Philosophical Works*, Leiden: Brill.
—— (2000) *Greek Philosophers in the Arabic Tradition*, Aldershot: Ashgate.
Hahn, L., Auxier, R. and Stone, L. (eds) (2000) *The Philosophy of Seyyed Hossein Nasr*, La Salle, IL: Open Court.
Ha'iri Yazdi, M. (1992) *The Principles of Epistemology in Islamic Philosophy: Knowledge by Presence*, Albany, NY: State University of New York Press.
—— (1987) *Al-Sahwa al-islamiyya fi mizan al-'aql* [Islamic Resurgence in the Balance of Reason], Cairo: Dar al-Fikr.
Hallaq, W. (1993) *Ibn Taymiyya against the Greek Logicians*, Oxford: Clarendon Press.
Hanafi, H. (1980) *Mawqifuna min al-gurath al-Gharbi* [Our Attitude Towards Western Heritage], Cairo: al-Markaz al-'Arabi lil-Bahth wa-al-Nashr.
—— (1982) 'Ibn Rushd sharihan Aristu' [Ibn Rushd as a Commentator on Aristotle], in *Dirasat Islamiyya* [Islamic Studies], Beirut: Bab al-tanwir, 157–206.
—— (1991) *Muqaddima fi 'ilm al-istighrab* [Introduction to the Science of Occidentalism], Cairo: al-Dar al fanniya.
Haq, S. N. (1996) 'The Indian and Persian Background', *HIP*, 52–70.
Hayoun, M.-R. and de Libera, A. (1991) *Averroes et l'averroïsme*, Paris: Presses Universitaires de France.
Heath, P. (1992) *Allegory and Philosophy in Avicenna, Ibn Sina: With a Translation of the Book of the Prophet Muhammad's Ascent to Heaven*, Philadelphia, PA: University of Pennsylvania Press.

Hourani, A. (1983) *Arabic Thought in the Liberal Age*, Oxford: Oxford University Press.

Hourani, G. (1971) *Islamic Rationalism: The Ethics of 'Abd al-Jabbar*, Oxford: Clarendon Press.

—— (1976) *Averroes: On the Harmony of Religion and Philosophy*, London: Gibb Memorial Trust.

—— (1985) *Reason and Tradition in Islamic Ethics*, Cambridge: Cambridge University Press.

Ibn Bajja (1945) 'Ibn Bajjah's Tadbiru'l-mutawahhid', trans. D. Dunlop, *Journal of the Royal Asiatic Society*: 61–81.

—— (1992) *Rasa'il ibn Bajja al-ilahiyya* [Ibn Bajja's Metaphysical Essays], ed. M. Fakhry, Beirut: Dar al-Jil.

Ibn Rushd (1959) *Kitab fasl al-maqal* [Decisive Treatise], ed. G. Hourani, Leiden: Brill.

—— (1961) *Averroes on the Harmony of Religion and Philosophy*, trans. G. Hourani, London: Luzac.

—— (1969) *Averroes' Commentary on Plato's Republic*, ed., intro. and trans. E. Rosenthal, Cambridge: Cambridge University Press.

—— (1978) *Averroes' Tahafut al-Tahafut (The Incoherence of the Incoherence)*, trans. S. Van Den Bergh, London: Luzac.

Ibn Sina (1959) *Avicenna's De Anima*, trans F. Rahman, London: Oxford University Press.

—— (1974) *The Life of Ibn Sina: A Critical Edition and Annotated Translation*, ed. and trans. W. Gohlman, Albany, NY: State University of New York Press.

—— (1984) *Remarks and Admonitions, Part One: Logic*, trans. S. Inati, Toronto: Pontifical Institute of Mediaeval Studies.

Ibn Tufayl (1972) Hayy ibn Yaqzan, *A Philosophical Tale*, trans. L. Goodman, New York: Twayne.

Ibn Warraq (2003) *Why I am Not a Muslim*, Amherst, NY: Prometheus.

Inati, S. (1996a) *Ibn Sina and Mysticism: Remarks and Admonitions*, London: Kegan Paul International.

—— (1996b) 'Ibn Sina', *HIP*, 231–46.

—— (1996c) 'Logic', *HIP*, 802–23.

Iqbal, Muhammad (1930) *The Reconstruction of Religious Thought in Islam*, London: Oxford University Press.

Iqbal, Muzaffar (2008) *Science and Islam*, Westport, CT: Greenwood.

Izutsu, T. (1971) *The Concept and Reality of Existence*, Tokyo: Keio Institute.

—— (2002) *Ethico-Religious Concepts in the Qur'an*, Montreal: McGill/Queens University Press.

'Abd al-Jabri, M. (1985) *Nahnu wa'l turat* [Tradition and Us], Beirut: Bab al-tanwir.

—— (1999) *Arab-Islamic Philosophy*, trans A. Abbassi, Austin. TX: University of Texas Press.

Jambet, C. (2006). *The Act of Being: The Philosophy of Revelation in Mulla Sadra*, trans. J. Fort, New York: Zone Books.

Janssens, J. (2006) *Ibn Sînâ and his Influence on the Arabic and Latin World*, Aldershot: Ashgate.

Jayyusi, S. (ed.) (1992) *The Legacy of Muslim Spain*, Leiden: Brill.

Kahteran, N. (2006) 'fitra', in O. Leaman (ed.), *The Qur'an: An Encyclopedia*, London: Routledge, 210–13.

Kalin, I. (2009) *Knowledge in Later Islamic Philosophy: Mulla Sadra on the Unity of the Intellect and the Intelligible*, New York: Oxford University Press.

Kant, I. (1959) *What is Enlightenment?*, in *Foundations of the Metaphysics of Morals and, What is Enlightenment?*, trans. Lewis White Beck, Indianapolis: Bobbs-Merrill.

Karsh, E. (2008) *Islamic Imperialism: A History*, Yale, CT: Yale University Press.

Kemal, R. and Kemal, S. (1996) 'Shah Waliullah', *HIP*, 663–70.

Kemal, S. (1991) *The Poetics of Alfarabi and Avicenna*, Leiden: Brill.

Kennedy-Day, K. (2003) *Books of Definition in Islamic Philosophy*, London: Routledge.

Khadduri, M. (1979) *War and Peace in the Law of Islam*, Baltimore, MD: Johns Hopkins University Press.

—— (1984) *The Islamic Conception of Justice*, Baltimore, MD: Johns Hopkins University Press.

Khalafallah, M. (1950) *Al Fann al- qasasi fi'l- Qur'an* [The Art of Narrative of the Qur'an], Cairo: Maktaba al-nahda al-misriyya.

Khalidi, M. A. (2005) *Medieval Islamic Philosophical Writings*, Cambridge: Cambridge University Press.

Kant, I. (1959) *An Answer to the Question 'What is Enlightenment?'*, trans. L. Beck, Indianapolis: Bobbs-Merrill.

Khomeini, R. (1981) *Islam and Revolution: Writings and Declarations*, trans. H. Algar, Berkeley, CA: Mizan Press.

Kılıç, M. (1996) 'Mysticism', *HIP*, 947–58.

al-Kindi, A. (1974) *Al-Kindi's Metaphysics: A Translation of the Treatise on First Philosophy*, trans. A. Ivry, Albany, NY: State University of New York Press.

Klein-Franke, F. (1996) 'Al-Kindi', *HIP*, 165–77.

Knysh, A. (1999) *Ibn 'Arabi in the Later Islamic Tradition: The Making of a Polemical Image in Medieval Islam*, Albany, NY: State University of New York Press.

Kohlberg, E. (1976) 'The Development of the Imami Shi'i Doctrine of Jihad', *Zeitschrift der Deutschen Morgenländischen Gesellschaft* 126: 64–86.

Kuşpınar, B. (1996) *Isma'il Ankaravı on the Illuminative Philosophy*, Kuala Lumpur: International Institute of Islamic Thought and Civilization.

Lahbabi, M. (1954) *Le personalisme musulman [Muslim Personalism]*, Paris: Presses Universitaires de France.

Lalani, A. (2006) 'Wali', in O. Leaman (ed.), *The Qur'an: An Encyclopedia*, London: Routledge, 682–6.

Lameer, J. (1994) *Al-Farabi and Aristotelian Syllogistics: Greek Theory and Islamic Practice*, Leiden: Brill.

Laroui, A. (1976) *The Crisis of the Arab Intelligentsia: Traditionalism or Historicism?*, Berkeley, CA: University of California Press.

Leaman, O. (1980a) 'Does the Interpretation of Islamic Philosophy Rest on a Mistake?', *International Journal of Middle Eastern Studies* 12: 525–38.

—— (1980b) 'Ibn Bajja on Society and Philosophy', *Der Islam* 57(1): 109–19.

—— (1985) *An Introduction to Medieval Islamic Philosophy*, Cambridge: Cambridge University Press.

—— (1988a) 'Continuity in Islamic Political Philosophy: The Role of Myth', *British Society for Middle Eastern Studies* 14(2): 147–55.

—— (1988b) 'The Philosophical Tradition', in T. Mostyn (ed.), *The Cambridge Encyclopedia of the Middle East and North Africa*, Cambridge: Cambridge University Press, 26–46.

—— (1991) 'Averroes, le Kitab al-nafs et la révolution de la philosophie occidentale', in *Le choc Averroes*, Paris: Maison des Cultures du Monde, 58–65.

—— (1992) 'Philosophy vs. Mysticism: An Islamic Controversy', in M. McGhee (ed.), *Philosophy, Religion and the Spiritual Life*, Cambridge: Cambridge University Press, 177–88.

—— (1994) 'Is Averroes an Averroist?', in F. Niewöhner and L. Sturlese (eds), *Averroismus im Mittelalter und in der Renaissance*, Zurich: Spur Verlag, 9–22.

—— (1995a) 'Averroes', in F. Niewöhner (ed.), *Klassiker der Religionsphilosophie: von Platon bis Kierkegaard*, Munich: C. H. Beck, 142–62.

—— (1995b) 'New Occasions Teach New Duties: Christian Ethics in the Light of Muslim Ethics', in C. Rodd (ed.), *New Occasions Teach New Duties?*, Edinburgh: T & T Clark, 219–31.

—— (1996a) 'Averroes and the West', in M. Wahba and M. Abousenna (eds), *Averroes and the Enlightenment*, Amherst, NY: Prometheus Books, 53–68.

—— (1996b) Entries on a variety of modern Muslim philosophers, in S. Brown, D. Collinson and R. Wilkinson (eds), *Biographical Dictionary of Twentieth Century Philosophers*, London: Routledge.

—— (1996c) 'Ghazali and the Ash'arites', *Asian Philosophy* 6(1): 17–27.

—— (1996d) 'A Guide to Bibliographical Resources', *HIP*, 117–36.

—— (1996e) 'Miskawayh', *HIP*, 25–7.

—— (1996f) 'Introduction', *HIP*, 1–10.

Leaman, O. (1996g) 'Introduction to the Jewish Philosophical Tradition in the Islamic Cultural World', *HIP*, 673–6.

—— (1996h) 'Islam', in J. Chambliss (ed.), *Philosophy of Education: An Encyclopedia*, New York: Garland, 311–16.

—— (1996i) 'Islamic Humanism in the Fourth/Tenth Century', *HIP*, 155–64.

—— (1996j) 'Jewish Averroism', *HIP*, 769–82.

—— (1996k) 'Orientalism and Islamic Philosophy', *HIP*, 114–38.

—— (1996l) 'Secular Friendship and Religious Devotion', in O. Leaman (ed.), *Friendship East and West: Philosophical Perspectives*, Richmond: Curzon, 251–62.

—— (1997a) *Averroes and His Philosophy*, 2nd edn, Richmond: Curzon (1st edn, 1988, Oxford: Clarendon Press).

—— (1997b) 'Averroes' Commentary on Plato's Republic and the Missing Politics', in D. Agius and I. Netton (eds), *Across the Mediterranean Frontiers: Trade, Politics and Religion, 650–1450*, Turnhout, Belgium: Brepols, 195–204.

—— (1997c) 'Ghazali and Averroes on Meaning', *Al-Masaq* 9: 179–89.

—— (1997d) 'Islamic Philosophy since Avicenna', in B. Carr and I. Mahalingam (eds), *Companion Encyclopedia of Asian Philosophy*, London: Routledge, 901–17.

—— (1997e) 'Logic and Language in Islamic Philosophy', in B. Carr and I. Mahalingam (eds), *Companion Encyclopedia of Asian Philosophy*, London: Routledge, 950–64.

—— (1997f) *Moses Maimonides*, rev. edn, Richmond: Curzon 1st edn, London: Routledge, 1990.

—— (1998a) 'The Future of Philosophy', in O. Leaman (ed.), *The Future of Philosophy: Towards the 21st Century*, London: Routledge, 113.

—— (1998b) 'Philosophy of Religion', in O. Leaman (ed.), *The Future of Philosophy: Towards the 21st Century*, London: Routledge, 120–33.

—— (1999a) *Key Concepts in Eastern Philosophy*, London: Routledge.

—— (1999b) 'Philosophical and Scientific Achievements in Islamic History', in F. Daftary (ed.), *Intellectual Traditions in Islam*, London: I. B. Tauris, 31–42.

—— (1999c) *Brief Introduction to Islamic Philosophy*, Cambridge: Polity.

—— (1999d) 'Madha baqi falsafa ibn Rushd?', in M. Mensia (ed.) *Ibn Rushd faylasuf al-sharq wa al-gharb*, Tunis: Beit al-hikma, 655–72.

—— (1999e) 'Institutionalising Research and Development Culture in the Islamic and Non-Islamic Worlds: Some Comparative Remarks, *Journal of Islamic Science* 15: 1–2, 95–108.

—— (1999f) 'Nursi's Place in the Ihya' Tradition', *Muslim World* 89 (3–4) (July–October): 314–24.

—— (2000a) 'Can Rights Coexist with Religion?', in G. Hawting, J. Mojaddedi and A. Samely (eds), *Studies in Islamic and Middle Eastern*

Texts and Traditions in Memory of Norman Calder, Journal of Semitic Studies Supplement 12, Oxford: Oxford University Press, 163–72.

—— (2000b) 'Islamic Philosophy and the Attack on Logic', *Topoi* 19/1: 17–24.

—— (2000c) 'Philosophical and Scientific Achievements in Islamic History', in F. Daftary (ed.), *Intellectual Traditions in Islam*, London: I. B. Tauris, 49–60.

—— (2002) *An Introduction to Classical Islamic Philosophy*, Cambridge: Cambridge University Press.

—— (2003a) 'The Search for Tradition: Islamic Art and Science in the Thought of Seyyed Hossein Nasr', in M. Faghfoory (ed.), *Beacon of Knowledge*, Louisville, KY: Fons Vitae, 305–15.

—— (2003b) 'Appearance and Reality in the Qur'an: Bilqis and Zulaykha', *Islam Araştırmaları Dergisi* 10: 23–37.

—— (2003c) 'Islam, the Environment and Said Nursi', in I. M. Abur-Rabi' (ed.) *Islam at the Crossroads*, Albany, NY: State University of New York Press, 255–62; reprinted and updated in C. Schmitt (ed.), *Islamische Theologie des 21. Jahrhunderts*, Stuttgart: Stuttgarter Stiftung für Wissenschaft und Religion, 2008.

—— (2003d) 'Political Thought beyond the Western Tradition', in A. Finlayson (ed.), *Contemporary Political Thought: A Reader and Guide*, Edinburgh: Edinburgh University Press, 523–58.

—— (2003e) 'The History of Philosophy and the Intentionalist Fallacy', *Journal of the History of Philosophy* 20 (4) (October): 361–71.

—— (2005a) 'How Aristotelian is Averroes as a Commentator on Aristotle?', in C. Baffioni (ed.), *Averroes and the Aristotelian Commentaries*, Istituto Universitario Orientale, Napoli, Guida, 23–33.

—— (2005b) 'Is Globalization a Threat to Islam? Said Nursi's Response', in I. Markham and I. Özdemir (eds), *Globalization, Ethics and Islam*, Aldershot: Ashgate, 121–6.

—— (2005c) 'Maimonides and the Development of Jewish Thought in an Islamic Structure', in G. Tamer (ed.), *The Trias of Maimonides*, Berlin: de Gruyter, 187–98.

—— (2006a) 'Arguments and the Qur'an', in O. Leaman (ed.), *The Qur'an: An Encyclopedia*, 55–66.

—— (2006b) 'Wali – Issues of Identification', in O. Leaman (ed.), *The Qur'an: An Encyclopedia*, 678–82.

—— (2006c) *Jewish Thought: An Introduction*, London: Routledge, chapters 5 and 8.

—— (2006d) *Islamic Aesthetics: An Introduction*, Edinburgh: Edinburgh University Press.

—— (2008a) 'The Developed Kalam Tradition', in T. Winter (ed.), *Cambridge Companion to Islamic Theology*, Cambridge: Cambridge University Press, 77–90.

—— (2008b) 'Philosophy', in A. Rippin (ed.), *The Islamic World*, Routledge, 278–88.

Lewis, B. (1993) *Islam in History: Ideas, People, and Events in the Middle East*, Chicago, IL: Open Court.

—— (1995) *Cultures in Conflict: Christians, Muslims and Jews in the Age of Discovery*, New York: Oxford University Press.

—— (2002) *What Went Wrong: Western Impact and Middle Eastern Response*, New York: Oxford University Press.

Lewisohn, L. (ed.) (1999a). *The Heritage of Sufism, vol. I: Classical Persian Sufism from its Origins to Rumi (700–1300)*, Oxford: Oneworld.

—— (ed.) (1999b). *The Heritage of Sufism, vol. II: The Legacy of Medieval Persian Sufism (1150–1500)*, Oxford: Oneworld.

Lory, P. (1996) 'Henry Corbin: His Work and Influence', *HIP*, 1149–55.

McGinnis, J. and Reisman, D. C. (eds) (2004) *Interpreting Avicenna: Science and Philosophy in Medieval Islam*, Proceedings of the Second Conference of the Avicenna Study Group (Islamic Philosophy, Theology and Science, 56), Leiden-Boston: Brill.

—— and —— (eds) (2007) *Classical Arabic Philosophy: An Anthology of Sources*. Indianapolis: Hackett.

Mahdi, M. (1970) 'Language and Logic in Classical Islam', in G. E. von Grunebaum (ed.), *Logic in Classical Islamic Culture*, Wiesbaden: Otto Harrassowitz, 51–83.

Maimonides, Moses (1963) *Guide of the Perplexed*, trans. S. Pines, Chicago, IL: University of Chicago Press.

Marenbon, J. (1996) 'Medieval Christian and Jewish Europe', *HIP*, 100–12.

Minc, A. (1993) *Le Nouveau Moyen Age*, Paris: Gallimard.

Mohamed, Y. (2006) 'Knowledge', in O. Leaman (ed.), *The Qur'an: an Encyclopedia*, London: Routledge, 347–53.

Morewedge, P. (1979) *Islamic Philosophical Theology*, Albany, NY: State University of New York Press.

—— (ed.) (1992) *Neoplatonism and Islamic Thought*, Albany, NY: State University of New York Press.

—— (1995) *Essays in Islamic Philosophy, Theology and Mysticism*, Oneonta, NY: Philosophy Department, State University of New York.

Morris, J. (2005) *The Reflective Heart: Discovering Spiritual Intelligence in Ibn 'Arabi's 'Meccan Illuminations'*. Louisville, KY: Fons Vitae.

Muhajirani, A. (1996) 'Twelve-Imam Shi'ite Theological and Philosophical Thought', *HIP*, 119–43.

Mulla Sadra (2003) *The Elixir of the Gnostics* (Iksir al-'arifin), trans. W. Chittick, Provo, UT: Brigham Young University Press.

Nanji, A. (1996) 'Isma'ili Philosophy', *HIP*, 144–54.

Nasir Khusraw (1998) *Knowledge and Liberation: A Treatise on Philosophical Theology*, ed. and trans. F. Hunzai, intro. P. Morewedge, London: I. B. Tauris.

Nasr, S. (1972) *Sufi Essays*, London: George Allen & Unwin.

—— (1978) *Sadr al-din Shirazi and his Transcendent Theosophy*, Tehran: Imperial Academy of Philosophy.

—— (1982) 'The Spiritual Significance of Jihad', *Parabola* 7(4): 14–19.

—— (1993) *The Need for a Sacred Science*, Richmond: Curzon Press.

—— (1996a) Ibn Sina's 'Oriental Philosophy', *HIP*, 247–51.

—— (1996b) 'Introduction', *HIP*, 11–20.

—— (1996c) 'Introduction to the Mystical Tradition', *HIP*, 367–73.

—— (1996d) *The Islamic Intellectual Tradition in Persia* , ed. M. A. Razavi, Richmond: Curzon.

—— (1996e) 'The Meaning and Concept of Philosophy in Islam', *HIP*, 2–16.

—— (1996f) 'Mulla Sadra: His Teachings', *HIP*, 643–62.

—— (1996g) 'The Qur'an and Hadith as Source and Inspiration of Islamic Philosophy', *HIP*, 273–9.

—— (1996h) *Religion and the Order of Nature*, Oxford: Oxford University Press.

—— (2006) *Islamic Philosophy from its Origin to the Present: Philosophy in the Land of Prophecy*, Albany, NY: State University of New York Press.

Nasr, S. H. and Razavi, M. A. (eds) (1999) *An Anthology of Philosophy in Persia*, 2 vols, New York: Oxford University Press.

Netton, I. (1982) *Muslim Neoplatonists: An Introduction to the Thought of the Brethren of Purity*, London: George Allen & Unwin.

—— (1989) *Allah Transcendent: Studies in the Structure and Semiotics of Islamic Philosophy, Theology and Cosmology*, London: Routledge.

—— (1992) *Al-Farabi and His School*, London: Routledge.

—— (1996) 'The Brethren of Purity (Ikhwan al-Safa')', *HIP*, 222–30.

Nursi, S. (1995) *The Flashes Collection*, trans. S. Vahide, Istanbul: Sözler Neşriyat.

Nuseibeh, S. (1996) 'Epistemology', *HIP*, 824–40.

Parush, I. (2004) 'Another Look at the Life of "Dead" Hebrew', in E. Greenspan and J. Rose (eds), *Book History*, University Park, PA: University of Pennsylvania Press, 171–214.

Pavlin, J. (1996) 'Sunni kalam and Theological Controversies', *HIP*, 105–18.

Peters, F. (1968) *Aristotle and the Arabs: The Aristotelian Tradition in Islam*, Albany, NY: State of New York University Press.

—— (1996) 'The Greek and Syriac Background', *HIP*, 40–51.

Peters, R. (1977) *Jihad in Medieval and Modern Islam*, Leiden: Brill.

Rahman, F. (1958) *Prophecy in Islam*, London: Allen & Unwin.

—— (1975) *The Philosophy of Mulla Sadra*, Albany, NY: State University of New York Press.

—— (1984) *Islam and Modernity: Transformation of an Intellectual Tradition*, Chicago, IL: University of Chicago Press.

Reinhart, K. (1995) *Before Revelation: The Boundaries of Muslim Moral Thought*, Albany, NY: State University of New York Press.

Ridgeon, L. (1998) *ʿAziz Nasafi*, Richmond: Curzon.

Rocha, C. (2006*) Zen in Brazil: The Quest for Cosmopolitan Identity*, Honolulu: University of Hawaiʼi Press.

Rosenthal, E. (1968) *Political Thought in Medieval Islam*, Cambridge: Cambridge University Press.

Rosenthal, F. (1994). *The Classical Heritage in Islam*, trans. E. and J. Marmorstein, New York: Routledge.

Rowson, E. (1996a) ʿAl-ʿAmiriʼ, *HIP*, 216–21.

—— (1996b) *A Muslim Philosopher on the Soul and its Fate: al-ʿAmiriʼs Kitab al-Amad alaʼl-Abad*, Chicago, IL: Kazi.

Sachedina, A. (1980) *The Just Ruler in Shiʿite Islam*, New York: Oxford University Press.

Mulla Sadra (1967) *al-Hikma al-mutaʿaliya fiʼl asfar al-ʿaqliyya al-arbaʿa* [Transcendental Wisdom about the Four Intellectual Journeys], ed. R. Lutfi, Tehran: Shirkat Dar al-Maʿarif al-Islamiyya.

—— (1992*) K. al-mashaʿir* [Book of Metaphysical Penetrations], trans. P. Morewedge as *The Metaphysics of Mulla Sadra*, New York: Society for the Study of Islamic Philosophy and Science.

Schimmel, A. (1975) *Mystical Dimensions of Islam*, Chapel Hill, NC: University of North Carolina Press.

—— (1994) *Deciphering the Signs of God: A Phenomenological Approach to Islam*, Edinburgh: Edinburgh University Press.

Shamsher Ali, M. (2006) ʿScience and the Qurʼanʼ, in O. Leaman (ed.), *The Qurʼan: An Encyclopedia*, London: Routledge, 571–6.

Shariʿati, A. (1980) *Marxism and Other Western Fallacies: An Islamic Critique*, trans. H. Algar, Berkeley, CA: Mizan Press.

Shayegan, Y. (1996) ʿThe Transmission of Greek Philosophy to the Islamic Worldʼ, *HIP*, 89–104.

Smart, N. (2008) *World Philosophies*, 2nd edn, ed. O. Leaman, London: Routledge.

Street, T. (2005) ʿLogicʼ, in P. Adamson and R. Taylor, *Cambridge Companion to Arabic Philosophy*, Cambridge: Cambridge University Press, 247–66.

Stroumsa, S. (1999) *Freethinkers of Medieval Islam*, Leiden: Brill.

al-Suhrawardi (1999) *The Philosophy of Illumination*, trans. J. Walbridge and H. Ziai, Provo, UT: Brigham Young University Press.

Taftazani, A. and Leaman, O. (1996) ʿIbn Sabʿinʼ, *HIP*, 34–9.

al-Tahtawi, R. (2004), *An Imam in Paris: al-Tahtawiʼs Visit to France (1826–31)*, trans. D. Newman, London: Saqi.

Thackston, W. (1982) *The Mystical and Visionary Treatises of Shihabuddin Yahya Suhrawardi*, London: Octagon.

Tusi, Nasir al-Din (1998) *Contemplation and Action: The Spiritual Autobiography of a Muslim Scholar*, ed. and trans. S. Badakhchani, London: I. B. Tauris.

Urvoy, D. (1996) 'Ibn Rushd', *HIP*, 330–45.

—— (1998) *Averroes: Les ambitions d'un intellectuel musulman*, Paris: Flammarion.

—— (2006) *Histoire de la pensée arabe et islamique*, Paris: Seuil.

Von Grunebaum, G. (ed.) (1970) *Logic in Classical Islamic Culture*, Wiesbaden: Harrasowitz.

Walbridge, J. (1992) *The Science of Mystic Lights: Qutb al-Din Shirazi and the Illuminationist Tradition in Islamic Philosophy*, Cambridge, MA: Harvard University Press.

—— (2000) *Suhrawardi and the Heritage of the Greeks*, Albany, NY: State University of New York Press.

Wansborough, J. (1977) *Qur'anic Studies*, Oxford: Oxford University Press.

Watt, W. (1985) *Islamic Philosophy and Theology: An Extended Survey*, Edinburgh: Edinburgh University Press.

Wild, S. (1996) 'Islamic Enlightenment and the Paradox of Averroes', *Die Welt des Islams* 36 (November): 379–90.

Wilson, C. (1996) 'Modern Western Philosophy', *HIP*, 1013–29.

Wittgenstein, L. (1953) *Philosophical Investigations*, trans. G. E. M. Anscombe, Oxford: Blackwell.

—— (1961) *Tractatus Logico-Philosophicus*, trans. D. Pears and B. McGuinness, London: Routledge & Kegan Paul.

Wolfson, H. (1976) *The Philosophy of the Kalam*, Cambridge, MA: Harvard University Press.

Zakariyya, F. (1988) *Al-haqiqa wa'l-wahm fi al haraka al-islamiyya al-mu'asira* [Fact and Illusion in the Contemporary Islamic Movement], Cairo: Dar al-Fikr.

Ziai, H. (1990) *Knowledge and Illumination: A Study of Suhrawardi's Hikmat al-ishraq*, Atlanta, GA: Scholars Press.

—— (1996a) 'The Illuminationist Tradition', *HIP*, 465–96.

—— 1996b) 'Mulla Sadra: His Life and Works', *HIP*, 635–42.

—— (1996c) 'Shihab al-Din Suhrawardi: Founder of the Illuminationist School', *HIP*, 434–64.

Zimmermann, F. W. (1986) 'The Origins of the So-Called Theology of Aristotle', in J. Kraye, W. F. Ryan and C. B. Schmitt (eds), *Pseudo-Aristotle in the Middle Ages: The Theology and Other Texts*, London: The Warburg Institute, 110–240.

Guide to Further Reading

Bibliographies

There is a guide to bibliographical resources below in Nasr and Leaman, and in Leaman 2006. Hans Daiber's various articles and books are particularly detailed in bibliography anyway, and his books on bibliography are very impressive. The articles on Islamic philosophy in the two recent encyclopedias of philosophy have respectable bibliographical material.

Borchert, D. (2006) *Encyclopedia of Philosophy*, 2nd edn, New York: Macmillan.
Craig, E. (1998) *Routledge Encyclopedia of Philosophy*, London: Routledge.
Daiber, H. (1999) *Bibliography of Islamic Philosophy*, 2 vols, Leiden: Brill.
—— (2007) *Bibliography of Islamic Philosophy*, Supplement, Leiden: Brill.
Leaman, O. (ed.) (2006) *Biographical Encyclopedia of Islamic Philosophers*, London: Continuum.

See also:
Georges C. Anawati (1968–70) 'Bibliographie de la philosophie médiévale en terre d'Islam pour les années 1959–1969', in *Bulletin de Philosophie Médiévale*, 10–12: 343–4.
—— (1967–2000) 'Bibliographie Islamo-arabe. Livres et articles sur l'Islam et l'arabisme parus, en langues occidentales, durant la période 1960–1966', in *Mélanges de l'Institut dominicain des études orientales (MIDEO)*, 9 (1967): 143–213; 24 (2000): 381–414.
Thérèse-Anne Druart and Michael L. Marmura (1990–7) 'Medieval Islamic Philosophy and Theology: Bibliographical Guide', in *Bulletin de Philosophie Médiévale* (32) 1990 (1986–9): 106–35; (35) 1993 (1989–92): 181–219; (37) 1995 (1992–4): 193–232; (39) 1997 (1994–6): 175–202.

For modern Islamic philosophy, see:
Nasr, S. H., and Leaman, O. (eds) (1996) 'The Modern Islamic World', *History of Islamic Philosophy*, London: Routledge, 1037–1169, in particular, M. Aminrazavi, 'Persia', 1037–50; M. Suheyl Umar, 'Pakistan', 1076–80; I. Abu-Rabiʿ 'The Arab World', 1082–1114; M. Campanini, 'Egypt', 1115–28; Z. Moris, 'South-East Asia', 1134–40; P. Lory, 'Henry Corbin', 1149–55; S. Akhtar, 'The Possibility of a Philosophy of Islam', 1162–9.
There is some useful reference material in Brown, S., Collinson, D. and Wilkinson, R. (eds) (1996) *Biographical Dictionary of Twentieth-Century Philosophers*, London: Routledge. Contains information on a number of modern Islamic philosophers. Relevant entries include: 'Arkoun, Mohammed', 30–1; 'Corbin, Henry', 159–60; 'Hanafi, Hasan', 305–6; 'Lahbabi, Muhammad Aziz', 431; 'Nagib Mahmud, Zaki', 562; 'Nasr, Seyyed Hossein', 563–4; 'Qadir, C. A.', 641; 'Rahman, Fazlur', 645–6; and 'Yazdi, Mehdi Hairi', 859.

Index

Ubiquitous terms in the book such as God, Islam and philosophy are not indexed.

Lightning Source UK Ltd.
Milton Keynes UK
UKOW05f0611050517
300550UK00011B/258/P